The Negro in the South Since 1865

SOUTHERN HISTORICAL PUBLICATIONS NO. 10

The Negro in the South Since 1865

Selected Essays in American Negro History

CHARLES E. WYNES, ed.

UNIVERSITY OF ALABAMA PRESS
University, Alabama

Second printing 1967

To
James Hugo Johnston,
Virginian, Scholar, and Friend

Contents

About the Authors

CLARENCE A. BACOTE is Professor of History at Atlanta University and is the author of several articles on the history of the Negro in Georgia.

MAXWELL BLOOMFIELD is Instructor of History at Ohio State University.

PHILIP DURHAM is Associate Professor of English at the University of California, Los Angeles. Together with EVERETT L. JONES he is the author of *The Negro Cowboys*.

JOHN HOPE FRANKLIN is Professor of History at the University of Chicago. Among his publications are *The Militant South; From Slavery to Freedom; Reconstruction After the Civil War;* and *The Emancipation Proclamation*.

DEWEY W. GRANTHAM, JR., is Professor of History at Vanderbilt University. He is the author of *Hoke Smith and the Politics of the New South* and *The Democratic South*.

Louis R. Harlan is Associate Professor of History at the University of Cincinnati and is the author of *Separate and Unequal: Public School Campaigns and Racism in the Southern Seaboard States, 1901-1915.*

Guion Griffis Johnson was formerly associated with the Institute for Research in the Social Sciences at the University of North Carolina. Among her publications are *Ante-Bellum North Carolina; Black Yeomanry;* and "The Ideology of White Supremacy."

Everett L. Jones is supervisor of the freshman English testing and placement program at the University of California, Los Angeles. Together with Phillip Durham he is the author of *The Negro Cowboys.*

Elsie M. Lewis is Professor and Chairman of the Department of History at Howard University.

Robert Moats Miller is Associate Professor of History at the University of North Carolina and is the author of *American Protestantism and Social Issues, 1919-1939.*

C. Vann Woodward is Sterling Professor of History at Yale University. Among his major publications are *Tom Watson, Agrarian Rebel; Reunion and Reaction; Origins of the New South, 1877-1913;* and *The Burden of Southern History.*

Charles E. Wynes is Assistant Professor of History at the University of Georgia. He is the author of *Race Relations in Virginia, 1870-1902* and the editor of *Southern Sketches from Virginia, 1881-1901.*

Introduction

Probably no area of United States history is more in need of fundamental research and interpretation, or re-interpretation, than is the history of the Negro American. For various reasons—some of them good ones—our best historians have seldom chosen to specialize in its investigation. In part, Negro history has suffered this neglect because of the simple dearth of historical materials—the personal papers, diaries, memoirs, newspapers, and the like—upon which research is based. Whether slaves or freedmen, or held in the position of "hewers of wood and drawers of water," Negroes rarely kept written records, and as a result the scholar lacks the necessary tools of his craft. Another reason, perhaps—a more subjective and sensitive one—is that the white scholar has been reluctant to identify himself and his professional future with the history of an oppressed race, one formerly held in slavery. What limited writing has been done has been too often left to those whites who are hostile to the Negro and his aspirations. By temperament and often by training, such whites are disqualified as serious and objective historians.

Unfortunately some grave shortcomings have also marred the work of the few Negroes who attempted the job. Many simply were not qualified because of their own material, social, cultural, and educational deprivation and their isolation from the American mainstream. But frequently, too, Negroes were so emotionally involved in "the cause" that it was impossible for them to write objectively and dispassionately even though objectivity is a prime requisite of historical writing. While it is undoubtedly true that "only a Negro can know what it is like to be a Negro in America," that fact is not necessarily an aid to writing good Negro history. It can be a distinct hindrance because it leads to becoming an advocate instead of an investigator. As a member of a minority group the Negro feels that he has been misunderstood and maligned; he wants to be heard; he wants more of the "good things" of America for himself. As a result, his product is sometimes polemic, not history.

Despite these criticisms, it is a fact that in recent years—certainly since the 1930's—the quality and quantity of history both by and about Negroes has improved tremendously, as John Hope Franklin writes in his article on "The New Negro History" (*Journal of Negro History*, XXXII [July, 1957], 89-97). One need only glance at the book review sections of the leading historical quarterlies to confirm Franklin's thesis.

When in the form of monographs, books, or texts, the best of these writings are to be found in all the better libraries where they are readily available for use by teachers, scholars, and graduate students alike. But, regrettably, if they happen to be in the form of articles in scholarly journals, a few months after their appearance they tend to become obscure, to be read only by a few specialists willing to make a diligent search for them. It is the aim of the editor of this book to rescue from this oblivion some of the articles on the history of the Negro since 1865 which in his opinion seem among the best and most significant to have appeared.

Of necessity, such a collection is uneven. There will be those who quarrel with my choice. Why did the editor include certain articles, and why did he fail to include others? I cannot undertake to explain why some articles are omitted, but I can attempt to justify in this introduction the selection which comprises the remainder of this book. Beyond that, I can only repeat that in my opinion these are *some* of the best articles which have appeared.

It might be wise to say a word first about the arrangement of the articles. The order decided upon, then, represents something of a compromise between the topical and the chronological. The subject matter might be broadly classified as either political or social history, with some obvious overlapping as in the story of Progressivism. Within each of these two classifications, the sequence is roughly chronological, exact chronological placement being impossible because the articles cover such varying spans of time.

The political section opens with an article by Elsie M. Lewis, entitled "The Political Mind of the Negro, 1865-1900." With the end of slavery and the prospect of a new status for all Negro Americans, what were the goals of their leaders for the Negro as a political factor in a democratic society? Not surprisingly, they sought full equality at the polls, for a free man without the right to vote was only half free. Finally in 1870, with ratification of the Fifteenth Amendment, this "natural right of free men" was accorded them. Disillusionment followed. Increasingly, both Negro leaders and the mass of Negro citizens lost faith in the Republican party, as it all but abandoned them, even before Reconstruction had come to an end. Some of them tried fusion with white Populists in the

1890's, while others, both before and after the 1890's, became Democrats out of desperation. But the great majority of Negroes continued, at least in sentiment, to identify themselves with the Republicans because, small hope though it was, that party remained their best hope. Yet some Negro leaders like Virginia's John Mercer Langston began to argue that the Negro should look to the courts, not the parties, for assurance of his rights. In the Federal courts, at least until well into the twentieth century, this course was equally futile. Even less justice was received from the state courts, although there were notable exceptions, as for instance, in North Carolina. (See Frenise A. Logan, *The Negro in North Carolina, 1876-1894,* Chapel Hill, 1964.) Because no party served the Negro, he interested himself more and more in class and race questions instead of those of more general national and regional importance.

In "Tom Watson and the Negro in Agrarian Politics," C. Vann Woodward is concerned with the transformation from liberal to reactionary of the Negro's first great Southern white political supporter, the only one the Negro had in 1890, at least in the sense of an active political leader. However, by 1917, Georgia's Tom Watson declared: "In the South we have to lynch him occasionally, and flog him, now and then, to keep him from blaspheming the Almighty, by his conduct, on account of his smell and his color." The great democratic champion, who in 1892 deplored the use of race demagoguery to divide poor white farmers from poor black farmers, employed that same demagoguery during the early years of the twentieth century against Catholics and Jews as well as Negroes. But Watson was not alone in this reactionary conversion, as is shown in the article described below on Virginia's Lewis Harvie Blair. The question remaining unanswered for both Watson and Blair is, "Why?"

Ironic as it may seem, most of the program of Negro segregation and proscription by statute was accomplished during the years of the national Progressive movement. In "The Progressive Movement and the Negro," Dewey W. Grantham, Jr., tells how, except for indirect benefits from some of the more general Progressive legislation, the Negro was excluded from Progressivism, which was, after all, for white men only. This was, he says, probably due to several factors: (1) Where Progressivism was strongest, as in Wisconsin for instance, Negroes were so few that their needs were overshadowed by problems which concerned a larger portion of the populace. (2) Many southern Progressives, such as the Vardamans and Hoke Smiths, were the very ones who advocated disfranchisement and repression of the Negro, or else they were paternalists of the "Old School," like Charles B. Aycock, Edwin A. Alderman, and Walter Hines Page, who for all their kindness, had no desire to tinker with a society that acknowledged white supremacy. (3) Philosophically, the whole nation was at this time accepting the scientific and pseudo-scientific ideas about the inferiority of colored peoples. Participation in the American Dream, as encouraged by Progressivism, was denied the Negro.

How did white Americans rationalize exclusion of the Negro from the Progressive crusade, and how did they justify to themselves exclusion of the Negro from a reform movement so highly charged with a sense of moral righteousness? Comparing earthy Populism with moralistic Progressivism, it seems that the more moralistic and religious the reform crusade, the less likelihood there is that it will include uplift of the Negro. After all, it was simple self-interest, not morality, which caused a significant portion of the white Populist movement to forget for a while "natural race antagonism," as black and white shared their common misery. The answer is that white Americans saw exclusion of the Negro from Progressivism as right and moral. Thomas Dixon, Jr., a liberal social gospel reformer, sophisticated social Darwinist, former lawyer, and Baptist min-

ister, insisted that in the society of man there could be no
"survival of the fittest" unless "fitness" was defined in moral
terms. He articulated the narrow white concept of Progressive
morality, chiefly through his racist novel, *The Leopard's Spots*
(1902). To Dixon, friend and onetime classmate of Woodrow
Wilson at Johns Hopkins University (See Raymond A. Cook,
"The Man Behind The Birth of a Nation," *The North Carolina Historical Review*, XXXIX [Autumn 1962], 519-540.), the
Negro was "an amoral creature . . . unable to discriminate between right and wrong." Why then should he be allowed to
pull down or even contaminate the society of a higher moral
order about to be perfected by white men? A muckraker in all
but name, Dixon mirrored the spirit of moralistic reform of
his age. The only difference was that his enemy was the "black
peril" instead of Wall Street, political bosses, and "malefactors
of great wealth."

Dixon, like Tom Watson and Lewis Harvie Blair, was another enigmatic Southern reformer and reactionary—an intellectual schizophrenic. A case study of his book is presented
here by Maxwell Bloomfield, in "Dixon's *The Leopard's Spots:*
A Study in Popular Racism." Strictly speaking, this article
should be classified as intellectual history. Here it is placed
at the end of the political section, serving as a bridge between
the political and social crusade which was Progressivism, and
more general social history.

Moving to the area of social history, the first article, by
Guion Griffis Johnson, is entitled "Southern Paternalism
Toward Negroes After Emancipation." While the title of this
article is somewhat misleading, the general reader as well as
the scholar will find it invaluable for understanding the white
South's attitude and thought on the Negro question. Basically,
the author says that Southern racial thought can be typed in
one of five categories: modified equalitarianism, benevolent
paternalism, separate but equal, separate but permanently un-

equal, and permanently unequal under paternal supervision. The author explains what is meant by each of these classifications and traces its development or decline, with quotations from white Southerners who typify each classification. This is a highly significant contribution to understanding the mind of the South.

In "Jim Crow Goes to School: The Genesis of Legal Segregation in Southern Schools," John Hope Franklin reminds us that while most of the South's segregation practices were not recognized by law until the decade of the 1890's or later, segregation in the public schools had existed ever since those schools were founded. This was the case even during Reconstruction except for a brief period of integration in the Louisiana and South Carolina schools. The idea was not peculiarly Southern, though, because before the Civil War segregation of Negroes in Northern schools was common. But wherever it was practiced, the perpetuation of Jim Crow in the public schools came to guarantee a lifetime of Jim Crow.

Histories of the post-Civil War Negro in the states of Mississippi, South Carolina, North Carolina, and Virginia have been published. Similar studies for the remaining states of the old Confederacy remain to be done. This need has been partly filled for Georgia, however, by Clarence A. Bacote's "Negro Proscription, Protests, and Proposed Solutions In Georgia, 1880-1908." In Georgia, as in the other Southern states, ultimate proscription of the rights of the Negro came much later than is commonly believed by the Southern public. It came with the extension of popular democracy, with the Farmers' Alliance and Populist movements, but not necessarily as a direct result of mass democracy. Negro reaction to growing proscription in Georgia and to the increasing incidence of lynching resulted in proposals of either: a back-to-Africa movement, an exodus to the North, or colonization in an all-Negro state to be set aside by the federal government in the Western

territories. Both the back-to-Africa and the domestic colonization schemes were completely unrealistic and doomed to failure from the start, and while many Negroes did go north, they
soon discovered that life beyond the Potomac was often quite
as difficult in its own way as life in the South. The result was
that the overwhelming mass of Georgia Negroes remained at
home and in their "place," as defined for them by the growing numbers of white supremacists.

The generation which knew Georgia's Tom Watson—once
champion and later scourge of the Negro—also knew another
of his kind, Virginia's Lewis Harvie Blair. A member of one
of the First Families of Virginia, Confederate veteran, and
wealthy Richmond businessman, Blair wrote a book in 1889
entitled *The Prosperity of the South Dependent Upon the
Elevation of the Negro.* Eloquent, pragmatically reasoned,
and yet compassionate, no better case has been made to this
day for an end to racial injustice and segregation. C. Vann
Woodward has edited and written a fine introduction to a
1964 edition of this volume, published by Little, Brown and
Company. The story of Blair's mental odyssey is told here by
Charles E. Wynes in "Lewis Harvie Blair, Virginia Reformer:
The Uplift of the Negro and Southern Prosperity."

The Old South knew that to educate a slave even slightly
was to sow the seeds of freedom within him. The New South
embraced this philosophy also, and sought to keep the freedmen and their descendants in hopeless, dependent ignorance.
Or, according to the old cliché, "Educate a Negro and you
spoil a good field hand." As for the education of whites,
Southern legislators were timid and fearful of the cost and
social changes to which mass education might lead and only
half embraced the cause of public education in the last third
of the nineteenth century. The twentieth century, however,
brought major changes. This story is told by Louis R. Harlan,
in "The Southern Education Board and the Race Issue in

Public Education." While public education in the South made great strides between 1900 and the outbreak of World War I, it was, as other aspects of Southern Progressivism, within the framework of racism and actually widened the gap between educational appropriations for white schools and Negro schools. The Negro was to be educated, if at all, in practical arts—in a word, trained. The Southern Education Board, nearly half of whose members were Northern philanthropists, weakly acquiesced to this policy apparently hopeful that education of Southern whites would eventually aid the Negro, as educated whites would supposedly be less prejudiced. The result was that the Board accomplished little or nothing in the area of Negro education. As Negroes became increasingly disillusioned, they combined with whites possessed of more moral fervor than members of the Southern Education Board to form the National Association for the Advancement of Colored People.

"Negro Cowboys," by Philip Durham and Everett L. Jones, is a unique piece of historical writing—perhaps the *most* unique and original article on Negro history available. If the reader wonders about its inclusion in a volume on the Negro in the South since 1865, the editor offers in explanation two reasons: one, its very uniqueness; and two, the fact that the Negro cowboys came out of Texas—a Southern and former Confederate state as well as a Western state—and to Texas most of them returned, for few stayed permanently on the Northern ranges. In the heyday of the open range, Negro cowboys were regularly found along all the famous cattle trails leading out of Texas to the railheads and market towns—the Chisholm, the Goodnight-Loving, and the Western Trail, among the best known. But today, in song and story, in the movies and on television, only the lean, tanned, and tall white cowboy rides the range, aided occasionally by such minorities as "good Indians," Mexican-Americans, and even the carica-

tured and pigtailed Chinese. Not a question of white supremacy or Jim Crow, it is as if the Negro American, the Negro
cowboy, was never there. He was, but history and time have
all but forgotten him.

"It is not too much to say that whoever wishes to become a
truly moral human being . . . must first divorce himself from
all the prohibitions, crimes and hypocrisies of the Christian
Church." This harsh prescription was written by a leading
Negro intellectual and reveals the dilemma in which Southern white Protestants find themselves today. For the uncomfortable truth is that many "love their church, but
not the Christ and His teachings." And when the teachings
of Christ conflict with the customs and mores of the community, of which the church is but a part, most Christians
prefer to risk the wrath of a righteous God in the hereafter
rather than that of their self-righteous fellow Christians in this
life. Truly Southern white Protestantism stands at a crossroads
where it can no longer benignly accept the fact as a part of
the "Southern way of life," that the most segregated hour of
the week is from 11:00 to 12:00 o'clock on Sunday morning, or
that, in the words of Mississippi Negro leader Aaron Henry,
"The most segregated school in the South is not the public
school but the Sunday school."

This Southern dilemma is presented and keenly but sympa-
thetically analyzed by Robert Moats Miller in "Southern Protestantism and the Negro, 1865-1965." It seems fitting that
this volume should end with such an essay since the South
has been characterized by at least one outside observer as "the
most simply and sincerely religious country that I was ever
in," and by Professor Miller who maintains that the " 'Protestant South' has always been more Southern than Protestant,
more secular than sacred."

It was the intent of the editor to include the following
articles in this volume: Patrick W. Riddleberger, "The Radi-

cals' Abandonment of the Negro During Reconstruction," *The Journal of Negro History*, VL (April 1960), 88-102; Vincent P. DeSantis, "The Republican Party and the Southern Negro," *The Journal of Negro History*, VL (April 1960), 71-87; and Robert Moats Miller, "The Attitudes of American Protestantism Toward the Negro, 1919-1939," *The Journal of Negro History*, XLI (July 1956), 215-240. All three are excellent articles and are recommended to the reader.

All of the essays have been edited for consistency in the capitalization of words such as *South, Southern, Fourteenth Amendment, Congress, President, Radicals, etc.*, except where they appear within quotations. The footnote style has also been made consistent. Any proof-reading errors in the original publication have, of course, been corrected. Otherwise the articles appear here unchanged. Therefore the editor assumes no responsibility for correctness of facts or for interpretation of the facts themselves.

In putting together this volume the editor is indebted, first, to the authors of the articles which appear here. Without their labors this volume would not be possible. I also wish to thank their respective publishers for permission to reprint the articles. In the process of selection I was ably assisted by one of my graduate students, Horace Calvin Wingo. For financial and typing assistance I am indebted to the Social Science Research Institute of the University of Georgia, and Mrs. Joanna G. Parsons and Mrs. Sandra Daniel.

The University of Georgia CHARLES E. WYNES

ELSIE M. LEWIS*

The Political Mind
of the Negro, 1865-1900

By the end of the Civil War a distinctive body of political thought was being advanced by a small group of Negroes in the United States. For the most part they were free Negro residents of the North. Such men as Frederick Douglass and the Reverend J. Sella Martin of New York, George T. Downing of Rhode Island, Peter H. Clark and John M. Langston of Ohio, and Martin R. Delaney and Robert Purvis of Pennsylvania formed the nucleus of the group. Douglass, of course, was better known to the American public than the others, but each was regarded with esteem in his home community. As a group, they represented the highest type of professional and intellectual achievement of the Negro in America. They were edu-

* From *The Journal of Southern History*, *XXI* (May 1955), 189-202. Reprinted by permission of the publisher.

cated, experienced in public affairs, and familiar with all the devices through which knowledge, ideas, and opinions are transmitted. Furthermore, they were ardent advocates of the nineteenth-century philosophy of equality and human rights, which they had vigorously championed during their long association with the antislavery movement. They had the competence to launch a movement designed to promulgate the ideas to which they were already committed.

During the war they had promoted a National Convention of Colored Men at Syracuse, New York, for the expressed purpose of consolidating thought and action among the members of their race. At the convention there were 144 delegates from eighteen states, seven of which were in the South. The convention established a National Equal Rights League, with state and local branches, to serve as the instrument through which unity of action and opinion could be effected. In addition, resolutions were passed which proclaimed the concept of equality and human rights and advocated political and civil rights for Negroes.[1]

As emancipation approached reality and President Lincoln initiated his plan of Reconstruction, these Negro leaders became more vigorous in their efforts and more determined that all the benefits of freedom should be accorded to their race. In their attempts to attain this goal they were supported by the Southern free Negro and the more intelligent of the newly emancipated freedmen. Largely through the influence of this increasing minority, who served as spokesmen for the ignorant masses, the agencies of thought and opinion were expanded and certain basic attitudes and ideas were nurtured and encouraged.

The capstone of this political ideology rested firmly on the theory of human rights expressed in the Declaration of Inde-

[1] *Proceedings of the National Convention of Colored Men held in the city of Syracuse, New York, October 4-7, 1864 with the Bill of Wrongs and Rights and Addressed to the American People* (Boston, 1864).

pendence. That is to say, the belief that all men were created equal, endowed by their Creator with certain inalienable rights—life, liberty, and the pursuit of happiness—formed the base upon which they built their claims for political recognition and status. It was the fundamental doctrine that all free men have a natural right to an existence worthy of a human being and that political institutions and government are the means by which that right is secured and maintained. Certainly, this was no new theory but a fundamental tenet which most Americans professed to accept. Furthermore, it was the principle which all reformers invoked in their democratic and humanitarian strivings. From this standpoint it was not illogical for colored men to use this traditional dogma as the justification for their being accorded full citizenship rights and privileges.

The right to vote was deemed essential not only because it afforded protection but primarily because it was considered the natural right of every free man. The authority for this belief was the Declaration of Independence. To black men the great charter of liberty meant exactly what it said. In their opinion slavery had imposed the unnatural condition of inequality on them; now that the shackles had been removed, they had been restored to their original condition of free men. Therefore, the elective franchise was their "natural, inalienable right." And if, as the Declaration implied, it was a natural right, to deny its exercise was a wrong to their nature as men.[2]

Inasmuch as life and the pursuit of happiness could not be secured "without adequate protection for the class or classes

[2] *Proceedings of the Colored People's Convention of the State of South Carolina held in Zion Church, Charleston, November, 1865 together with the Declaration of Rights and Wrongs; An Address to the People, A Petition to the Legislature and a Memorial to Congress* (Charleston, 1865); *Proceedings of the Convention of Colored People of Virginia held in the city of Alexandria, August 2-5, 1865* (n.p., 1865); Nashville *Colored Tennessean,* August 12, 1865; New Orleans *Tribune,* May 23, July 4, November 7, 1865, December 6, 1866.

that are deprived of the rights and immunities enjoyed by the most favored," the elective franchise was necessary, argued Dr. R. B. Roundanez, wealthy "Creole" editor of the New Orleans *Tribune*. He concluded that protection and political rights were correlative because "the man who has no rights of his own, has no real protection." The deductions of Roundanez were sanctioned by the Convention of Colored Men in Virginia, the Equal Rights League of New Orleans, and Oscar J. Dunn, first Negro lieutenant-governor of Louisiana.[3]

To reinforce these assumptions other colored men in their addresses and conventions called attention to the fact that "governments derive their just powers from the consent of the governed," and to be governed without having a voice in the selection of political officials was tyranny. So was it contrary to American political principles to be taxed without being represented. In the mind of John M. Langston any abridgement of this doctrine was unconstitutional. Political rights constituted the inherent sovereignty of the people, and where there was no acknowledged sovereignty there could be no binding power. Hence, Langston and Martin Delaney maintained that it was tyranny to force black men to pay taxes when they had no sovereignty to delegate their wishes to their elected representatives.[4]

It was evident that Negroes were identifying themselves with the crusade the "patriots of 1776" had waged for their natural rights to life, liberty, and the pursuit of happiness. In much the same spirit the Negro veterans of the Civil War declared that they had fought for liberty and defended their country against the enemy in every war in which the United States had been engaged. The blood of loyal, patriotic black men had

[3] New Orleans *Tribune*, August 5, June 11, July 18, October 6, 1865.
[4] John M. Langston, *Freedom and Citizenship, Selected Lectures* (Washington, 1883), 109-11, 119-20; Washington *New National Era*, February 3, March 10, 1870.

been shed at Boston during the Revolutionary War, at New
Orleans with General Andrew Jackson in the War of 1812, and
more recently at Richmond and Fort Pillow. How, then, could
it be, they asked in 1866 at their National Convention, meeting in Washington, D. C., that "you will enfranchise the red
headed rebel traitor who struggled four years using his slaves,
his power and his all to destroy the Government and still keep
disfranchised four million of your loyal population whose only
offense is their skins are black"?[5] The Civil War veterans were
not alone in expressing sentiments of patriotism and nationalism. It was not unusual for colored newspaper editors, orators,
and various assemblies to declare that they were "native born
Americans," "loyal Americans," or to announce with pride,
"this is our country," and to reaffirm loyalty by claiming, "we
have defended it with our blood."[6]

Even when assertions of love of country were not made or
claims of national rights specifically advanced, Negro leaders
found support for their demands in what had been done in the
past. The North Carolina Convention of Colored Men reminded President Johnson that as free persons they had ex-
ercised the right of suffrage until 1835.[7] Others were quick to
point out that free men of color had voted in many states of
the South until the first quarter of the century and had re-

[5] New Orleans *Tribune,* October 31, 1865.

[6] *Proceedings of the First Annual Meeting of the National Equal
Rights League held in Cleveland, Ohio, October 19-21, 1865* (Philadel-
phia, 1865); *Address from the Colored Citizens of Norfolk, Virginia to
the People of the United States, June 5, 1865* (New Bedford, Mass.,
1865); *Proceedings of the Colored People's Convention of the State of
South Carolina . . . November, 1865;* New Orleans *Tribune,* May 19,
26, June 11, July 25, November 7, 1865, October 5, December 6, 1866;
*Memorial to Honorable Senate and House of Representatives of the
United States Assembled from the Pennsylvania Equal Rights League,
February 20, 1866* (Philadelphia, 1866); *Proceedings of the Freedmen's
Convention of Georgia assembled at Augusta, January 10, 1866* (n.p.,
1866).

[7] New York *Daily Tribune,* May 19, 1865; New Orleans *Tribune,*
May 31, 1865.

tained the privilege in many states of the North. From this premise they reasoned that if one was free, he was entitled to the ballot.

Furthermore, these champions of rights for their race charged that color had been neither a consistent historical nor legal basis for the denial of the franchise. According to Langston, mulattoes had been granted the right to vote in Ohio by a state supreme court decision in 1859 notwithstanding a constitutional provision to the contrary.[8] Despite "visible admixture" laws in some states, colored men were reputed to have voted. In view of such inconsistencies Langston and his associates questioned the principle upon which these discriminations were made. They could find none. The United States Constitution contained no provision that could be interpreted to exclude them, and Attorney General Edward Bates in 1862 had ruled that African descent was not incompatible with citizenship. If, however, "color is to mark the line which shall be drawn about the ballot box," the colored men of Missis.ippi and Missouri requested that "a statute shall clearly define the castes and shades of complexions which shall be permitted within or expelled from its royal precincts."[9]

A further appeal for full citizenship rights was made by pointing to the superiority of American democratic ideals and institutions. To relegate any group of persons to an inferior position was contrary to republican and democratic concepts. The editor of the New Orleans *Tribune* pointed out that it was the boast of America that hereditary privileges were unknown and "all discrimination on account of birth or origin is repugnant to the principles of our Government and to American manners and custom." Yet, the "African race is enveloped in a law of proscription." To assign any group of persons to an inferior condition in a country where self-made

[8] Langston, *Freedom and Citizenship,* 101-02, 104-05.
[9] New Orleans *Tribune,* November 7, 1865; *An Address by the Colored People of Missouri to the Friends of Equal Rights* (St. Louis, 1865).

men were regarded with more respect than those born in af-
fluence and prosperity was un-American. All the members of
his race wanted, Roundanez declared, was to be given a fair
chance—"each unobstructed to find his own level according to
his education and means."[10] Here was a plea for reality of opportunity, for the full growth within the power of the individual.

Colored men also tended to introduce ethical teachings to
bolster their argument. They emphasized the Christian uni-
versals of the fatherhood of God and the brotherhood of man
as the guide for all human relations.[11] The equality and democracy they had in mind had their foundations in natural
rights and in the religious faith that God had created all human beings equal, each the peer of the other, and that He
intended each individual to achieve his highest potential.

Under the provision of the Radical Reconstruction program
Negroes in the South were permitted to vote. This privilege,
however, was not extended to those men of the North to whom
the franchise was not already accorded. Neither was it generally assumed that Negro suffrage was assured until the passage
of the Fifteenth Amendment. With the ratification of this
amendment enfranchisement was considered a *fait accompli*.
Negroes rejoiced that the concepts of the Declaration of Independence had become an integral part of the organic law of
the land. Now, they cried, America had become a government
of the people, for the people, and by the people. Innumerable
ratification meetings, conventions, and celebrations were held
throughout the spring and autumn of 1870. Resolutions were

10 New Orleans *Tribune,* July 8, 1865.
11 *Ibid.,* July 8, December 3, 1865; Washington *New National Era,*
February 24, 1870; *Proceedings of the State Convention of Colored Men
of the State of New Jersey, Trenton, New Jersey, July 13-14, 1865*
(Bridgeton, N. J., 1865); *Proceedings of the Convention of Colored
People of Virginia . . . Alexandria;* New Orleans *Tribune,* November
21, 1865.

passed, addresses made, and columns in Negro newspapers filled with expressions of praise and thanksgiving.[12]

Although Negro leaders were elated over the prospect of enfranchisement, they were at the same time beset by fears. In the first place, they knew that the majority of the freedmen was ignorant. They needed to be instructed not only in the actual process of voting but educated to assume the responsibilities and duties of citizenship. Early in 1867 Dr. R. I. Cromwell, an educated free Negro who had emigrated to New Orleans, addressed a long letter to "The Colored People of Louisiana and the Ten Rebel States." His purpose was "to instruct, interest and enlighten freedmen and new voters."[13] Peter H. Clark, Martin R. Delaney, James Lynch, and others lectured the new voters on the duties and responsibilities of citizenship, the necessity of using the ballot wisely, and the importance of understanding the nature of politics.[14]

A second disturbing factor to the more astute colored men was the fear that the right of suffrage might be lost. They knew that not all men, Northern or Southern, were committed to the experiment of Negro suffrage. Moreover, they were none too sure that the party which had promoted their enfranchisement had not been motivated by political expediency rather than principles. Consequently, they were uncertain as to the extent to which the party would go to uphold their privileges and rights in the face of opposition. Unlike J. Willis Menard of New Orleans, John M. Langston was willing to reserve his final judgment and let time tell whether the right to vote had been extended to his people for political reasons. He was inclined to believe that "The Republican party was forced by a pressure they could not resist to enfranchise the Negro—It was

[12] Washington *New National Era,* April 7, 21, 28, May 5, 1870.
[13] New Orleans *Tribune,* April 14, 1869.
[14] Washington *New National Era,* February 10, 17, 24, March 10, April 14, May 5, 1870, April 16, 1871; New Orleans *Tribune,* December 23, 1866.

because they could not stand without them."[15] Menard, however, was positive that those who were professing friendship
for the Negro were doing so for party ends. In fact, he thought
his race had suffered from their agitation. This free Negro
Creole believed that "suffrage is a second consideration" for
Negroes and that "security of life, liberty and property . . .
is the first and most urgent want of the colored race in the
South."[16] If by 1870 some were skeptical of the Republican
party, the Colored National Labor Convention was very critical of its program. This assembly concluded that "The Government, in giving the Negro his freedom has given him the
freedom to starve, and in giving him the ballot-box has given
him a coffin."[17] The attitude of the convention was that the
Republican administration had meant well but had been ill-
advised. It had attempted to make men independent voters
but had left them prey to conditions that made this goal impossible. The newly enfranchised freedmen were compelled to
look "to their rebel masters for their very existence." Political
equality, then, in the opinion of the National Labor Convention, was meaningless without corresponding economic independence.

By 1871 Southern Negro leaders were convinced that the
ballot was of no avail if life and property were jeopardized. At
their Southern States Convention they requested the national
government to protect them. The most provocative speech of
the convention was made by John T. Quarles of Georgia. He
made an eloquent plea for the enforcement of laws for protection and the "just remuneration of the laborer." He declared,
"free labor must be secured, maintained and developed";
either the Southern people must uphold the laws of their states

[15] Washington *New National Era*, April 14, 1870.

[16] New Orleans *Tribune*, November 6, 1866.

[17] *Proceedings of the Colored National Labor Convention in Washington, December 6-10, 1870* (Washington, 1870); Washington *New National Era*, January 19, 1871.

or the national government must do so. For the latter to act
meant constant interference in local matters which, in his
opinion, was not satisfactory. He preferred to invoke the moral
sentiment of the South because "experience teaches us that
laws are powerless in the face of public sentiment."[18]

It was soon evident to Negro leaders that whatever may have
been the motives for their enfranchisement, its exercise was impossible without the protection of their civil rights. Since they
were powerless and the state administrations were recalcitrant,
it was the obligation of the federal government to guarantee
and insure their rights. Thus, Negroes became committed very
early to a policy of federal control and extension of federal
power—a point of view from which they did not depart
throughout the nineteenth century.

When the Republican national administration was slow to
act in extending protection, it was criticized. From 1871 to
1875 there was a sustained movement to force action.[19] Men
continued to talk of the duty of the party and of the power of
the Negro vote. Some Negroes in their disillusionment accused
the administration of acquiescing in the violence and outrages
committed on them, while others cried that the party had
turned its back on them.[20] A few voices, like those of J. Sella
Martin and W. U. Saunders of Baltimore, advocated severing
all party allegiance. In fact, they renounced the party and
supported the Liberal Republican ticket in 1872. Even P. B. S.

[18] *Proceedings of Southern States Convention of Colored Men, Columbia, South Carolina, October 18-25, 1871* (Columbia, 1871), Appendix.
[19] Washington *New National Era,* September 28, 1871, January 11,
18, 21, December 27, 1872, August 7, December 9, 11, 18, 25, 1873,
February 5, 12, 19, 1874; New Orleans *Semi-Weekly Louisianian,* April
6, August 20, October 1, 1871, February 13, August 14, 1875; New
Orleans *Weekly Louisianian,* March 30, 1870, March 26, 1871, February
29, March 30, April 14, 1872; *Congressional Record,* 43 Cong., 1 Sess.,
407-10, 565-67, 4782-86.
[20] Washington *New National Era,* December 25, 1873, January 15,
22, May 7, June 25, 1874; New Orleans *Weekly Louisianian,* December
14, 1872, October 3, 1874, March 6, June 5, 1875.

Pinchback, then lieutenant-governor of Louisiana, and George T. Downing expressed sympathy with the Liberal Republican movement.[21] Nevertheless, they remained loyal to Grant as did the majority of colored men.

Contrary to the general belief the more intelligent Negroes did not give their support unreservedly to the Republican party. They attacked the Radical program, "carpetbaggers" and "scalawags," Northern leaders, and party policies throughout the last third of the nineteenth century. The New Orleans *Tribune* and the Washington *New National Era* outspokenly disapproved of carpetbaggers. These journals denounced these "new masters" of the freedmen for sowing seeds of discord among the Negroes on the basis of color and education.[22] The most scathing attack came in 1871 from Martin R. Delaney, who had migrated from Pennsylvania to Charleston, South Carolina.[23] He not only censured the carpetbaggers for deliberately dividing colored people but charged them with building their whole program on "deception, lying, cheating and stealing." In his opinion they were generally a class of men who were of the "lowest grade of Northern society, Negro haters at home . . . who could not have been elected to any position of honor or trust in their homes." Aristide Mary and Pinchback of New Orleans also considered carpetbaggers unworthy of support.[24] According to Pinchback, who was also editor and publisher of the *Louisianian,* Negroes "as a race are between the hawk of Republican demagogism and the buzzards of Democratic prejudices. The aspirants for position in

[21] New Orleans *Weekly Louisianian,* April 4, June 25, July 20, 1872, January 25, August 23, 1873; Washington *New National Era,* June 22, July 13, 1871, June 20, July 4, 11, 25, September 15, 1872, January 16, 1873.
[22] New Orleans *Tribune,* May 19, 1867; Washington *New National Era,* February 17, 24, 1870.
[23] New Orleans *Semi-Weekly Louisianian,* September 14, 1871; Washington *New National Era,* August 31, 1871.
[24] Washington *New National Era,* December 28, 1871, July 18, August 15, 1874; New Orleans *Weekly Louisianian,* May 9, October 10, 1874.

our party threaten us with excommunication if we do not follow every jack o'lantern who raises his feeble light, and the
Democrats invite us to annihilation if we turn away from
these Republican jack o'lanterns." He concluded, "Truly ours
is a great risk."[25]

The risk was indeed great in the opinion of certain colored
men after Rutherford B. Hayes's election to the Presidency.
Again Pinchback raised his voice in his newspaper in 1878 to
criticize the Republican program, but more to express his re-
gret that his race had failed to accept the policy he had suggested in 1874. He claimed that he had seen the signs of "the
shameful surrender of the Southern state Government . . .
while the 'Man on Horseback,' " U. S. Grant, was president
and the Republican party had a two-thirds majority in both
houses of Congress. For him the failure of Congress to pass the
Force bills, the omission of the school clause from the Civil
Rights bill, and the refusal to seat Negro contestants in Congress had been portents of the Republican party's conciliation
policy. When that trend became evident, he had advocated co-
operation with white Southerners. Such a policy, he claimed,
would have been possible in 1874, but four years later it would
require "more sagacity and skill than the race had ever demonstrated."[26]

The majority of colored leaders remained silent on Pinchback's proposal, but they were consistent in their criticism of
the Republican party. From 1877 to 1900 Negroes were dis-
gruntled, first, because of the party's failure to grant them
offices and a share of the patronage, and, second, because of
the failure of the national administration to guarantee them
protection of their political and civil rights.

The issue of officeholding and patronage was not a new one.
This sentiment had been revealed during the Reconstruction

[25] New Orleans *Semi-Weekly Louisianian,* August 3, 1871.
[26] *Ibid.,* December 14, 1878.

period. By 1883 Southern Negroes were saying: "We are the Republican party . . . but are only so regarded when our votes are counted."[27] In general, each Republican President between 1877 and 1900 was enjoined, and then criticized for his failure to appoint a Negro to an important position. Men like John M. Langston, Frederick Douglass, Blanche K. Bruce, Peter H. Clark, and D. Augustus Straker called on the chief executives of the nation to ascertain their views on the subject.[28]

Just as Negroes had been zealous in their drive for office-holding and patronage, so were they equally insistent on the the issue of federal protection of their rights. They were, however, not belligerent in their demands but conciliatory. Congress and the President were requested to enforce the law and uphold the Constitution of the United States. It is significant that the formulas for protest did not change. The equalitarian principle of the Declaration of Independence and the democratic ideal of individual opportunity were once more the cornerstones upon which colored men laid their claims. Again and again they declared: "We ask but an equal chance before the law, no more, no less," or "we do not ask for class legislation. We have had enough of that."[29]

Although the basic premises for full citizenship rights and privileges did not change, the proposals did. No longer were

[27] Huntsville (Ala.) *Gazette,* April 14, 1883.
[28] *Ibid.,* November 12, 1881, July 8, 22, September 2, 23, 1882, January 20, February 10, March 31, April 14, 28, 1883, April 11, August 15, 1885, February 6, April 14, October 16, 1886, February 26, 1887, November 12, 1888.
[29] *Proceedings of Civil Rights Meeting at Lincoln Hall, October 22, 1883* (Washington, 1883), 2-3, 4-8, 11-13; John M. Langston, "The Sparta of Office," MS. of speech delivered at mass meeting of colored citizens, 1883 (Fisk University Library); Washington *Bee,* April 1, May 12, June 23, 1883, June 12, 1886, October 2, 1886-June 1, 1889, *passim;* Cleveland *Gazette,* 1888-1900, *passim;* Washington *National Leader,* January 3, 1885, December 8, 1888, January 19, February 2, 9, March 9, 1889; Huntsville (Ala.) *Gazette,* March 31, April 14, 1883, April 11, 1885, April 14, October 16, 1886, February 26, 1887, November 24, December 22, 1888, March 23, 31, April 13, May 11, June 1, 1889.

colored leaders sure that through action within the Republican party their rights would be secured. Elder leaders such as Douglass and Langston admitted the failure of the Republican party but offered no solution.[30] Langston, however, did recommend a proposal that had been advocated in 1871 by the Colored Southern States Convention, that is, to seek redress for wrongs through state and federal courts in spite of the decision of the United States Supreme Court in the Civil Rights Cases (1883). He recommended the establishment of an organization, similar to the old Equal Rights League, that would prosecute cases and assist colored people to secure their rights through the courts. The funds for the agency would be raised through individual contributions.[31] It was left to T. Thomas Fortune, editor of the New York *Age,* to suggest a new course of political action. At the Colored National Press Association Convention in 1882 Fortune outlined his plan.[32] He believed that the Negro should be an independent force in politics, an independent voter. He was convinced that the Republican party was powerless to insure protection; therefore, he did not deem "it binding upon colored men further to support the Republican party when other more advantageous affiliations can be formed." Yet, he said:

No colored man can ever claim truthfully to be a Bourbon Democrat. It is a fundamental impossibility. But he can be an independent, a progressive Democrat. . . . [He] must think less of the party and more of himself, give less heed to a name and more to principles. . . .

[30] Washington *National Leader,* January 18, April 27, 1889; John M. Langston, "Our Emancipation, Our Progress and Our Future assured alone in regenerated Popular Feeling as sustained by Public Law, 1891," MS. (Fisk University Library).

[31] John M. Langston, "The Liberation and Demands of the Colored American, 1891," MS. (Fisk University Library); *Proceedings of Southern States Convention of Colored Men, Columbia, South Carolina, October 18-25, 1871.*

[32] T. Thomas Fortune, *Black and White; Land, Labor and Politics in the South* (New York, 1884), 112-46, *passim;* Washington *Bee,* February 10, 17, June 26, 1883; New York *Age,* 1882-1883, *passim.*

When colored voters differ among themselves and find themselves
on both sides of the local political contests, they will begin to find
themselves of some political importance, their votes will be sought,
cast, and counted.

What Fortune was advocating was heresy to many colored men,
and a storm of protest raged among Negro leaders. Frederick
Douglass considered the movement ridiculous. To be independent meant to be neutral, and that was no remedy because
a "man can not serve two masters in politics."[33] Notwithstanding the opposition among the older leaders, the movement for
independence in voting gained momentum. Southern leaders
like W. A. Pledger of Atlanta, Georgia, and Charles Hendley
of Huntsville, Alabama, advised colored men to support third-
party and fusion tickets, especially if they favored the interests
of the Negro. Pledger joined the Prohibition party, Hendley
the Fusion party in Alabama, while Negroes in Virginia, North
Carolina, Mississippi, and Tennessee co-operated with fusion
tickets in their states.[34] In some Northern states Negro Democratic organizations were formed.[35] Active support was given
to the Democrats in the campaigns of 1884 and 1892. In fact,
Cleveland received considerable praise from the colored press.[36]
George T. Downing, Robert Purvis, Peter H. Clark, Henry M.
Turner, now a bishop in the African Methodist Episcopal

---

[33] Washington *Bee*, February 10, March 3, 1883; Huntsville (Ala.)
Gazette, May 8, 1886.

[34] Washington *Bee*, April 14, 1883, October 30, November 13, 1886,
April 23, December 3, 1887; Huntsville (Ala.) *Gazette*, September 1,
1881, November 4, 1882, May 17, August 9, 1884, September 5, 1885,
May 15, June 19, October 2, 30, 1886.

[35] Washington *Bee*, April 28, 1886, May 26, July 7, 21, 1888; Wash-
ington *National Leader*, December 8, 1888; Milwaukee *Wisconsin Afro-
American*, October 8, 15, November 8, 1892; Martinsburg (W. Va.)
Pioneer Press, September 6, 1890.

[36] Huntsville (Ala.) *Gazette*, January 16, June 12, December 11, 25,
1886, January 15, 1887; Washington *Bee*, August 14, 21, 1886, July 2,
1887, August 11, October 20, December 10, 22, 1888; New York *Age*,
1884-1886, 1894-1896, *passim*.

Church, Bishop John Brown, T. Thomas Fortune, and Monroe Trotter threw their support to Cleveland.[37]

It is difficult to ascertain the extent of this defection among the masses of Negroes, but it is evident that many disillusioned Negroes did break from their traditional party allegiance, though perhaps not in as great a number as colored Democrats claimed. Moreover, it is probable, as Editor Calvin Chase of the Washington *Bee* said, that the young colored voter had no affection for the Republican party but rather understood that "the attitude in both parties is about the same" with regard to his race. Chase hoped that history would guide the young, intelligent Negro so that he would "shift for himself, make his own terms, exercise his own intelligent discrimination and seek such combinations as will promote the welfare of his people."[38]

In the quest for full citizenship those Negroes who were articulate exhibited no concern for any issues that did not affect their status. They ignored or failed to understand the great issues of the economic revolution that was transforming America and creating complex new problems. Furthermore, they evidenced little interest in foreign affairs except where colored peoples were involved, as in Haiti, Santo Domingo, and Cuba.[39] America's policy regarding the Spanish administration of Cuba was criticized. Negroes chided their government for condemning Spanish brutality in Cuba when its black citizens at home were being lynched, murdered, and denied rights by their white fellow Americans.[40] There was a tendency to identify

[37] Milwaukee *Wisconsin Afro-American,* October 8, 15, November 19, 1892; Milwaukee *Northwestern Recorder,* March 1893; Huntsville (Ala.) *Gazette,* May 3, 1884; Washington *Bee,* November 20, 1886; New York *Globe,* March 10, 1883.

[38] New York *Globe,* September 4, 1886.

[39] Washington *New National Era,* February 3, 17, March 17, 24, 1870, January 5, 1871; Washington *National Leader,* July 18, August 31, 1889.

[40] Cleveland *Gazette,* November 19, December 3, 10, 24, 1898; Richmond (Va.) *Planet,* March 25, 1899.

their struggle with other minority groups. Thus, some support was given to the woman's rights movement, those who resisted Chinese exclusion, and the Irish struggle against the British.[41]

The goal of the Negro remained the complete recognition of his rights. He was irrevocably committed to the principles of democracy and equality as expressed in the Declaration of Independence and Christian dogma. New conditions and new problems gave rise to new proposals, but the formula for solution remained the same: It was the responsibility of government to insure and guarantee each of its citizens opportunity for life, liberty, and the pursuit of happiness through the enactment and enforcement of law.

[41] Washington *New National Era*, January 27, May 12, July 21, October 20, 27, 1870; New Orleans *Weekly Louisianian*, May 30, 1874; Washington *Bee*, September 10, 1887.

C. VANN WOODWARD*

Tom Watson and the Negro in Agrarian Politics

"Consider the advantage of position that Bryan had over me," once wrote Thomas E. Watson, with the vehemence that characterized his later utterances. "His field of work was the plastic, restless, and growing West: mine was the hide-bound, rock-ribbed Bourbon South. Besides, *Bryan had no everlasting and overshadowing Negro Question to hamper and handicap his progress: I HAD.*"[1] There is no doubt that Watson thought of the Negro problem as the nemesis of his career. He wrestled with it mightily all his days. At the outset he came to grips with

*From *The Journal of Southern History,* *IV* (February 1938), 14-33. Reprinted by permission of the publisher.

[1] *Jeffersonian,* January 20, 1910. This weekly paper underwent several changes in title and place of publication. For a while it was called *Watson's Weekly Jeffersonian;* then *"Watson's"* and later *"Weekly"* were dropped from the title. It was published at Atlanta, Thomson, and Augusta.

it boldly and courageously, and in the end he took refuge in every retreat and subterfuge known to Southern politicians.

Born of a slaveholding family of planters in the upper part of the Georgia black belt in 1856, Watson spent an impoverished childhood growing up among the most violent scenes of Reconstruction in the state. The Negroes were in the majority in his county and the adjoining one, and the Ku Klux Klan did its work in that section with remarkable thoroughness.[2]

The class that seized power in Georgia after the overthrow of the Reconstruction regime was neither the old planter oligarchy nor the small farmer. It was the rising class of industrial capitalists, aggressively led by the so-called "Bourbon Triumvirate": the millionaire industrialist, Joseph E. Brown, extensively interested in coal, iron, and railroads; General John B. Gordon, promoter of an astonishing multiplicity of railroad, mining, publishing, insurance, and land schemes; and Alfred H. Colquitt, a representative of the large planter class who was heavily interested in railroads and a participant in several of Gordon's schemes. These three men bandied the highest offices of the state back and forth among themselves from 1872 to 1890. Strict submission was demanded from all classes in the name of "White Supremacy."

In 1880 the small farmer democracy of the rural counties revolted from the "ring-rule" of the industrial capitalists. A major cause of resentment was the sudden resignation from the Senate of Gordon, Colquitt's appointment of Brown to the vacant seat, and Colquitt's candidacy to succeed himself as governor. At the Democratic convention before which Colquitt sought renomination, Tom Watson, then a red-headed youth of twenty-three, made his political debut in the role he played for the next thirty years. In a stirring speech he called for a revolt from the rule of the industrial clique even if it meant

[2] C. Mildred Thompson, *Reconstruction in Georgia, Economic, Social, Political, 1865-1872* (New York, 1915), 366.

splitting the white man's party.[3] The ensuing contest was said to have been "such a tornado of violence as to make all previous disturbances mere child's play."[4] In its effort to employ the Negro vote, the party of white supremacy revived the corrupt methods of the Carpetbaggers as well as its own development, the Ku Klux Klan. "Those of us who were in the thick of that fight," recalled Watson, "will never forget the wild enthusiasm, the whoop and hurrah, with which the Negro, roused from his sleep of more than twelve years, rushed back into political activity."[5] Although the agrarian insurgents seem to have polled a majority of the white vote, they were overwhelmed by the Negro vote brought out by their opponents.[6] From this first experiment in revolt the discontented whites learned that any serious opposition against the business man's domination would be met by the same methods that were used to overthrow the Reconstruction regime, plus some of the methods of the Carpetbaggers themselves.

The career of agrarian rebellion that Watson opened brilliantly in 1880 was virtually closed to him throughout the next decade. The business man and the industrial capitalist were in the saddle, and behind these leaders Georgia plunged forward into the adventure of industrial revolution with a rush of eager enthusiasm that swept aside all restraints. The farmer's troubles were forgotten and his leaders were ignored. Many of the farmers, indeed, were persuaded by the eloquence of Henry W. Grady, the most articulate spokesman of the industrialists, to support the business man's regime. Grady believed that the self-made business man had "sunk the corner-

[3] Atlanta *Daily Constitution*, August 7, 1880.
[4] Isaac W. Avery, *History of Georgia, 1850-1881* (New York, 1881), 555.
[5] Quoted by William H. Skaggs, *The Southern Oligarchy* (New York, 1924), 141.
[6] Rebecca L. Felton, *Memoirs of Georgia Politics* (Atlanta, 1911), 273-74; Avery, *History of Georgia*, 591; Atlanta *Daily Constitution*, September 29, October 9, 1880.

stone of the only aristocracy that Americans should know";[7]
yet he always had a sympathetic word for the farmer. Toward
the end of the eighties the farmers, ripe for renewed revolt,
began to join the National Farmers' Alliance by the thousands.
Grady bent every effort to mollify their discontent and pledge
their loyalty to the industrialist regime. Addressing a great
convention of the Alliance in Atlanta in 1889, he told the
farmers, "There is no room for divided hearts in the South."
Because of the threat of Negro domination all white men
were morally obliged to vote together "without regard to
class."[8] Grady's program meant strict subordination of class
conflict in the South in the interest of the *status quo* of a
business man's regime identified in the popular mind with
white supremacy. There were those, he admitted, who believed
that "the South should divide, the color line be beaten down,
and the southern States ranged on economic or moral questions
as interest or belief demands." This, he asserted, was "the
worst in my opinion that could happen." The only "hope and
assurance of the South" was "the clear and unmistakable domination of the white race." "What God hath separated let no
man join together. . . . Let no man tinker with the work of
the Almighty."[9]

Impressed by such solemn admonitions, the farmer, for the
time being, agreed to subordinate his interests to the demands
of racial solidarity. Grady's death in December, 1889, however,
marked the passing of an era. The following year there occurred a party revolution that filled the offices with men
pledged to the Farmers' Alliance platform. The heir to Grady's
editorial chair took comfort in the reflection that, "After all,
business is the biggest thing in this country. When the princes
of commerce and industry say to the politician that they must

7 Atlanta *Daily Constitution,* August 15, 1880.
8 *Ibid.,* October 25, 1889.
9 Joel Chandler Harris (ed.), *Henry W. Grady: His Life, Writings and
Speeches* (New York, 1890), 99-101.

let dangerous experiments alone they will be heard and obeyed." Furthermore, "There are some things more important than reforms that merely affect the pocket"—namely, white supremacy.[10] The farmer, on the other hand, soon began to despair of gaining his reforms through the old party and to show signs of leaving it to found a party of his own.

Tom Watson, the most outspoken champion of the Alliance platform in the state, was overwhelmingly elected to Congress from the tenth district in 1890. Chosen as a nominee of the Democratic party, he nevertheless felt that his first obligation was to Alliance principles. He therefore refused to enter the Democratic congressional caucus and pledge himself to support a candidate for the speakership who was known to be an enemy of those principles. After canvassing his district he openly broke with the old party and threw in his lot with the Alliance-elected Western congressmen to organize the People's party. As its official leader in the House, and its first member from the South in Congress, Watson was the logical man to formulate the Populist policy toward the Negro. The Farmers' Alliance had already laid the groundwork for the agrarian experiment in interracial co-operation by organizing a million and a quarter Negroes in the Colored Farmers' Alliance.[11] On this foundation Watson sought to construct a political alliance between the races in the South.

According to Watson's plan, the third party was to recruit its ranks from the farmers of all classes and both races and from the working class of both races in the cities. He framed his appeal in this way: "Now the People's Party says to these two men, 'You are kept apart that you may be separately fleeced of your earnings. You are made to hate each other because upon that hatred is rested the keystone of the arch of financial despotism which enslaves you both. You are deceived

10 Atlanta *Constitution*, January 8, 13, 1890.
11 John D. Hicks, *The Populist Revolt* (Minneapolis, 1931), 114-15.

and blinded that you may not see how this race antagonism
perpetuates a monetary system which beggars both'."[12]

Watson believed that interracial co-operation for economic
and political reform was impossible in either of the old parties.
"The Republican Party represented everything which was
hateful to the whites," he declared; "The Democratic Party,
everything which was hateful to the blacks." A new party was
therefore an absolute necessity. This appeal for united action
was framed in terms of economic realism rather than in
the language of idealism. "Gratitude may fail; so may sympathy and friendship and generosity and patriotism; but in
the long run, self-interest *always* controls. Let it once appear
plainly that it is to the interest of a colored man to vote with
the white man, and he will do it." The same rule applied to
the white man's attitude toward the black. "The People's
Party will settle the race question," he announced. "First, by
enacting the Australian ballot system. Second, by offering to
white and black a rallying point which is free from the odium
of former discords and strifes. Third, by presenting a platform
immensely beneficial to both races and injurious to neither.
Fourth, by making it to the *interest* of both races to act together for the success of the platform."[13]

This bold program called for a reversal of many of the
articles of Grady's racial creed, as well as the altering of prejudices and traditions deeply ingrained in Southerners. In place
of race hatred, political proscription, lynch law, and terrorism,
it was necessary to foster tolerance, friendly co-operation, justice, and political rights for the Negro.

Georgia's lynching record in those years stood highest
among the states. It should be the object of the Populist party,
said Watson, to "make lynch law odious to the people."[14]
The state platform of the People's party in 1896 carried a

[12] Thomas E. Watson, "The Negro Question in the South," *Arena*
(Boston, 1889-1909), VI (1892), 548.
[13] *Ibid.*, 544-47.
[14] Atlanta *People's Party Paper*, November 3, 1893.

plank denouncing lynch law, Ku Kluxism, and terrorism, and demanding justice for the Negro. Another plank called for the abolition of the iniquitous convict lease system, which fell heaviest upon the blacks.[15] Negroes became prominent as organizers of the new party and several found high office in the party organization. At the state convention of the party in 1894 Watson seconded the nomination of a Negro "as a man worthy to be on the executive committee of this or any other party from the State at large." "Tell me the use of educating these people as citizens," he demanded, "if they are never to exercise the rights of citizens. (Applause.) Tell me the sense of saying to them. 'You have rights only so long as you live under the benign guardianship of the Democratic party.' (Laughter and applause.)"[16] In the same spirit of racial amity Watson frequently mentioned praiseworthy accomplishments of the Negro race at home and abroad. There was the "manly" conduct of the king of a South African tribe who courageously resisted the encroachments of Cecil Rhodes and British imperialists. Again there was the "good work" of a Negro member of the legislature who was exposing the brutalities practiced upon the convicts leased to Senator Joseph E. Brown's coal mines.[17]

In 1890 the Conservative party in the Lower South began the process of constitutional amendment with the avowed purpose of disfranchising the Negro—thus driving another wedge between the races in the lower classes of society. Discontented whites protested that the amendments might be turned with equal success to the work of disfranchising poor and illiterate members of their own race, and they offered convincing evidence that this was being done.[18] In 1895 Ben Tillman led

[15] Atlanta *Constitution,* August 7, 1896.
[16] Atlanta *People's Party Paper,* May 25, 1894.
[17] *Ibid.,* December 2, 1892; December 29, 1893.
[18] Joseph C. Manning, *The Fadeout of Populism* (New York, 1928), 59; Skaggs, *The Southern Oligarchy,* 142-45.

the movement for a disfranchising amendment in South Carolina. Tom Watson wrote an indignant denunciation of the
proposal:

> All this re-actionary legislation is wrong.
> There can be no sound principle, consistent with our democratic
> theory of government, which says that a negro worth $300 is a better
> citizen than one worth $200.
> Nor is there any satisfactory reasoning to support the claim that
> a negro who can read is better fitted to vote than some who cannot
> read.
> The whole scheme of the democrats of South Carolina is to per-
> petuate the rule of their party. . . .
> Old fashioned democracy taught that a man who fought the battles
> of his country, and paid the taxes of his government, should have a
> vote in the choosing of rulers and the making of laws.[19]

No one was more keenly aware of the overwhelming odds
against the racial aspect of his social program than Tom Watson himself. On the very outset of the Populist movement he
wrote despairingly in an article in the *Arena:*

> You might beseech a Southern white tenant to listen to you upon
> questions of finance, taxation, and transportation; you might demon-
> strate with mathematical precision that herein lay his way out of
> poverty into comfort; you might have him "almost persuaded" to
> the truth, but if the merchant who furnished his farm supplies (at
> tremendous usury) or the town politician (who never spoke to him
> excepting at election times) came along and cried "Negro rule!" the
> entire fabric of reason and common sense which you had patiently
> constructed would fall, and the poor tenant would joyously hug the
> chains of an actual wretchedness rather than do any experimenting
> on a question of mere sentiment. . . . The Negro has been as valu-
> able a portion of the stock in trade of a Democrat as he was of a
> Republican.[20]

Again and again Watson was called upon to meet the Democrats' charge that he was advocating "social equality," encour-
aging "Negro domination," and promoting disloyalty to

[19] Atlanta *People's Party Paper,* November 8, 1895.
[20] Watson, "The Negro Question in the South," *loc. cit.,* 541.

"White Supremacy." He ridiculed these charges as the stale tricks of demagogues and denied their implications. "The question of social equality does not enter into the calculation at all," he declared. "This is a thing each citizen decides for himself." He repeatedly told blacks and whites that he did not advocate social mixing of the races, that he thought it better for both to stay apart. "But when it comes to matters of law and justice," he emphasized, "I despise the Anglo-Saxon who is such an infernal coward as to deny legal rights to any man on account of his color for fear of 'negro domination.' 'Dominate' what? 'Dominate' how? 'Dominate' whom?" It was from his "very pride of race" that there sprang his "intense scorn of that phantasm manufactured by the political bosses and called 'negro domination.' " "Away with such contemptible timidity counsel," he cried. Nor could he see what threat to white supremacy lay in teaching the Negro tenant that he was "in the same boat as the white tenant; the colored laborer with the the white laborer." "Why cannot the cause of one be made the cause of both?" he asked. "Why would this be dangerous? I can see very well where it is dangerous to Ring Rule, to Bossism, the iron rule of the Money Power."[21]

The Negroes responded to Watson's message with great enthusiasm. They thronged to his rallies by the thousands and stood side by side with white farmers listening to him speak from the same platform with speakers of their own race. A favorite device of Watson was to pledge the white listeners to defend the Negro's constitutional rights, making them hold up their hands and promise. Never before or since have the two races in the South come so close together politically. The Negroes, it should be emphasized, continued their support of Populism in the face of as much or more intimidation and violence than they encountered from the Democrats during

[21] Thomas E. Watson, *The Life and Speeches of Thomas E. Watson* (2nd ed., Thomson, Ga., 1911), 128-29; *id.*, "Address to My Fellow Citizens of Georgia," Atlanta *People's Party Paper,* March 17, 1892.

Reconstruction. Negro speakers who campaigned for Watson or other Populist candidates did so at the risk of their lives.

"Political campaigns in the North," wrote a veteran of Alabama Populism, "even at their highest pitch of contention and strife, were as placid as pink teas in comparison with those years of political combat in the South."[22] The pattern of violence, always characteristic of the South, took its shape mainly from the intensification of economic strife by the complexity of race.

One of the most effective workers for Watson's cause was H. S. Doyle, a young Negro preacher of intelligence and courage. In the face of repeated threats upon his life, Doyle made sixty-three speeches in behalf of Watson's candidacy for Congress during the campaign of 1892. Toward the close of that campaign he was threatened with lynching at Thomson and fled to Watson for protection. Watson installed him on his private grounds and sent out riders on horseback for assistance. All night armed farmers poured into Thomson. The next morning the streets were "lined with buggies and horses foaming and tired with travel." All that day and the next night farmers continued to assemble until "fully two thousand" Populists crowded the village—arms stacked on Watson's veranda. Prominent among them was the Populist sheriff of McDuffie County. They marched to the courthouse under arms, where they were addressed by Doyle and Watson. "We are determined," said the latter, "in this free country that the humblest white or black man that wants to talk our doctrine shall do it, and the man doesn't live who shall touch a hair of his head, without fighting every man in the People's party." The farmers remained on guard for two nights.[23]

[22] Manning, *Fadeout of Populism*, 5, 142-44.
[23] *Contested Election Case of Thomas E. Watson vs. J. C. C. Black from the Tenth Congressional District of Georgia* (Washington, 1897), 669, 683, 717, 793-94; Atlanta *Constitution*, October 25, 26, 1892; Augusta *Chronicle*, October 26, 1892.

The spectacle of white farmers riding all night to save a Negro from lynchers was rare in Georgia. So shocking was the incident to the Democratic press that one paper was sure that "Watson has gone mad," and another declared that "the whole South, and especially the tenth district [of Georgia] is threatened with anarchy and communism" because of the "direful teachings of Thomas E. Watson."[24] While Doyle was speaking at Louisville, Georgia, a week later, a shot intended for him struck a white man in the back and killed him. Two days later when Watson and Doyle spoke at Davisboro they were accompanied by a guard of forty men carrying Winchester rifles. In the county where the previous murder occurred a Negro was killed the following week by white Democrats. At Dalton a Negro man who had spoken for the Populists was called out of his home and murdered by unknown men, and at Rukersville five Negro Populists were shot down at the polls by men to whom they were said to have belonged in slavery days. The verdict of "justifiable homicide" in such cases was rarely contested, and then futilely. One estimate had it that fifteen Negro Populists were killed in Georgia during the state election in 1892.[25]

"After that," testified Doyle in regard to the Thomson incident, "Mr. Watson was held almost as a savior by the negroes. The poor ignorant men and women, who so long had been oppressed, were anxious even to touch Mr. Watson's hand, and were often a source of inconvenience to him in their anxiety to see him and shake hands with him, and even to touch him."[26]

[24] Augusta *Chronicle,* October 25, November 6, 1892; Atlanta *Constitution,* October 28, 1892.

[25] Harlem (Georgia) *Farmer's Light,* October 20, 1892; Atlanta *People's Party Paper,* October 14, 28, 1892; *Contested Election Case of Thomas E. Watson vs J. C. C. Black,* 781; Augusta *Chronicle,* November 4, 8, 10, 1892.

[26] *Contested Election Case of Thomas E. Watson vs. J. C. C. Black,* 782.

The sincerity of Watson's appeal to the Negro has been called into question—as has the sincerity of any appeal to the Negro vote. Whatever his motives, nothing that Watson did in this period reflects upon his fidelity. It is interesting to note in passing that W. E. B. Du Bois, a Negro leader not given to uncritical enthusiasm for Southern politicians, was sufficiently convinced of the sincerity of Watson to regard the failure of his movement as a calamity for the Negro race.[27]

The question of what substantial benefit the Negroes derived, or might have reasonably expected to derive, from their loyal and hazardous support of Tom Watson presents some difficulties. In the first place, although Watson waged his fight for Populism with astounding courage and perseverance, and although a majority of the voters seem to have been with him, Populism never achieved power in Georgia, and its program was therefore never put to test. Moreover, in his battle against industrial capitalism Watson sought to align within his ranks all agrarian forces, whether landowners, tenants, or laborers. The Populist ideology was that of the landowner, and at that time the landowning farmers about equaled the landless farmers. On the other hand, the great majority of Negro farmers owned no land. That class contradictions were not magically resolved in the Populist-agrarian potpourri is indicated by various signs. Once the Colored Farmers' Alliance proposed to call a general strike of Negro cotton pickers. Colonel L. L. Polk, president of the National Farmers' Alliance (white) did "not hesitate to advise our farmers to leave their cotton in the fields rather than pay more than 50 cents per hundred to have it picked." The Negroes were attempting "to better their condition at the expense of their white breth-

[27] W. E. B. Du Bois, "Georgia: Invisible Empire State," in Ernest Gruening (ed.), *These United States* (2nd Ser., New York, 1926), 339-40.

ren. Reforms should not be in the interest of one portion of our farmers at the expense of another."[28]

It was fairly plain that what material benefit the landless Negro might expect from Populism must perforce accrue to him from the general improvement to which agrarian interests might aspire through the Populist program of checking the greed of industrial capitalism by government ownership and monetary legislation. The benefits, however substantial, would come indirectly.

More immediate, however, were the political and social profits that the Negro derived from his Populist experience. Tom Watson was perhaps the first native white Southern leader of importance to treat the Negro's aspirations with the seriousness that human strivings merit. For the first time in his political history, the Negro was regarded neither as the incompetent ward of white supremacy, nor as the ward of military intervention, but as an integral part of Southern society with a place in its economy. Grady's assertion in 1889 that "the Negro as a political force has dropped out of serious consideration" was absurd in 1892. Moreover, it was now possible for the Negro to escape the dilemma of selling his vote to the Democrats or pledging it blindly to the Republican bosses. Under the tutelage of Watson and the Populists, also, a part of the Southern white people were learning to regard the Negro as a political ally bound to them by economic ties and a common destiny, rather than as a slender prop to injured self-esteem in the shape of white supremacy. Here was a foundation of political realism upon which some more enduring structure of economic democracy might have been constructed. The destruction of that foundation constitutes a tragic chapter in Southern history.

[28] Editorial in Raleigh *Progressive Farmer,* September 15, 1891. See, also, Washington *National Economist,* September 26, 1891.

The story of how Tom Watson abandoned his dream of uniting the Southern masses of both races against industrial capitalism, and came to be regarded as the leading exponent of racial bigotry, and of how the Southern white masses followed the same course, is a part of the story of how Southern Populism went to seed. It is a small part of the larger story, but a significant part.

"Politically I was ruined," wrote Watson of his predicament after the debacle of Populism in 1896. "Financially I was flat on my back. How near I came to loss of mind only God who made me knows—but I was as near distraction, perhaps, as any mortal could safely be. If ever a poor devil had been outlawed and vilified and persecuted and misrepresented and howled down and mobbed and hooted and threatened until he was well nigh mad, I was he."[29] Time after time since the election of 1892 he had been defeated by the old Reconstruction practices of terror, fraud, chicanery, and intimidation. A part—but only a part—of the methods used to defraud the Populists had been the corruption of the Negro vote, especially in the cities.

Embittered by frustration and by what he considered a betrayal within his own ranks in 1896, Watson retired from public life for a period of eight years. His silence reflected the discouragement of the Populist masses. Twice during this period Watson emerged to denounce the Spanish-American War and to speak for a child-labor amendment, but otherwise he confined his activity to historical writing and law practice. Aroused by the triumph of the reactionary element of the Democratic party that resulted in the nomination of Alton B. Parker, Watson accepted the Populist nomination for president in 1904. His nation-wide campaign reawakened Populist hopes and provided the only diverting element in a dull election, but he was bitterly disappointed in the small vote

[29] Editorial in *Watson's Jeffersonian Magazine* (Atlanta, Thomson, 1907-1917), X (1910), 818. *"Jeffersonian"* was deleted from the title of this magazine in March, 1912.

he received in the South. His next move was to found *Tom Watson's Magazine* in New York and plunge into the muckraking and reform movement with the hope of mobilizing reformers and progressives for Populism.

More and more Watson was coming to regard the Negro as the perennial stumbling block in his path. In 1892 he declared that "The argument against the independent political movement in the South may be boiled down into one word—NIGGER."[30] He scoffed at the argument then. Now in the reform movement he met the same argument. To the plea for government ownership John Sharp Williams and other conservatives replied, as Watson interpreted them: "The North, the East, and the West may adopt Government Ownership of railways, but the South never will—because of the negro." With any other reform, industrial or political, the reply was the same, according to Watson. "No matter what direction Progress would like to take in the South she is held back by the never failing cry of 'Nigger!'

"It sickens me to the very soul to witness the unscrupulous skill, on the one hand, and childlike ignorance and prejudice, on the other, which make the negro question the invincible weapon of Bourbon Democracy in the South."[31]

About this time Watson shifted his position on the Negro and put forth his second answer to the political-racial dilemma that Grady propounded in the eighties. He might be said to have "backed into" the reactionary position, for while still clinging to his older views, he embraced the very doctrine he professed most to despise.

In his campaign for the presidency in 1904 Watson had been met from one end of the South to the other by a revival of the Democratic dialectic of the nineties: "the ominous shadow of

[30] Atlanta *People's Party Paper,* August 26, 1892.
[31] Editorial in *Tom Watson's Magazine* (New York, 1905-1906), II (1905), 19.

negro domination." Elsewhere he ridiculed the cry, but in Georgia he met it with a challenge and a promise to his Democratic enemies. He was "not at all afraid of any negro domination," and never had been. Furthermore, he believed that "the cry that we are in danger from 'the nigger' is the most hypocritical that unscrupulous leadership could invent." What could the Negro do? He had been disfranchised in nearly every state in the South except Georgia. There he had been "white primaried." If the Democrats were honest in their fears, why did they not write the principle of the white primary into the state constitution, as other states had done? He would tell them: "In Georgia they do not dare to disfranchise him [the Negro] because the men who control the Democratic machine in Georgia know that a majority of the whites are against them. They need the negro to beat us with." The white primary, being nothing but a party rule, could be shelved at any time the machine needed to vote the Negro. He therefore pledged his support, and the support of the Populists, to any antimachine Democratic candidate running upon a suitable platform that included a pledge to "a change in our Constitution which will perpetuate white supremacy in Georgia."[32]

Watson's offer did not long go begging. Early the following year a serious rift opened in the Democratic party between the conservative machine, led by Clark Howell, and the opposing wing, led by Hoke Smith. Both men sought Watson's assistance in their race for governor in 1906.[33] Smith outbid his opponent, however, by writing what Herbert Quick pronounced "the most radical platform ever adopted, with perhaps one exception, by a state convention of either of the two great parties of these times."[34] Containing demands for several reforms

[32] Speeches of the 1904 campaign, Watson MSS., University of North Carolina Library, Chapel Hill; Atlanta *Constitution,* September 2, 1904.

[33] Clark Howell to Watson, August 4, 1905; Hoke Smith to Watson, September 16, 1905, Watson MSS.

[34] Herbert Quick, "Hoke Smith and the Revolution in Georgia," *The Reader* (New York, 1902-1908), X (1907), 241.

aimed at direct popular government together with demands
for stringent control and regulation of railroads and corporations, Smith's platform might have been written by a Populist. In curious juxtaposition with these reforms, the following
pledge appeared permanently in Smith's paper: "THE ELI-
MINATION OF THE NEGRO FROM POLITICS . . . BY
LEGAL AND CONSTITUTIONAL METHODS . . . WITH-
OUT DISFRANCHISING A SINGLE WHITE MAN."

With some difficulty Watson was finally persuaded to join
hands with his former enemy. "Hoke Smith is trying to do
what we want done and cannot do ourselves," he announced
to the Populists. With his assistance Smith defeated Howell
in the most bitterly fought race since the nineties. Race hatred
was keyed to an unprecedented pitch, and lynching flourished.
An unforeseen sequel to the campaign was the Atlanta race
riot of 1906, the most hideous the state ever experienced. However remote Watson's connection with it, that tragedy was a
milepost in the road he now traveled, and others not unlike
it lay before him.

In rationalizing his desertion of his Negro allies Watson had
argued that only by such a sacrifice could Populism triumph
in the South. "The white people dare not revolt so long as
they can be intimidated by the fear of the negro vote," he explained. Since the "bugaboo of negro domination" was removed,
however, "every white man would act according to his own
conscience and judgment in deciding how he should vote."[35]
There was another consideration that he did not mention.
With the Negro vote eliminated, Watson and the white Populists stood in much the same relation toward the two factions
of the Democratic party as the Negro had previously occupied
toward Populists and Democrats: they held the balance of
the power.

Somehow the white Populist revolt, for which Negro disfran-

[35] Atlanta *Journal*, July 27, 1906.

chisement was to prepare the way, never did occur. True, Watson made some pretense of running for president in 1908, but the main exception he took to the candidacy by Bryan was the liberal Democratic attitude toward the Negro. He stressed the Japanese problem of the West Coast as the chief bond of union between his old agrarian allies of the West and his own section—which had its Negro problem. Western Populists could not understand his position on the Negro and fell away from him, as did also his Progressive friends (for example, Upton Sinclair) in the East. He changed the name of his magazine, which was becoming narrowly sectional in interest, to *Watson's Jeffersonian Magazine* and moved its headquarters from New York to Hickory Hill, his home.

Likewise on the local front the Populist revolt failed to materialize. Although Smith accomplished wonders in fulfilling his reform pledges, frequently consulting the wishes of his Populist ally, Watson became convinced that Smith was attempting to undermine his power by destroying the "county-unit system," which gave rural counties an advantage out of proportion to their population. *"The evil of pure democracy,"* proclaimed Watson, recalling Calhoun, *"is that the minority have no protection from the majority."*[36] In 1908 he shifted his support to Joseph M. Brown, son of his old enemy Joseph E. Brown, and defeated Smith. That Brown, besides being a defender of the county-unit system, was also an outspoken champion of railroads and corporate interests, as well as a bitter critic of organized labor and reformers, did not seem to trouble Watson. Instead, he took pleasure in reflecting that "we hold the balance of power in the country counties and the country counties rule the state."[37] Thenceforth he succeeded in establishing himself as a virtual boss of state politics by shifting this balance of power from one faction of the Democrats to the other.

[36] *Jeffersonian,* April 2, May 3, 1908.   [37] *Ibid.,* November 12, 1908.

The next stage in the development of Watson's policy toward the Negro followed from his conclusion that he had been wrong in supporting Smith's disfranchisement program. The opponents of the measure had been correct, he decided, in holding that it would eliminate illiterate whites and encourage literate Negroes. The idea developed into an issue in one of his campaigns against Smith and took on exaggerated proportions in his mind: "it gives the negro the balance of power," he maintained. "It brings back the danger of negro domination. It imperils white supremacy. . . . It is a stimulant to them to learn to read and write." Therefore all such half measures were inadequate and more drastic action was demanded in face of the menace. "The hour has struck for the South to say that the Fifteenth Amendment is not law, and will no longer be respected." The Republican party was split against itself and the South and West "find that their interests coincide on the race question." "This is a white man's civilization, and the white man must maintain it."[38]

At this point in the development of his ideology Watson had arrived somewhere near the position that Mr. Justice Taney announced in 1857: that the Negro had "no rights or privileges but such as those who held the power and the government might choose to grant them." This was as reactionary a policy as any serious leader of the South dared advance in Watson's period. Yet he was destined to carry his position even further toward reactionism.

At the seat of Watson's confusion was the fact that he was still thinking in the capitalist-agrarian conflict pattern of the nineties in an era where that dichotomy no longer applied. He still thought of the farmers as solidly aligned against the industrialists, and ignored or sought to explain away the rift in the agrarian ranks clearly implied by the great increase in tenancy between 1890 and 1910. The fact that he now esti-

[38] *Ibid.*, September 8, 1910.

mated his wealth at $258,000, counted himself one of the largest planters in the state, and had twice as many tenants on his roll books as his father owned slaves did not prevent his thinking of himself as a "farmer." As for a certain agitator who was "demanding that land ownership be restricted to his own narrow notions" and seeking to "sow discord and strife between landlord and tenant," Watson put him down as *"A Contemptible little Demagogue."*[39] It was nonsense to say any industrious tenant could not acquire land: some farmers simply "prefer to rent." Privately he confessed the fear that Socialism would "sweep the rural districts like a prairie fire if not opposed in time,"[40] and publicly he did his bit in opposing the doctrine by a voluminous series of articles and pamphlets attacking Socialism and defending rent, interest, and land ownership as "not only just but sacred." Daniel De Leon, answering the attack in a series of articles, remarked that "Mr. Watson and his 'Niggers' have their hands in each others' wool." "Hit the Junker," he said, "and the capitalist will yell—we are seeing the spectacle in Great Britain in the matter of the House of Lords; hit the capitalist, and the Junker will shriek—we are seeing the spectacle in Mr. Watson's deportment."[41]

One way of concealing the cleavage in the agrarian ranks was to identify tenancy, landlessness and dependency with the Negro—who was by this time politically incapacitated, friendless, and generally accepted as an incompetent ward of white supremacy. Calling attention to the alleged increase of impertinence, rape, and social ambitiousness on the part of Negroes, Watson now advocated a policy of repression so severe and so firm that "the great mass of the negroes would gradually reconcile themselves to the condition of a recog-

[39] *Ibid.*, February 17, 1910.
[40] Watson to Dr. John N. Taylor, April 23, 1910, Watson MSS.
[41] Daniel De Leon, *Watson on the Gridiron* (New York, 1911), 20, 31, 39.

nized peasantry—a laboring class."[42] It is clear from the context that Watson employed the word "peasantry" in the sense of the word "peonage." Shortly after he was chosen vice president of the Confederacy, Alexander H. Stephens said of the new nation: "Its corner-stone rests upon the great truth that the negro is not equal to the white man; that slavery—subordination to the superior race—is his natural and normal condition." Tom Watson, who occupied Stephens' old chair in Congress for a term in the nineties, held much the same idea in 1910 that his predecessor had held in 1861.

In the course of Watson's gyrations as political boss of the state, his traditional battle against plutocracy, corporate interests, and industrial capitalism underwent a gradual transformation. As his interests narrowed to sectional issues the enemies became exclusively "Yankee" corporations and "Northern" capitalists. Then little or nothing was heard of them at all. In their place was substituted "The Roman Catholic Hierarchy: The Deadliest Menace to Our Liberties and Our Civilization"; Socialism, which would reduce all women "to the same level of sexual depravity"; and the Northern Jew, Leo Frank, who had violated Southern womanhood, whose rich Jewish friends on Wall Street had corrupted Georgia courts, who, in fact, deserved to be lynched—and was.

Perennially defeated in their ancient feud with industrial capitalism, the Southern agrarian masses joined in Watson's later crusades with great enthusiam. They were more exciting, the victories more immediate, and the enemy more vulnerable. Socialists could be jailed, priests booed, and Jews lynched.

For his attacks upon the Negro, Watson reserved a peculiar venom lacking in his other crusades. Perhaps the explanation lay in the fact that of all his later victims the Negro was the

[42] Thomas E. Watson, "The Negro Question," *Watson's Jeffersonian Magazine*, I (1907), 1032-40.

only one that he had once befriended—and later betrayed. Few
if any Southern politicians rivaled Watson in his insistence
upon *"the superiority of the Aryan"* and the "HIDEOUS,
OMINOUS, NATIONAL MENACE" of Negro domination.
These onslaughts were sometimes prefaced by the conventional tribute to a Negro mammy,[43] and the familiar claim—
"If there is any human creature that I do understand it is
the Southern negro." The attacks usually involved a sex
theme and necessitate only a few examples to make clear
their trend:

> They will ravish girls who have hardly passed babyhood; they
> will go in squads, surprise some white man, and take turns lying
> with his wife, in his presence: they will grab a white girl at her
> door, gag her, drag her away to the negro section, violate her re-
> peatedly all night long, then brutally kill her, and throw her la-
> cerated body into the street. They will rape an old woman who is
> so bent and enfeebled by age that she can hardly walk with the
> aid of a stick. The very animals in the stables are not safe from their
> bestiality.[44]

One of the few Southern politicians who chose to ignore
the outcry created by the Roosevelt-Booker Washington
luncheon (Watson was one of the President's luncheon guests
himself a few years after), he later pursued the Negro leader
relentlessly. Washington, said Watson, was as "imitative as
an ape; was as bestial as a gorilla"; and was once "chased out
of a white woman's sleeping apartment in New York *and
beaten as he ran from street to street.*"[45] In his publications
Watson frequently condoned the lynching of a Negro, and
in fact openly advocated the practice. *"Lynch law is a good
sign,"* he wrote; *"it shows that a sense of justice yet lives
among the people."* He himself would no more hesitate to

[43] Thomas E. Watson, *Bethany: A Story of the Old South* (New York,
1904), 15.
[44] *Id., Sketches* (Thomson, Ga., 1912), 40.
[45] Harlem (Georgia) *Columbia Sentinel,* November 7, 1919.

help lynch a Negro rapist than he would to "shoot a mad dog, a wolf, or a rattlesnake." "In the South," he explained, "we have to lynch him [the Negro] occasionally, and flog him, now and then, to keep him from blaspheming the Almighty, by his conduct, on account of his smell and his color."[46] Georgia had managed to retain pre-eminence in lynchings over her sister states by a safe margin ever since the nineties, but in this period, the second decade of the century, that pre-eminence was annually written in two figures, while her closest rivals trailed with one.

It was a far cry from the Jeffersonian equalitarianism and humanitarianism of the nineties to the Watson of 1920. His changing attitude toward the Negro was symptomatic of the changing racial views and policies of agrarian politics in the South.

[46] *Jeffersonian,* January 2, May 15, 1913; January 4, 1917.

DEWEY W. GRANTHAM, JR.*

The Progressive Movement
and the Negro

The Progressive movement in the United States affected
the whole of American life during the two decades before
World War I. Walter E. Weyl noted that "men in the Middle
West, in the Far West, in the East and South; men in the
factory and on the farm; men, and also women . . . are looking at America with new eyes, as though it were the morning
of the first day." William Allen White, himself one of the
Progressives, remembered that reform was everywhere:

A sudden new interest in the under dog was manifest in the land.
. . . Some way, into the hearts of the dominant middle class of
this country, had come a sense that their civilization needed re-
casting, that their government had fallen into the hands of self-

* From *The South Atlantic Quarterly*, *LIV* (October 1955), 461-77.
Reprinted by permission of the publisher.

The Progressive Movement and the Negro 63

seekers, that a new relation should be established betwen the haves
and the have-nots . . . because we felt that to bathe and feed the
under dog would release the burden of injustice on our conscience.

Yet, despite the comprehensive nature of their proposed reforms, American liberals of the Progressive era gave little attention to the status of the Negro, which all agreed represented one of the nation's social and political problems. This
omission in the Progressive program poses the provocative
question of why. By such indices as ownership of property,
rate of literacy, entry into new occupations, and development
of social and cultural institutions American Negroes made
substantial advances during the four decades following Appomattox. The material progress and industrial leadership
epitomized by the Atlanta Compromise and the efforts of
Booker T. Washington won increasing endorsement of whites
both North and South and apparently improved the relations
between the two races. But the progress, particularly after
1877, was exasperatingly slow and painful, and Negroes remained in large part landless, uneducated, and diseased—the
downtrodden bottom rail.

As the new century opened, the difficulty of reconciling the
American ideals of democracy and legal processes with the
prejudices of the dominant groups was outlined in sharp
relief. The heavy lynching tolls of the 1890's continued into
the twentieth century, and Negroes were often victims of
antiquated convict leasing and chain-gang practices, of peonage, and of inferior accommodations on public carriers and
in public places. Furthermore, the process of legal disfranchisement by the Southern states was well on the way to completion, and even where the Negro retained the right to vote,
he could not participate in the Democratic primaries that
really controlled Southern elections. In many ways the thirty-
year period after 1877 was an era of retrogression for the
Negro. Walter Hines Page wrote of the Southern Negro in
1907, "I'm afraid he's a 'goner.' " To liberals the Negro prob-

lem posed a challenge, but a challenge that might be ration-
alized and explained away or evaded.

Generalization about the nature of Progressivism is not
without hazards. The Progressives were reformers, but reform
could mean "all sorts of things"; Ralph H. Gabriel has called
it "a potpourri of social theories and beliefs." A writer in
1912 observed that Progressivism was "inchoate and speaks
with many voices. To many men it means many things."
Whatever the regional and individual variations among
Progressives, they were optimists who held fast to the idea
of progress. The evils and imperfections that had come
with the powerful economic tides of a changing America
could be removed through the agency of the state. The
rules must be changed somewhat, but not radically; economic power must be responsible to the government, and
"new weapons of democracy" must make the government responsible to the people. There must be legislation to improve
the lot of the working man, to restrain monopoly and abolish special privilege, to widen the electoral franchise and institute direct democracy. Man was fundamentally good and
rational; if dealt with fairly he would deal justly with his fellow men. The Progressives believed, as William Allen White
wrote, that if the underdog were given "a decent kennel,
wholesome food, regular baths, properly directed exercise,
[and if someone would] cure his mange and abolish his
fleas, and put him in the blue-ribbon class, all would be well."

If Progressives were convinced of the possibility of progress,
if they advocated the abandonment of laissez-faire and the
use of positive government to promote that progress, if they
desired to help the depressed elements in the nation's population and to answer "the simple demand for fair dealing,
[and] for exact justice between man and man," it is pertinent to ask what they did about the nation's major minority
problem. As individuals and as members of philanthropic
groups many Progressives considered the Negro question at

some length and made significant contributions to the amelioration of the conditions that created the problem. To answer the question "What did American liberals do about the Negro in a political way?" requires a longer examination.

Progressive reformers appeared first on the municipal level; their attention was largely focused on breaking the control of the political machines, on effecting tax reforms, and on establishing a more wholesome relationship between public utilities and city governments. Mark Fagan and George L. Record, for instance, strove to improve the educational, health, and recreational facilities of Jersey City, but they fought their most vigorous battles for tax reform and control of public utilities. Tom Johnson made Cleveland "the best governed city in America," but his major efforts were to secure municipal ownership of street railways and to equalize the city's taxes. Joseph W. Folk flashed into the national limelight because of his sensational exposures of the corrupt alliance between business and government in St. Louis. In California the Los Angeles nonpartisan movement aimed at breaking the control of the Southern Pacific machine. Negroes as well as whites might benefit from reduced street railway fares, from tax reassessment, and from better school facilities, but the most spectacular municipal reforms did not occur in the South, where most Negroes were concentrated, and when good government movements did reach Southern cities, Negroes seldom shared equally in such reforms. At any rate, the Negro question was incidental to other reforms supported on the city level during the Progresssive period.

Much the same was true of Progressivism on the state level. Robert M. La Follette of Wiconsin was a democrat in the best sense of the word; he possessed a genuine concern for the rights and dignity of the individual and a keen desire to promote the welfare of the depressed man. La Follette, like most Progressives, felt that most political issues had a moral answer, but he saw that economic power was the keystone in the arch of American society. Therefore it was necessary to solve in some fashion the problem of the misuse of economic power, whether by aggregations of powerful business corporations, as in Wisconsin, or by strong organizations of labor, as in California. For this reason Progressives across the land concentrated their efforts toward handling the problem of the monopolization of economic forces; their belief in democracy led them to sponsor numerous democratic devices in an effort to make economic power responsible to political authority. There were state and regional variations, but in all states where Progressivism was strong Progressive leaders concentrated on the problem of dealing with powerful organizations of capital or labor and widening the base of a political democracy to nourish the state government.

The concern of political reformers on the state and local levels with the regulation of privilege and monopoly and their efforts to forge new "weapons of democracy" did not prevent them from attacking many specific problems involving social welfare. There were laws to abolish child labor, to regulate the working conditions of women, to provide for workmen's compensation, to increase the appropriations for public education, and to establish more adequate institutions for the care of unfortunates. Negroes might benefit from all of these reforms, but the fact was there were relatively few Negroes outside of the South before the World War, and the Progressive movement was most effective in other regions. The Negro question for such non-Southern Progressives was thus a theoretical question or at most a national problem. Meanwhile, state and local Progressives focused their attention on their own pressing concerns.

There were reform governors and liberal leaders in the South during the Progressive period. Attempts were made there to regulate more effectively railroads and other corporations, to provide tax reforms, to abolish free passes and corrupt lobbying practices. Primary elections came into widespread use, and corrupt-practices legislation was enacted. The convict-leasing system was abolished, beginnings were made in the regulation of child labor, legislation to control the liquor traffic was adopted, and increased appropriations were made for public education and health facilities, agricultural services, and state care of unfortunates. Negroes undoubtedly profited from much of this reform program despite the fact that most of its political sponsors were aiming at "Progressivism for whites only." But while the Negro might benefit from such reforms, their passage often cost his race a heavy price. This was true because the strongest group of Southern Progressives —those who sponsored the major reforms—were insurgent politicians who came to power not only because they denounced the corporations and sponsored a program of neo-Populism but also because many of them made the race issue their chief stock-in-trade and led such anti-Negro movements as that of disfranchisement. The strongest supporters of these political leaders were the most rabid negrophobes. The Vardamans and Hoke Smiths might have represented "a genuine movement for a more democratic government in the South," as Ray Stannard Baker contended, but their democracy was for whites only and did great harm to the cause of the Negro and to good relations between blacks and whites.

Among another group of Southern liberals during the Progressive era were such men and women as Charles B. Aycock, Edwin A. Alderman, Walter Hines Page, Edgar Gardner Murphy, and Julia Tutwiler: men and women who worked for education, good government, the regulation of child labor, prohibition, and help for the Negroes. Believing that the South's hope lay in industrial and educational progress, they were more conciliatory toward the corporations than were the agrarian Progressives and less enthusiastic about vigorous government, although in their humanitarianism and middle-class approach they were similar to Progressives in other regions. Clearly, their restraint in dealing with the race

question, their constructive work for education, and their
espousal of such reforms as the abolition of child labor and
of the convict-leasing system made a greater contribution to
the progress of Negroes than did the work of the more radical
agrarian leaders. But they were unwilling and unable to sponsor reforms for the Negro that would drastically change the
relationship of the two races in the South. Furthermore, while
their concern for social justice might be real, most of them
were not in politics, and they were often opposed to the
agrarian Progressives who were in power. Their interest in
the advancement of the Negro might be genuine, but it was
also paternalistic and philanthropic; their solution lay within the framework of white supremacy.

Thousands of people in the South wished the Negro well,
but, as a contemporary Progressive noted, "The South is psy-
chologically cramped." The ideology of white supremacy was
all pervasive, and few were the Southerners who would
answer in the affirmative Ray Stannard Baker's question,
"Does democracy really include Negroes as well as white
men?" Baker himself spoke of "a vigorous minority point of
view," which he labeled the "broadest and freest thought" of
the South: "a party of ideas, force, convictions, with a definite constructive programme." Yet the philosophy of this group
rested on the maintenance of "racial integrity," the "gospel
of industrial education," and disfranchisement. Charles H.
Brough, professor of Economics and Sociology at the University of Arkansas, spoke for them when he declared: "As the
sons of proud Anglo-Saxon sires, we of the South doubt seriously the wisdom of the enfranchisement of an inferior race."
These "liberals" expressed their belief in progress for the
Negroes, but, as Brough said: "I believe that by the recognition of the fact that in the Negro are to be found the essential
elements of human nature, capable of conscious evolution
through education and economic and religious betterment,
we will be led at last to a conception of a world of unity,

whose Author and Finisher is God." Even Edgar Gardner Murphy, one of the Southerners most concerned with social justice, held Negroes to be a "backward and essentially unassimilable people," whom the "consciousness of kind" would forever set apart from the whites, whatever the race's advancement.

If the race problem was a national concern, as some people said it was, what were the attitudes of the national parties and political leaders as the twentieth century ushered in the Progressive period? Party pronouncements avoided the Negro question or at most had little to say on the subject. The Populist platform of 1896 condemned "the wholesale system of disfranchisement adopted in some States as unrepublican and undemocratic." The Socialist Labor platform in 1896 called for the equal right of suffrage without regard to color. The Republicans condemned lynching and termed "revolutionary" certain devices designed to overthrow the Fifteenth Amendment. In 1904 they called for a Congressional investigation to determine whether the vote had been unconstitutionally limited in any state and threatened proportionate reductions in representation if such restrictions were found to exist. In 1908 they asked for the enforcement of the Civil War amendments while reminding Negroes that the Republican party had been their "constant friend" for fifty years. These promises, it soon developed, were about as far as the party was willing to go on the Negro problem. The truth was that the Republicans had all but deserted the Negro. The Democratic position was well stated in the party's platform in 1904. While criticizing Republican imperialism for following one set of laws "at home" and another "in the colonies," the Democrats declared: "To revive the dead and hateful race and sectional animosities . . . means confusion, distraction of business, and the reopening of wounds now happily healed."

The literature of the muckrakers gave attention to the

position of the Negro. Disfranchisement, sharecropping, peonage, racial segregation, the Negro's failure to obtain justice
in the courts, lynchings, and race riots were seized upon as
worthy materials by such writers as Richard Barry, Benjamin
O. Flower, and William English Walling. Ray Stannard
Baker's articles in the *American Magazine,* though perhaps
not muckraking in the strict sense of the term, were widely
read and were published in book form in 1908 under the
title *Following the Color Line.* But Americans failed, somehow, to get very excited about muckraking materials on the
Negro, and the Negro question proved a poor second to such
topics as corporation evils and political corruption.

If the muckrakers failed to arouse widespread interest in
the status of the American Negro, the same could not be said
of President Theodore Roosevelt. Roosevelt expressed a deep
concern for the Negroes, and his actions and his utterances
stimulated avalanches of editorial copy. The President's close-
ness to Booker T. Washington, his denunciation of lynching
and disfranchisement, and his announced determination to see
that the Negro received his due generated a wave of hope
among liberals on the race question and among the Negroes
themselves. But what could Roosevelt do? As he wrote Albion
W. Tourgée in the fall of 1901, "I have not been able to think
out any solution of the terrible problem offered by the presence of the negro on this continent. . . ." He had decided,
however, that "the only wise and honorable and Christian
thing to do is to treat each black man and each white man
strictly on his merits as a man." His objective for the Negro
came to be "cautiously, temperately, and sanely, to raise him
up."

In practice even this modest goal was beset with difficulties.
Roosevelt might appoint only "reputable and upright colored
men to office," as was his constant claim, but by doing so he
alienated the whites in the South who were otherwise attracted
to the Republican party. He was interested in building up the

Republican party in the South and therefore anxious "not to shock southern sentiment," although, as he wrote Lyman Abbott, it would be a serious mistake to let Southerners "think that they were blameless, or to let them cast the blame on anyone else." The mounting pressure on the part of white Republicans in the South for a lily-white party led Roosevelt to seek middle ground. His philosophy was well stated in a letter to Booker T. Washington in June, 1904: "The safety for the colored man in Louisiana is to have a white man's party which shall be responsible and honest, in which the colored man shall have representation but in which he shall not be the dominant force—a party in which, as is now the case in the Federal service under me, he shall hold a percentage of the offices but in which a majority of the offices shall be given to white men of high character who will protect the negro before the law." This was to remain essentially Roosevelt's position. He contended that his administration through the federal courts had accomplished a good deal to break up Negro peonage in the South and to secure equal facilities for Negroes on interstate carriers, but he saw little hope of federal action to enforce the Fifteenth Amendment, and in 1908 opposed including such a threat in the Republican platform. The principal hope of the Negro, he declared, must lie in the sense of justice and good will of Southerners, for the Northern people could do little for him. But Southerners, he found, continued to show a "wrong-headedness and folly" about the race question, while men like Oswald Garrison Villard and Charles Francis Adams, who had a genuine interest in promoting the Negro cause, had in the President's opinion "frittered away their influence" until they had no weight with either party.

Theodore Roosevelt's correspondence reveals the enigmatic quality of the Negro problem in his mind during the first dozen years of the century. Like his contemporaries, he never found an adequate solution, although he probably gave more thought to it than most other political leaders on the national scene. The "condition of violent chronic hysteria" on the subject in the South baffled him, and at times he felt that the region never made any progress on the race problem unless forced by outside pressure. Yet in the end he was not sure that his own efforts, which were certainly interpreted in the South as outside pressure, had been of much avail. He agreed with Owen Wister that the Negroes as a race and in the mass were "altogether inferior to the whites," and that the progress of the race would be slow and painful, but he did believe that progress was possible. After his action in the Brownsville affair, he became increasingly suspicious of the more radical Negro leaders and of what he called "shortsighted white sentimentalists." By the middle of his second administration, many Negroes and their white supporters had become convinced that they could expect little in the way of positive aid from Roosevelt. Nevertheless, the President was right when he wrote in 1908: ". . . I have stood as valiantly for the rights of the negro as any president since Lincoln. . . ."

The election of William Howard Taft promised small encouragement for a positive program to advance the cause of Negroes. Taft was a peaceful man and refused to ruffle the political waters by making anything of the race question.

But, as the strong tides of Progressivism began to roll through the major parties on the national level, advocates of Negro progress began to experience a new optimism and a faith that Progressive ideals might also include the Negro. For a time the greatest expectations centered in the Progressive revolt in the Republican party and in Theodore Roosevelt's embryonic Progressive party with its liberal promises of positive federal action to promote the social welfare. Here, such leaders as W. E. Burghardt Du Bois felt, was "a splendid chance for a third party movement, on a broad platform of votes for Negroes and the democratization of industry." But when Roosevelt decided to endorse the organization of the new party on a lily-white basis in the South, in the hope that a strong, permanent party might thus be established in that region, he lost the support of many Negroes, including such leaders as Du Bois. The former President attempted to straddle the perplexing issue by advocating one policy for the North, where it was possible "to bring the best colored men into the movement on the same terms as the white men," and another for the South, where "actual conditions and actual needs and feelings" dictated a traditionally Southern approach. Roosevelt still believed that the Negro's best hope lay with the "intelligent and benevolent" whites of the South. "We have made the Progressive issue a moral, not a racial issue," he declared.

With their hopes thus dashed, where could Progressive Negro leaders turn? The Republicans under Taft provided no hope for a Progressive era. With some misgivings, many of the more militant Negro leaders accepted the New Freedom of Woodrow Wilson, aware of the danger posed by the South's part in the Wilson movement and of Wilson's own background, but encouraged by the liberalism that he represented and by certain promises he was understood to have made. One Negro reminded Wilson in the summer of 1913, "We enlisted with the delight of children at play under your standard and fought a good fight. . . ." Having helped elect the new President, Negroes turned to his administration for a share of the patronage and for additional evidences of justice to their race. The editor of the New York *Age* expressed the attitude of many Negroes when he wrote: "The race, as a whole, is not so deeply concerned in the question of the appointment of Negroes to office as it is [in] the attitude President Wilson will assume—whether he will give a helping hand to a struggling people or whether he will co-ooperate with those who believe that it is humane and American to do all in their power to keep the Negro down, thereby hindering the progress of the Nation."

Negro leaders were soon disappointed by Woodrow Wilson's course. The new President's attitude toward the Negro, as Arthur S. Link has said, was characteristically Southern. While he abhorred Southern demagogues who made the race issue a bête noire, his feeling toward the Negro was at best one of tolerance and kindliness, strongly paternalistic. He soon found that it was difficult enough to carry the South with him in the enactment of his major program and that to make an issue of the race question would jeopardize measures which he considered much more important than a frontal attack on a difficult minority problem. Thus it was that he allowed racial segregation among federal employees in certain of the federal departments, refused to make many Negro appointments, and failed to appoint a federal commission to investigate the Negro situation as some people urged. Southerners in Washington, led by James K. Vardaman, were vociferous in their demands that no Negroes be appointed to federal positions. When the news of one Negro appointment spread, Thomas Dixon wrote to Wilson to say, "I am heartsick over the announcement that you have appointed a Negro to boss white girls as Register of the Treasury." The President's reply was reassuring to white Southerners: "We are handling the force of colored people who are now in the departments in just the way they ought to be handled. We are trying—and by degrees succeeding—a plan of concentration which will put them all together and will not in any one bureau mix the two races." Wilson explained his dilemma to Oswald Garrison Villard in August, 1913: "It would be hard to make any one understand the delicacy and difficulty of the situation I find existing here with regard to the colored people." Emphasizing such matters as the tariff and antitrust legislation, Wilson viewed the Negro problem as a peripheral issue and one that was increasingly irritating. He desired to avoid "a bitter agitation" and to hold things "at a just and cool equipoise."

The disillusionment on the part of Negro leaders was rapid and eventually complete. Booker T. Washington wrote in late summer, 1913: "I have recently spent several days in Washington, and I have never seen the colored people so discouraged and bitter. . . ." The Negro press, Negro leaders, and men like Villard protested, but the President remained aloof. By 1916 Du Bois felt that the political situation was hopeless.

Still, many of the more moderate Negro leaders, such as Robert R. Moton of Tuskegee, admired Wilson for his accomplishments and for the idealism that permeated his addresses. Moton wrote Wilson late in 1916, "I realized that it was embarrassing and perhaps unwise for you to make any reference to the race question as it might perhaps hazard in some way the other important policies of your administration, but now that your election is assured and your policies are pretty definitely established and accepted by the nation as a whole, I am wondering if you could refer in some way to the ten or eleven millions of Negroes in our country." The President promised to do his best, but he was not optimistic. ". . . the truth is," he wrote, "that I have not been able to form a confident judgment as to what would be effective and influential." Nor did he form such a judgment.

The East St. Louis riot of July 1917, brought heated demands to the Wilson administration for action against such "unchecked savagery." The lynchings in 1918 and the discriminations against Negroes in the armed forces brought further protests, while the President's course on the race question at the Paris Peace Conference was also criticized by some Negro spokesmen. Wilson publicly announced his abhorrence of lynching and commended the valor of the Negro soldiers, but he gave no indication that he considered the Negro problem of primary importance. It seems fair to say that he never conceived of the Negro question in a broad sense as a federal problem. At any rate, the more extreme

Negro leaders would have echoed the statement of a Philadelphia Negro, James S. Stemons, who wrote Woodrow Wilson in November, 1920: "The verdict of the masses, regardless of race or creed or clan, has long been that while you were vigorously preaching one thing you were, when expedience demanded it, as vigorously practicing the direct opposite."

If sectionalism and racial prejudice frustrated any possibilities of direct action on the Negro question by Woodrow Wilson's New Freedom and Theodore Roosevelt's New Nationalism, the same was true even of the Socialist party in its consideration of the problem. Socialists in the South proved no more tolerant on the race question than non-Socialists, and this prejudice was not restricted to the South. Victor Berger, for instance, declared in 1902: "There can be no doubt that the negroes and mulattoes constitute a lower race—that the Caucasians and indeed even the Mongolians have the start on them in civilization by many thousand years—so that negroes will find it difficult ever to overtake them." About the best the Socialists could do was to advertise Socialism as exclusively an economic movement, having nothing to do with social equality. Indeed, moderate Socialists contended that the races did not want to live together and that capitalism was at fault, since it forced them to do so. Eugene Debs opposed all discrimination, and the left-wing Socialists urged that racial prejudice be wiped out. But the Socialist party in the period before World War I made no real opposition to Negro discriminations as such.

It will be helpful at this point to differentiate between certain practical considerations that entered into the failure of Progressives to deal with the race question and the more fundamental philosophical background that conditioned their attitudes toward the Negro. As for the practical considerations, the fact was that the Negro problem prior to the World War was still essentially sectional. A great majority of the Negroes were still concentrated in the South, and the leading Progressives, such as Robert M. La Follette, Hiram W. Johnson, and Albert R. Cummins, operated in other regions. They never really came in contact with the Negro question, at least in a situation where they could make a direct contribution to its solution. They could adopt academically a liberal position on the question, and they sometimes took an incidental stand in Congress, but that was all. Such matters as suffrage and the whole broad question of social legislation were still considered the primary responsibility of state and local governments, although the Progressives generally emphasized a more vigorous central government. Many of the Progressives, however, were averse to centralized power, as was true of supporters of Wilson's original program. Another consideration was the inability of Negro leaders and their most zealous white supporters to agree upon a positive program or upon the means necessary to advance their cause.

To explain the philosophical limitations of the Progressive movement in facing the Negro question in American democracy is more difficult. It would appear paradoxical that a philosophy which emphasized the worth and the dignity of man and which laid stress on the democratic process should reveal this blind spot in regard to what was really a complete refutation of its most sacred premises.

One of the keys to this apparent enigma is to be found in the attitude of Americans during the period between 1898 and 1918 toward imperialism and the so-called "backward" races that were the subjects of imperialism. Progressives were no more willing to accord equal civil and social rights to the people recently subjugated by the American republic than were the majority of Americans. Most of them agreed with the imperialistic views of Theodore Roosevelt and Albert J. Beveridge, although many of them were probably influenced in their views on the subject by the mastery Roosevelt held over them. Roosevelt was emphatic in stating his position: ". . . I have the impatient contempt that I suppose all prac-

tical men must have for the ridiculous theorists who decline
to face facts and who wish to give even to the most utterly
undeveloped races of mankind a degree of self-government
which only the very highest races have been able to exercise
with any advantage." If the Filipinos were inferior and entitled to the privileges of American democracy only after a
long apprenticeship, was not the same true of Orientals on
the West Coast and of Negroes in the South? There was,
moreover, what Southerners described as the "dreadful epi-
sode of Reconstruction" to provide apparent documentation
of the Negro's backwardness supplemented by the widely
circulated accounts of his continued degradation in the post-
Reconstruction years. Once having accepted the ideology of
the new imperialism, it was difficult to escape the logic of
the Southerners' position. As Benjamin R. Tillman said,
chiding the Republicans for their imperialism: "Your slogans
of the past—brotherhood of man and fatherhood of God—
have gone glimmering down through the ages." The con-
quered, it seemed, had overcome the conquerors.

Fortunately for Republican and Progressive theoreticians,
the new sciences or pseudo-sciences, with their theories of the
multiple origin of the races and the notion of retarded races,
seemed to provide a scientific explanation that would justify
imperialism, while history itself seemed to prove the superiority of Western culture. As for the democratic concept that
governmental authority rested on the consent of the governed,
Senator Beveridge pointed out that this was true only where
the governed were capable of self-government. Lyman Abbott
said the important thing was not government by the "consent of the governed" but government for the "benefit of the
governed." Thus American imperialism could be viewed as
a crusade to free backward people from their antiquated over-
lords and to set them on the road of progress under the tutelage of a benign and liberal government.

At home there was powerful evidence that Negroes, re-

tarded as was their race, were making headway. This evidence
was particularly apparent in the Booker T. Washington
School, the material gains of which could not be doubted.
Here was progress, tangible and capable of being measured;
more important perhaps, progress based on a philosophy
that received the whole-hearted endorsement of the middle-
class heart of America—and of Progressives. It emphasized
philanthropy and practical education, and it sought to avoid
conflict between employer and employee, between class and
class, and between race and race. It eschewed politics and
worked within a framework that received the enthusiastic ap-
proval of the Southern whites. Thus it provided an opening
for the powerful Northern philanthropic organizations, which
were eager to help the Negro and to work with the more
moderate Southern white leaders. So persuasive was the Washington philosophy that it received widespread support
throughout the country. A non-Southerner such as Bourke
Cockran could appeal for justice for the Negro in one breath
and advocate the repeal of the Fifteenth Amendment in the
next, while Ray Stannard Baker could say some years later
that the North "wrongly or rightly, is today more than half
convinced that the South is right in imposing some measure
of limitation upon the franchise." In 1909, in the words of
Hilary A. Herbert, "Intelligent public opinion at the north
is at this writing so thoroughly with us that there is now no
longer any danger of interference with us from Washington,
either legislative or executive, so long as we do not, by harsh
or unjust treatment of the negro, now at our mercy, alienate
the sympathies of the majority section of our union." The
Progressive *New Republic's* solution followed the course
charted by Booker T. Washington. "The greatest service
which can be rendered the Negro to-day," declared its editors
in 1916, "is to be dispassionate about it. It is, after all, only
a problem like any other. There is no need to keep alight the

old fire upon the abolition altar, or to blow into flames smoldering embers upon the ruined hearth of the old South."

Another element in the Booker T. Washington philosophy was the idea of self-advancement, the belief that the Negro must make his own way and demonstrate his own abilities to get ahead in the contest of life. This idea found easy lodgement in the Progressive rationale. It was implicit in much of Theodore Roosevelt's writing. Even such a zealous believer in Negro rights as Moorfield Storey counseled "patience, courage, and faith." "The prejudice against you today," asserted Storey, "is no stronger than the prejudice which Jews and Irish have overcome." "You are all soldiers in a great army fighting for the future of your race. . . ." Negroes must now work out their own destiny, declared Charles Francis Adams in 1908. "It is for the Afro-Americans, as for the American descendant of the Celt, the Slav, or the Let, to shape his own future, accepting the common lot of mankind."

This was not as inconsistent with the Progressive philosophy as might appear at first glance. Despite its humanitarian outlook and its interest in moral issues, the Progressive movement aimed at "the equalizing of opportunity" by an approach that was essentially negative. As Herbert Croly wrote in *The Progressive Democracy* (1914): " . . . the expectation was that if the concentrated economic system could be checked and disintegrated, small local producers, both agricultural and industrial, would have a much better chance of prosperity." The Progressives, then, hoped to produce a condition in which men might be free to prove their merit. If the Negro could make his way on the economic front, political and civil rights would take care of themselves.

Such were the main philosophical components that influenced the attitude of Progressives toward the Negro problem. To this explanation might be added what Herbert Croly described as the "Promise of American Life," an apt phrase with which he summed up the American faith in progress and in the peculiar destiny of America. That is, Americans believed their nation to be progressive regardless of its shortcomings.

In *The New Democracy* (1912) Walter Weyl called the Negro question "the mortal spot of the new democracy." But he noted that Americans wanted to avoid the issue; to illustrate his point he discussed Negro suffrage: "To-day, millions of men, discouraged by the dwindling but still large residuum of Negro ignorance, discouraged by the passion which seeps like a torrid wind over every phase of the question, seek to avoid the question of Negro suffrage. . . ." In reality Northerners and Republicans—and Progressives as well—had adopted attitudes toward Negroes and other colored races not unlike those of the South. What George W. Cable had written about the Negro question a generation before still seemed apropos. "The popular mind in the old free States," he had written, "weary of strife at arm's length, bewildered by its complications, vexed by many a blunder, eager to turn to the cure of other evils, and even tinctured by that race feeling whose grosser excesses it would so gladly see suppressed, has retreated from its uncomfortable dictatorial attitude and thrown the whole matter over to the States of the South."

The Progressive movement had certainly touched a responsive chord in the ranks of American Negroes, although it was true, as Walter Weyl said, that "The race is too poor, weak, ignorant, and disunited to make effective protest." Negro leaders, however, did protest, and many of them were inspired to believe that the Progressives really intended to battle abuses and to urge democracy on all fronts. Negro leaders themselves were divided and uncertain. As Du Bois wrote, "We all believed in thrift, we all wanted the Negro to vote, we all wanted to abolish lynching, we all wanted assertion of our essential manhood; but how to get these things—there, of course, must be wide divergence of opinion."

The Progressive movement came to be associated by the more militant Negro leaders with the Booker T. Washington school of thought. The failure of Roosevelt and then of Wilson to include the Negroes in their agendas for progress, the death of Washington, and the frustration of Negro aspirations in the World War precipitated a new unity among Negro leaders and an acceptance of the philosophy of the National Association for the Advancement of Colored People. In conclusion it may be said that the Progressive movement, or perhaps it would be more accurate to say the climate of Progressivism, did bring some advances for American Negroes. There were the indirect benefits of Progressive legislation and gains deriving from humanitarian agencies. But in a larger sense the Progressive movement passed over the Negro question and, ironically, by doing so helped to promote the militant approach to the problem that most Progressives would have abhorred.

MAXWELL BLOOMFIELD*

Dixon's *The Leopard's Spots:*
A Study in Popular Racism

The first fourteen years of the twentieth century constituted a major reform period in American history. In politics,
economics and the arts new ideas and practices emerged to
shatter nineteenth-century pre-conceptions. Crusading journalists led the way in calling for a revitalized democracy to
bridge the dangerous gulf separating the very rich from the
very poor. Increasingly public opinion was directed toward
the elimination of class barriers by absorbing both laborer
and capitalist, immigrant and old-stock native, into an expanded form of democratic state which should minister to the
welfare of all.

* From *The American Quarterly*, *XVI* (Fall, 1964), 387-01. Reprinted by permission of the publisher.

Yet during these same years, when mass audiences responded to the idealism of class solidarity and human brotherhood, relations between Negroes and whites in America grew more embittered and violent. By 1909 the National Association for the Advancement of Colored People had been organized to combat a mounting wave of race riots and lynchings in both North and South. What caused this upsurge of racial intolerance in an otherwise reform-minded era? A study of the most popular anti-Negro propagandist in pre-World War I America suggests that middle-class liberalism was by no means incompatible with attacks on allegedly "inferior" racial groups.

Thomas Dixon, Jr., was thirty-eight years old in 1902, when his first novel, *The Leopard's Spots,* made him a best-selling author overnight. In his earlier years he had followed a variety of occupations, each of which contributed in recognizable fashion to his development as a propagandist. Born on January 11, 1864, in the village of Shelby, North Carolina, he grew up during the turbulent Reconstruction era, when black-and-tan governments dominated state politics with the aid of federal troops. One of his earliest recollections was of a parade of the Ku Klux Klan through the village streets on a moonlight night in 1869. As the white-hooded riders swept past his window in ghostly silence, young Dixon shivered with fear. But his mother reassured him: "They're our people— they're guarding us from harm."[1] Later he learned that his maternal uncle, Colonel Leroy McAfee, was chief of the Klan in Piedmont, North Carolina. The romantic colonel made a lasting impression on the boy's imagination, which was equally influenced in another direction by his father, the Reverend Thomas Dixon, a well-known Baptist minister.

At the age of nineteen Thomas Jr. graduated from Wake

[1] Thomas Dixon, "American Backgrounds for Fiction: North Carolina," *Bookman,* XXXVIII (January 1914), 513.

Forest College and secured a scholarship to Johns Hopkins
University in Baltimore, Maryland, then the leading graduate
school in the nation. As a special student in history and politics he undoubtedly felt the influence of Herbert Baxter
Adams and his circle of Anglo-Saxon historians, who sought
to trace American political institutions back to the primitive
democracy of the ancient Germanic tribes. The Anglo-Saxon-
ists were staunch racists in their outlook, believing that only
latter-day Aryan or Teutonic nations were capable of self-
government.[2]

After a year's study at Johns Hopkins Dixon remained un-
decided about a future career. He thought briefly of becoming
an actor but a disastrous experience with a traveling Shakes-
pearean company soon changed his mind. The group, whose
specialty was *Richard III,* found itself stranded in the back-
woods settlement of Herkimer, New York, when the manager
slipped off into the woods with the cash box. Thereafter
Dixon returned to North Carolina and took up the study of
law, a profession which offered considerable scope for his-
trionics without the hazards of one-night stands.[3]

While attending classes at Greensboro Law School (1884-
86) he engaged actively in local politics and was elected to
the North Carolina legislature. His maiden speech aroused
the interest of Walter Hines Page, editor of the Raleigh *State
Chronicle* and a prominent spokesman for the "New South,"
who reported on Dixon for his readers. By 1886 the fledgling
lawmaker seemed destined for a promising political career.
Within a matter of months he graduated with honors from
law school, got married, and was admitted to the state bar.
Then abruptly he changed his mind. Displaying what one
early biographer termed a "characteristic restlessness," he

[2] On Adams, see: Richard Hofstadter, *Social Darwinism in American
Thought* (Boston, 1955), 173-74.
[3] "Chronicle and Comment: Thomas Dixon," *Bookman*, XX (February
1905), 498-500.

abandoned the law in October 1886 to become a Baptist minister like his father.[4]

The crowded years of preaching and traveling which followed (1887-99) marked a watershed in Dixon's life. During this time he built up a stock of basic ideas which he continued to endorse, without serious modification, until his death in 1946. He also achieved remarkable success as a platform personality. Toward the close of his ministry he was reportedly attracting larger congregations than any other Protestant preacher in the country. While this personal acclaim did not prevent him from deserting the pulpit after 1900, it did indicate that he had already gained some invaluable experience in the art of mass persuasion.

Certainly his rise to prominence as a churchman was spectacular enough. He began his preaching career in Goldsboro and Raleigh, but within a year he was invited to occupy a Baptist pulpit in Boston, Massachusetts. Then, in 1889, he accepted a call to become pastor of the Twenty-third Street Baptist Church in New York City. Here his audiences soon outgrew the church and, pending the construction of a new People's Temple, Dixon was forced to hold services in a neighboring YMCA. A vivid impression of his platform appearance at this time has been recorded by the journalist A. C. Wheeler, who attended one of the YMCA meetings:

It was Sunday evening. I found the large hall with its old-fashioned gallery choked with the congregation that had outgrown its church edifice proper and taken refuge here. After the preliminary musical services a young man came down to the front of the platform, and made an extemporaneous prayer and read a portion of the Scriptures from a small Bible which he held in his hand. In the view which I had of him he appeared to be six feet three in stature and almost weirdly gaunt. He did not stand erect in the parade sense, and his long limbs betokened an enormous sinewy power rather than grace or symmetry. His dark, spare, close-shaven

[4] E. F. Harkins, *Little Pilgrimages Among the Men Who Have Written Famous Books. Second Series* (Boston, 1903), 113-31.

face, his plentiful coal-black hair, carelessly pushed backward from his temples, his strong, almost cadaverous jaw, and his black, deep-set, and scintillant eyes made up a personality that arrested my interest at once. It was a type of man especially forged for hard, earnest, fearless work in some direction.[5]

Dixon's personal magnetism accounted, in some degree, for his increasing fame as a metropolitan preacher. But more important was the gospel he brought to his hearers. In the name of the urban masses, he attacked the stand-pat Christianity of well-to-do churchgoers. True religion, he insisted, was a matter of conduct rather than of pious formulae. Christ's "creed was His life." And Christ worked to save all men, not merely a favored few. Dixon aligned himself with the liberal reformers of the Social Gospel Movement in demanding justice for the immigrant, the slum-dweller, the "weak and helpless." He called for an active commitment to human brotherhood and warned that the continued indifference of city churches to the plight of the lower classes might lead to eventual social revolution in America:

I hear the coming tread of a generation of men who not only know not the name of Jesus Christ, but who do not even know the name of the government in which they were born; who do not know the flag under which they are supposed to march as citizens, who one day may stand before a staggering State and challenge it to make good its own life before the stern tribunal of the guillotine, the dagger, the torch, and the dynamite bomb! Those children growing up in those districts without Christ or the knowledge of truth, or the influence of civilization, cannot be left alone with impunity. If you do not love them they will make you look after them to save your own life, bye and bye. . . . The time will come in the life of the men who tear up their churches and move them to the grand boulevards of the north, when a heavy hand may knock at their barred doors and ask them the reason for their existence.[6]

[5] *Dixon on Ingersoll: Ten Discourses Delivered in Association Hall, New York, by Rev. Thomas Dixon, Jr.* (New York, 1892), 11-12.
[6] Thomas Dixon, Jr., *The Failure of Protestantism in New York and Its Causes* (New York, 1896), 27-28.

Nor could this grim reckoning be sidestepped by any appeal to self-regulating economic laws. While Dixon accepted the theory of evolution, particularly as interpreted by Herbert Spencer and John Fiske, he refused to recognize any of its deterministic implications. The material universe, he argued, was a free world. "It was created by the free play of divine law upon matter." God, a "superior intelligence," set the forces of nature to work in a uniform way, but the outcome of the evolutionary process depended upon the creative action of man.

Alone of all animals, man possessed free will, which gave him the power to transcend his environment and to control the brute struggle for existence in the interest of the weak and the oppressed. Without such human intervention there could be no genuine "survival of the fittest." This concept, which Dixon regarded as the vital force in evolution, had for him a specialized meaning quite different from that espoused by conservative Darwinists. Dixon defined "fitness" in moral terms, rejecting mere strength or physical endurance as a criterion. Human progress he traced to the development of character in man; that is, to man's free choice of good in the face of evil. But character, as the measure of an individual's right to survive, could not be monopolized by any limited class. Every man had the power to choose between good and evil, because every man was endowed with free will. Thus, in Dixon's hands, the theory of evolution took on a broadly democratic form, implying the preservation and uplift of the masses.[7]

"Jesus declared that weakness shall rule strength," Dixon observed in 1892. "Now the only history of the world is the history of the weak—the dark, vulgar crowd that used to have

[7] *Dixon on Ingersoll*, 84, 86-87, 160-61. See also Thomas Dixon Jr., *Living Problems in Religion and Social Science* (New York, 1889), 50-70.

no history." Together religion and science were working to democratize the world, bringing the benefits of self-government and self-discipline to the lower classes everywhere. The spread of political democracy, rooted in the idealism of Christian brotherhood, seemed "resistless." Democracy was "a race movement . . . an age movement . . . the first manifest destiny of the world."[8]

In none of his early writings did Dixon display any hostility toward the Negro or even hint that the blessings of democracy should be restricted to white men only. As late as 1896, in his most influential religious polemic, *The Failure of Protestantism in New York and Its Causes,* he declared: ". . . I thank God that there is not to-day the clang of a single slave's chain on this continent. Slavery may have had its beneficent aspects, but democracy is the destiny of the race, because all men are bound together in the bonds of fraternal equality with one common love."[9]

Within the next few years, however, this sympathy for the black man gave way to quite different feelings, as Dixon found himself caught up in the expansionist enthusiasm that accompanied the Spanish-American War. The defeat of Spain opened new areas in the Caribbean and the Pacific to American control, including the Philippine Islands. But it also posed a novel governmental problem: What should be the relationship between American democracy and a backward colored race like the Filipinos? To Dixon and other staunch imperialists the answer seemed clear: democracy was unsuited to a semibarbarous people who lacked the judgment and self-control to manage their own affairs. At the same time the United States could not abandon its newly acquired possessions without violating a moral duty to help civilize the in-

[8] *Dixon on Ingersoll,* 124; Dixon, *Failure of Protestantism,* 51.
[9] Dixon, *Failure of Protestantism,* 52. For a similar viewpoint, expressed several years earlier, see: *Dixon on Ingersoll,* 150.

habitants. So the Filipinos and other backward natives must be governed without their consent until such time as they proved capable of absorbing the white man's culture and utilizing his political institutions.

Inevitably the assertion of white supremacy in the new dependencies led to disturbing afterthoughts about race relations in continental America. By 1900 Dixon had re-examined the position of the Negro in American democracy and concluded that a racial crisis of national dimensions was in the making. Putting aside his earlier fears of a revolutionary immigrant mob, he resigned his pulpit in order to launch a nationwide nondenominational crusade against the "black peril." The moral fervor which had made him one of the foremost preachers in the country was now enlisted in the cause of Anglo-Saxon supremacy. As one Negro critic shrewdly charged, Dixon set out to "frighten a heedless world into the belief that the end is at hand . . . to warn your race to flee from amalgamation, as from the wrath to come."[10] The first fruit of the new gospel was *The Leopard's Spots.*

This novel was at once the earliest and greatest of all Dixon's propaganda works. Into its writing went the logic of the lawyer, the social criticism of the reformer, the zeal of the religious prophet and an actor's sense of dramatic incident and timing. Subsequent books, notably *The One Woman* (1903) and *The Clansman* (1905), reached an even wider audience, but none was so representative of the full range of the author's ideas and attitudes. Without exaggeration it may be said that all of the major themes which Dixon was to develop in a score of works scattered over the next forty years may be found, clearly outlined, in *The Leopard's Spots.* As a purveyor of ideas he drew upon a limited store which he saw no need to modify with the passing of time. To read

[10] Kelly Miller, *As to The Leopard's Spots: An Open Letter to Thomas Dixon, Jr.* (Washington, D.C., 1905), 16.

The Leopard's Spots, then, is to apprehend the whole corpus of Dixon's work.

"I claim the book is an authentic human document and I know it is the most important moral deed of my life," he wrote. "It may shock the prejudices of those who have idealized or worshipped the negro as canonized in 'Uncle Tom.' Is it not time they heard the whole truth? They have heard only one side for forty years."[11] Dixon's side of the race issue presented the Negro under two aspects: as an historical problem peculiar to the South and, more importantly, as a contemporary menace to white civilization in every section of the country. He first sought to justify, as a matter of historical necessity, the suppression of the Negro as a political force in the South. Then he added a new dimension to the problem by carrying his readers northward for a look at the threat which the black race allegedly offered to an urban-industrial society. By the time he rested his case Southern racism had been lifted from its traditional context and made a vital component in the new American sense of world misson and imperial destiny. It was no accident that Dixon subtitled his story of racial tensions in the New World "A Romance of the White Man's Burden."

From cover to cover the book is permeated with a strong sense of national pride. "I love mine own people," declares the politician-hero Charles Gaston. "I hate the dish water of modern world-citizenship."[12] Gaston speaks for a strong, centralized democratic state, the product of four years of bloody fighting between North and South. While the Civil War was ostensibly fought over the question of Negro slavery, in reality, according to Dixon, it represented a contest between two antagonistic forms of government—a democracy *versus* a republic.

The Old South stood for the aristocratic ideals of the

[11] Harkins, *Little Pilgrimages,* 121.
[12] Thomas Dixon, Jr., *The Leopard's Spots* (New York, 1902), 441.

Founding Fathers who had set up a union of republics dominated by the well-to-do propertied classes. In time, however,
the laboring men of the North began to challenge this class
government. As their numbers grew ever larger through continued immigration, Northern workers came to demand
greater political power and a government more directly responsive to their interests. They set in motion a democratic
revolution which the South was bound to resist, since it implied the eventual grant of equal rights to four million irresponsible Negroes "but yesterday taken from the jungle."
Slavery, then, was but one aspect of the broader struggle of
the masses against the classes—of democracy against aristocracy
—in America. And in seeking to halt "the resistless movement
of humanity from the idea of local sovereignty toward nationalism, centralization, solidarity," the South courted inevitable defeat.[13]

Dixon does not mourn the passing of the slaveholding aristocracy. He identifies himself with the new forces in Southern life: the rising industrialist, the reform-minded lawyer,
the poor white farmer of the back country. These groups do
not look to the past; they welcome the spread of middle-class
democracy. And it is as a democrat par excellence that Dixon
appeals to the reading public. Even the setting of his story,
North Carolina, has a symbolic value in this respect. It was
"the typical American Democracy" which "had loved peace
and sought in vain to stand between the mad passions of
the Cavalier of the South and the Puritan fanatic of the
North."[14]

Protected by its dangerous coastline from direct contact
with the Old World, North Carolina had been an early frontier area, attracting the most venturesome and freedom-loving

---

[13] *Ibid.*, 332. Dixon developed this argument at greater length in his
fictionalized biography of Jefferson Davis, *The Victim* (New York,
1914), 74-76, 85-87.
[14] Dixon, *Leopard's Spots*, 5.

spirits from neighboring colonies. Most of Dixon's heroes
claim descent (as did he) from sturdy Scotch-Irish pioneers
who fought all encroachments on their liberties and who
led the way in declaring independence from Great Britain.
They represent old-stock, hardworking, Protestant Americans,
in other words, products of the same frontier conditions
which shaped the thinking of their counterparts in every
section of the Union. Dixon makes it clear, then, that his
characters can not be dismissed as reflecting only "the Southern mind." What they have done to combat the "black peril,"
he insists, any genuine American would have done under similar circumstances.

The story purports to cover the effects of Negro emancipation in North Carolina over a thirty-five year period, from
1865 to 1900. Beginning with a long look at the evils of Reconstruction, Dixon paints a lurid picture of political and
moral corruption, as carpetbaggers and scalawags join hands
with Negro voters to seize control of the state government
and to launch a reign of terror against the former white
ruling classes. Crimes multiply against persons and property
until the beleaguered whites introduce their own brand of
terrorism to keep the Negroes from the polls and to rescue
their state from "African barbarism." A localized struggle
between two political parties thus takes on the aspect of an
epic battle for racial survival.

In Darwinian terms Dixon describes the North Carolina
Democrats as the defenders of Anglo-Saxon civilization, fighting for the prerogatives of white men everywhere. Their interests are identical with those of their Northern kinsmen,
who can not appreciate the true state of affairs because of the
lies being fed to them by radical Republican demagogues.
Thaddeus Stevens and the other Radical leaders are bent
upon destroying Southern civilization through a policy of
racial amalgamation, which will enable them to perpetuate
their control indefinitely over a degenerate mulatto race.

But of course the sinister plans of the Republicans come to naught, thanks to the efforts of those fearless fighters for racial integrity, the men of the Ku Klux Klan. As Dixon describes the Klan, it resembles a glorified Boy Scout troop beefed up with the romanticism of Walter Scott:

> The simple truth is, it was a spontaneous and resistless racial uprising of clansmen of highland origin living along the Appalachian mountains and foothills of the South, and it appeared almost simultaneously in every Southern state produced by the same terrible conditions. . . . This invisible Empire of White Robed Anglo-Saxon Knights was simply the old answer of organised manhood to organised crime. Its purpose was to bring order out of chaos, protect the weak and defenceless, the widows and orphans of brave men who had died for their country, to drive from power the thieves who were robbing the people, redeem the commonwealth from infamy, and reestablish civilisation.[15]

It must be noted, however, that the Klan which Dixon so idealized was the original organization, and that only. He had no sympathy with later attempts to revive the Klan as an instrument for the persecution of racial and religious minorities other than the Negro. His novel, *The Traitor* (1907), attacked the unauthorized use of Klan costumes and organizational machinery by a group of young firebrands who sought to carry out personal vendettas after the genuine Klan had been formally dissolved in the early 1870's. And in 1924, during the heyday of the white-robed Knights in their twentieth-century reincarnation, Dixon again issued a sharp protest against latter-day bigotry. *The Black Hood* (1924) reworked much of the material on the downfall of the Klan which had previously appeared in *The Traitor;* but this time Dixon took care to make one of his heroes a Christlike Jewish merchant. "Remember this, Nathan," he wrote, in reference to the indiscriminate terrorism practiced by the "new" Klu Klux Klan, "you are an American citizen. If you

[15] *Ibid.*, 150-51.

are not safe, I am not safe. Freedom is a mockery. We have no republic—"[16]

This concern for the rights of non-Negro minorities points up the peculiarly American framework within which Dixon developed his racist doctrines. For him "Anglo-Saxon supremacy" meant something quite different from what it meant to European agitators or even to racially-minded New England Brahmins. The onetime preacher to the urban poor never lost his concern for their welfare. Dixon drew no line between Slav and Teuton, between the "new" immigrant from southern and eastern Europe and the old pioneering stock from the northwestern areas. Like the most progressive minds of his generation, he believed that the American melting-pot was still capable of assimilating the most diverse ethnic strains without danger to the fundamental soundness of the national character. Only educate the newcomers to their obligations as American citizens, he urged, and all would be well. Here was no elitist cant, then, but a broadly democratic outlook which places Dixon squarely in the liberal tradition.[17]

The Negro alone found no place in an "Anglo-Saxon" America. To understand why Dixon wished to exclude him is to grasp both the strength and the weakness of Progressive democracy. For Dixon was no isolated crank, but a representative spokesman of his time. However irrational and instinctive his negrophobia may have been, he sought to justify it on scientific and humanitarian grounds. He used liberal arguments to buttress a reactionary creed, and therein lay his appeal to a reform-minded generation.

The Reconstruction chapters of *The Leopard's Spots* serve as a mere prologue to the rest of the book, in which Dixon addresses himself to the larger issue: why does the Negro

[16] Thomas Dixon Jr., *The Black Hood* (New York, 1924), 150; Thomas Dixon Jr., *The Traitor* (New York, 1907).
[17] Dixon dealt with the immigrant problem most extensively in his novel, *The Fall of a Nation* (New York, 1916).

continue to pose as grave a threat to honest democratic government in 1900 as he did back in 1865? Or, to put it another
way, why cannot education—the traditional liberal answer to
the immigrant problem—transform the Negro as well into a
responsible American citizen? Dixon's answer is that the black
man is a hopelessly inferior type of being, closer to the jungle
animal than to the white man who first uprooted him from
his African home. No amount of training or good will can
lift him from the lowest rung of the evolutionary ladder or
make him the equal, in any respect, of the proud Anglo-
Saxon. Between the two races stretches an unbridgeable gulf
of thousands of years of antithetical race history. The real
tragedy of the Negro does not lie in the years of slavery he
endured on Southern plantations, morally indefensible as
the ante-bellum regime may have been. Rather his backwardness stems from his "race's inheritance of six thousand
years of savagery in the African jungle." During that immense
time span, while the Anglo-Saxon was steadily enlarging his
power over man and nature, the Negro remained sunk in
barbarism. He could not progress in the evolutionary scale
because he lacked the inner resources which Dixon's earlier
forays into Darwinism had convinced him were the measure
of racial fitness. As the Rev. John Durham, Dixon's alter
ego in *The Leopard's Spots,* explains to a Negro critic: "You
have shown no power to stand alone on the solid basis of
character."[18]

The Negro is an amoral creature, then, unable to discriminate between right and wrong. The power to make a free and
intelligent moral choice has been denied to him by his Creator, leaving him a permanent cripple in the evolutionary
struggle for existence. At his best he is a good child, for

[18] Dixon, *Leopard's Spots,* 308. *Cf.* Dixon's remarks in his last novel,
The Flaming Sword (Atlanta, 1939), 24-26, 39-43, 190, 271-77, 319,
which seeks to chronicle the "Conflict of Color in America from 1900
to 1938."

whom one may feel a genuine affection (as Dixon did) akin
to the love of a master for a loyal dog. But just as a dog must
be told what to do if he is to be of use in a human society,
so the Negro must be guided and controlled by his Anglo-
Saxon superiors, on whose shoulders rests the burden of
civilizing him, so far as his limited capacities will permit. Any
attempt to reverse the laws of nature by artificially equalizing the relations between the two races can only lead to the
disintegration of the white man's world. The danger is particularly acute in a democracy such as the United States,
where equality is a driving force which can not well be confined to a single area of racial contact, such as politics:

> The beginning of Negro equality as a vital fact is the beginning
> of the end of this nation's life. There is enough negro blood here
> to make mulatto the whole Republic. . . . You younger men are
> growing careless and indifferent to this terrible problem. It's the
> one unsolved and unsolvable riddle of the coming century. *Can
> you build, in a Democracy, a nation inside a nation of two hostile
> races?* We must do this or become mulatto, and that is death. Every
> inch in the approach of these races across the barriers that separate
> them is a movement toward death. You cannot seek the Negro vote
> without asking him to your home sooner or later. If you ask him
> to your house, he will break bread with you at last. And if you
> seat him at your table, he has the right to ask your daughter's
> hand in marriage.[19]

Here was the ultimate horror, as far as Dixon was concerned: the prospect of eventual social equality for the Negro.
For, however deficient the black man might be in the ways of
civilization, he was plentifully endowed with a primitive sex
appeal. In Dixon's eyes the sex impulse was an irrational and
elemental force common to man and animal alike. It represented the "herd instinct," against which civilized man struggled to assert his individual will in defense of his home and
family. Marriage, like evolution, was a test of character, and

[19] Dixon, *Leopard's Spots*, 242.

the African's lack of moral scruples made him a peculiar danger to family life.

By way of illustration, Dixon pointed to the untamed passions of the Negro as the major cause of miscegenation in the South. In *The Sins of the Father* (1912), he explored this argument to its final absurdity as he recounted, through 462 anguish-packed pages, the pursuit of the noble Anglo-Saxon, Colonel Norton, by the voluptuous Cleo, a mulatto girl whose jungle antecedents are thrust upon the reader at every turn. Cleo is a "tawny young animal," "a young leopardess from an African jungle." She is so feline that her eyes glow in the dark, a circumstance that occasions no surprise to the long-suffering colonel. He falls prey at last to her barbaric charms, but achieves a belated moral victory by taking his own life in atonement for his betrayal of racial purity.[20]

This frantic dread of sexual encounter, grotesque as it appears in Dixon's novels, did follow logically from his evolutionary theories. In terms of his personalized brand of Darwinism—

I happen to know the important fact that a man or woman of Negro ancestry, though a century removed, will suddenly breed back to a pure negro child, thick lipped, kinky headed, flat nosed, black skinned. One drop of your blood in my family could push it backward three thousand years in history.[21]

— the strict segregationist policy he outlined for the nation could well seem both necessary and forward-looking.

Why, he demanded, should the Negro continue to be treated as a ward of the federal government, now that his support was no longer needed to preserve the Union? The Spanish-American War had proved the loyalty of the South and restored a sense of Anglo-Saxon solidarity to the entire country, as rich and poor, Catholic and Protestant, immigrant and

[20] Thomas Dixon, *The Sins of the Father* (New York, 1912), 25, 195, 229.
[21] Dixon, *Leopard's Spots*, 393-94.

native, flocked to the colors. Overnight America had become
a world power, called by God to join the other Anglo-Saxon
nations in the great work of uplifting backward peoples everywhere through the exercise of a beneficent imperialism. The
implications which this new-found racial mission entailed for
the Negro were spelled out with Scriptural intensity:

> We believe that God has raised up our race, as he ordained
> Israel of old, in this world-crisis to establish and maintain for
> weaker races, as a trust for civilisation, the principles of civil and
> religious Liberty and the forms of Constitutional Government.
> In this hour of crisis, our flag has been raised over ten millions
> of semi-barbaric black men in the foulest slave pen of the Orient.
> Shall we repeat the farce of '67, reverse the order of nature, and
> make these black people our rulers? If not, why should the African
> here, who is not their equal, be allowed to imperil our life?[22]

Self-preservation alone dictated that the Negro be recognized as an irresponsible force whose very presence en-
dangered the stability of a democratic society. Immediate
steps must be taken to deprive him of his constitutional rights
as a citizen through the repeal of the Fourteenth and Fifteenth
Amendments. Then he must be held at arm's length until
such time as he might be returned to his African homeland.
Dixon thus proposed, as a final solution to the race problem,
the old rallying-cry: "Back to Liberia!" He turned a deaf ear
to critics who protested that, apart from all other considerations, Liberia could scarcely absorb such a mass colonization
project, being roughly equal in size and population to his own
state of North Carolina. Even so, such geographical details
could wait upon a future generation. What mattered at present was to persuade the American masses to undertake the
great crusade against Negro equality and to "fight it out on
this line, if it takes a hundred years, two hundred, five hundred, or a thousand."[23]

Dixon's fire-eating sentiments attracted a wide audience at

[22] *Ibid*, 435.   [23] *Ibid*, 439.

home and abroad. The first edition of *The Leopard's Spots,* comprising 15,000 copies, was exhausted on publication. Thereafter sales continued to soar until reviewers classified the work as a "mob novel," a category reserved for books whose circulation figures reached several hundred thousand.[24] English and German editions brought the problem of the American Negro to still more readers overseas.

Wherever it appeared, *The Leopard's Spots* aroused a storm of controversy, as responsible critics, both white and colored, attacked its pseudo-science in the name of human dignity and minority rights. They exposed the fanatical race hatred which lurked behind Dixon's Darwinian pronouncements, a passionate negrophobia that did incalculable harm in aggravating racial tensions during the era of progressive reform.[25] But they failed to note the significant relationship between Dixon's vicious propaganda and the moralistic literature of the Progressive movement.

In an extreme form, Dixon's novels dramatized one of the major unresolved dilemmas which plagued American reformers at the turn of the century: how to reconcile majority and minority interests within the framework of a democracy. The muckrakers, the most vocal exponents of reform, generally sidestepped the issue by assuming that they spoke for an undivided popular will. In their fiction and factual articles they attacked specific minority groups (or "vested interests") in the name of a democratic majority. Favorite targets included: the big businessman, the white slaver, the paid lobby-

[24] See, in particular: Henry Dwight Sedgwick, *The New American Type and Other Essays* (Boston and New York, 1908), 27-50; "Mr. Dixon Once More," *Independent,* LV (September 3, 1903), 2116-18.

[25] Representative viewpoints, pro and con, include: Harkins, *Little Pilgrimages,* 113-31; Miller, *As to The Leopard's Spots,* 1-21; B. O. Flower, "Books of the Day," *Arena,* XXVIII (August 1902), 217-18; "Books Reviewed," *Critic,* XLII (January 1903), 84; W. H. Johnson "The Case of the Negro," *Dial,* XXXIV (May 1, 1903), 299-302; Ernest Crosby, *Garrison the Non-Resistant* (Chicago, 1905), 109-15.

ist, the saloonkeeper, the labor agitator and the socialist fire-brand. The battle lines were sharply drawn: on one side, the virtuous "people"; on the other, a sinister minority whose very existence threatened the "people" with some specific evil—political, economic or social. Looking forward to the advent of an exclusively middle-class society, the muckrakers demanded either the extinction or strict control of dangerous minorities.

And Dixon pursued a similar line in all of his racist novels. He, too, was a muckraker in all but name, specializing in the "black peril" rather than "Wall Street" or "the demon rum." Like other publicists who sought to exalt the majority will as an authoritative, quasi-religious symbol, he had no sympathy for the give-and-take which must necessarily characterize the genuine democratic process. But his muddled thinking reflected the uncertainties of an entire generation, apprehensive about American strength in world affairs yet intoxicated by the recent acquisition of far-flung colonial populations. For a brief moment racism could be reconciled with the American dream of a middle-class millennium. Then the moment passed; the dream shattered against the grim realities of World War I; and the nation moved onward to new visions that were less grandiose but better attuned to the true nature of man, whose limitations no race—not even the proud Anglo-Saxon—could disavow.

Dixon found himself an anachronism in the postwar world. While he continued to write, publishing some ten books in the 1920s and 1930s, he never again made the best-seller lists. His arguments, reiterated over and over again, took on the mildly comic flavor associated with the literary relics of a bygone era. But in one respect his work possesses an enduring value independent of his reputation as a writer. For Dixon was the first "mob novelist" to dramatize the Negro problem as a national, rather than a sectional, issue and to insist that its solution was a matter of grave concern for all Americans.

In this connection, the remarks made by one of his critics half a century ago bear special meaning for a present-day audience:

A vital question: why is it that so many Northern readers are so ready to accept today a line of argument which would have met with instant rejection, throughout the entire North, a few years ago? The answer is not far to seek. For good or for ill, that fine enthusiasm for the doctrine of equal political rights for all who are called upon to submit to the jurisdiction of our government is no longer a dominant sentiment in any part of our country. George William Curtis unquestionably voiced the general feeling when he went from platform to platform at the close of the [Civil] war, declaring amid wild applause that his doctrine was "the immediate jewel of our national soul," and that its consistent acceptance was the most essential triumph of "the Good Fight." The shameful facts of a mismanaged Reconstruction policy dealt that inspiring belief its first serious blow, but left it still in possesion of the field. Its effective extrusion came only when the vicissitudes of a foreign war drove a popular administration into an attitude essentially irreconcilable with any such belief. The natural opponents of the policy which Mr. Dixon represents were thus disarmed. The psychological moment was at hand, and right shrewdly has it turned to account, both by the political leaders, and by Mr. Dixon, their most effective literary apologist. It is a dangerous and ill-defined path which we have thus taken, and safe egress at the other side of the morass depends upon wiser leadership than we have as yet developed; but whether it was formerly so or not, the North must now bear with the South its equal share of responsibility for these dangers.[26]

[26] W. H. Johnson, "The Ku Klux Klan in Fiction," *Critic and Literary World,* XLVI, (March 1905), 278.

GUION GRIFFIS JOHNSON*

Southern Paternalism toward Negroes after Emancipation

By the turn of the twentieth century racial adjustment in the South had become fixed in a biracial social and economic order. The paternalistic concepts of slavery had become neatly placed within the framework of emancipation.[1]

In 1896 the United States Supreme Court had placed its blessing upon segregation in *Plessy* v. *Ferguson* and had established the separate-but-equal doctrine which was to endure

* From *The Journal of Southern History*, XXIII (November 1957), 483-509. Reprinted by permission of the publisher.

[1] Paternalism as used in this essay is conceived as being systems of value premises and specific practices based on these premises which seek to define and determine the relation of whites and Negroes in all aspects of life in the manner of a father dealing with his children. It should be pointed out that there are both kind and cruel fathers. Southern paternalism toward the Negro was graduated between the extremes of benevolence and malevolence.

for more than half a century. The opinion in this case declared that segregation laws were valid exercises of the police
powers of the state and that they did not imply racial inferiority. As to the plaintiff's argument "that the enforced
separation of the two races stamps the colored race with a
badge of inferiority," the court held: "If this be so, it is not
by reason of anything found in the acts, but solely because
the colored race chooses to put that construction upon it."[2]

As stated by Bishop Charles Betts Galloway at the Conference for Education in the South held in Birmingham in
1904, the position of Southern whites was as follows:

First.—In the South there will never be any social mingling of
the races. Whether it be prejudice or pride of race, there is a middle wall of partition which will not be broken down.

Second.—They will worship in separate churches and be educated in separate schools. This is desired alike by both races, and
is for the good of each.

Third.—The political power of this section will remain in present hands. Here, as elsewhere, intelligence and wealth will and
should control the administration of governmental affairs.

Fourth.—The great body of the negroes are here to stay. Their
coerced colonization would be a crime, and their deportation a
physical impossibility. And the white people are less anxious for
them to go than the negroes are to leave. They are natives and
not intruders.[3]

This hard core of paternalistic thought had emerged by the
time the Southern states had begun to feel safe from the
threat of federal intervention. The correlative rights and
duties of the strong and weak, reminiscent of ante bellum arguments based on Filmer and Burke, were now applied to
the white and black races. The superior white race, with its
roots deep in the experiences of law and government, had
the obligation of teaching the inferior Negro race, with its
history of "four thousand years of barbarism," the precious

[2] 163 U. S. 537, 16 Sup. Ct. 1138, 41 L. Ed. 256 (1896).
[3] Charles B. Galloway, *The Negro and the South* (New York, 1904),
8.

knowledge of citizenship. The weaker race had corresponding obligations: implicit obedience, deference, loyalty, and hard work. John Adams, John C. Calhoun, Thomas Carlyle, and all the proslavery advocates of the late ante bellum period added to the thinking of the South as it outlined what was soon to become "race orthodoxy."[4]

It was held that segregation actually protected the Negro's best interests. It was his duty, therefore, to conform to it and thereby best serve the general welfare. Discrimination was the very basis of good government because it was the only means by which equality among equals might be obtained and good government itself preserved. Government existed for the best people—the intelligent, educated and wealthy. In a society where all are equally free and share alike in political privileges, there are some more fit for the exercise of good government than others. The more fit constituted the men of the upper classes who had time for leisure and study. Wherever there was any large proportion of the un-educated, laboring class present, the possibilities of republi-canism were hampered; but in a community, such as the South, where the menial labor was performed by a particular race, such as the Negro, devoted only to labor and excluded from political participation, the tendency was toward the elevation of the remainder of society. Conferring suffrage upon the freedmen was tantamount, therefore, to conferring social equality.

Since the slaves had been freed, it was the duty of the strong white race to prepare them, if possible, for ultimate political participation through education. The debates on how this education was to be financed and what kind of education was best suited to the Negro were to be some of the most bitter which followed the Civil War.[5] The position which a South-

[4] *Cf.* Thomas Pearce Bailey, *Race Orthodoxy in the South* (New York, 1914).
[5] See Horace Mann Bond, *The Education of the Negro in the Ameri-*

ern white man took on Negro education was often a mark either of race orthodoxy or heresy and certainly determined his category of thinking on paternalism. No American writer after 1865 who has tried seriously to analyze the race problem has failed to find some comfort in the hope of education. The extent of his hope has usually depended upon his concept of the theory of progress.

The theory of progress was itself undergoing a vast change at the very time that racial equalitarianism was being incorporated into the Federal Constitution. It soon came to be held that if particular races of men seemed less advanced than others, it was because they had not progressed as far on the scale of evolution. Thus, the progression theory was capable of proving the incapacity of the Negro for immediate citizenship. Auguste Comte's theory of progress in the philosophical school, Thomas Malthus' concepts in economic theory, and Charles Darwin's implications of inborn instincts furnished Southerners with convenient hypotheses with which to modify their old paternalism.

At least five categories of paternalistic value premises emerged after emancipation. These categories have been set up on a hypothetical scale ranging from concepts most favorable to the personal welfare of the individual Negro to those least benevolent. On a scale ranging from one to ten, one might be called extreme negrophilism and ten might be extreme negrophobia. The five paternalistic concepts would probably fall between points two and eight. They might be labeled for convenience in referring to the categories: (1) modified equalitarianism, (2) benevolent paternalism, (3) separate but equal, (4) separate and permanently unequal, (5) permanently unequal under paternal supervision. These categories of white attitudes from which were evolved procedures for dealing with the Negro had no inherent relation-

---

can Social Order (New York, 1934); E. Franklin Frazier, *The Negro in the United States* (New York, 1949), chs. xvii-xviii.

ship to the long-range, ultimate good of the Negro. Stated briefly, these attitudes were based upon the following assumptions:

1. Modified equalitarianism: The Negro is a retarded race which only needs education and the sympathetic treatment of the white race to rise eventually to the level of the superior race.

2. Benevolent paternalism: The Negro is a retarded race which performs the menial work of the South and, therefore, deserves the most benevolent considerations of the superior white race.

3. Separate but equal: The Negro is an inferior race which can be greatly improved by education but must be separated from the superior white race for the best interests of both.

4. Separate and permanently unequal: The Negro is a permanently inferior race which can be somewhat improved by education. He must be forever segregated but permitted to rise in his own society within the limits of his capacities.

5. Permanently unequal under paternal supervision: The Negro is a permanently inferior race on which it is a waste of money to attempt education but Negroes can fill the need for unskilled labor when supervised by whites and should be protected as long as they keep their place.

Modified equalitarianism. The paternalistic thinkers most favorable to the general welfare of the individual Negro believed in the power of education to lift him out of his retardation. The chief difference between the strong and the weak was the matter of education and opportunity. Like Thomas Jefferson, the equalitarians thought that the only way for American republicanism to be preserved was through an enlightened citizenry. War had emancipated the slave, and the organic law both of the federal Constitution and of the states had now declared him to be a citizen entitled to the ballot and to education. This group of Southern thinkers would get on with the business of making an intelligent citizen of the freedman. A North Carolina legislative resolution of 1877 concluded:

. . . we recognize the full purport and intent of that amendment to the constitution of the United States which confers the rights of suffrage and citizenship upon the people of color, and of that part of the constitution of North Carolina conferring equal educational privileges upon both races: . . . we are disposed and determined to carry out in good faith these as all other constitutional provisions.[6]

At the time this resolution was adopted, forces were already at work which were to defeat an equalitarian program. There were, however, a few in the South who secretly agreed with Northern advocates when they referred to the Negro as a "lamp blacked white man," needing only educational and economic opportunities to prove his capacities to be equal to those of whites. This was a varied group which came from the old planter aristocracy, sons of planters educated in the leading Northern schools where they had come under the influence of exponents of the theory of progress, those motivated by Christian ethics who had thought slavery a moral wrong, and upward moving groups from the lower middle class who had not forgotten the doctrines of the American Revolution.

Lewis H. Blair, born of Virginia planter aristocracy, argued in 1889 like Edmund Ruffin[7] of ante bellum Virginia that the Negro was as good a worker as the white man when properly directed. Blair declared that the prosperity of the South was dependent upon the elevation of the Negro. One by one he answered all the objections of Southern whites to admitting the Negro to full and equal participation in the main stream of society. Basic to his thinking was the assumption

6 North Carolina General Assembly, *Session Laws,* 1876-1877, 590.
7 Edmund Ruffin, *The Political Economy of Slavery* [Washington, 1857?]. Ruffin, however, believed implicitly in "the intellectual inferiority of the black race." See 15.

that the Negro had all the potentialities of the white man. The Negro, he said, had been forced into a caste status from which he must be rescued if the South was ever to become prosperous and share in the wealth of the world. Blair wrote:

Before we can make men of depraved and degraded human beings, be they negro, semite, or even Caucasian, and therefore efficient producers of wealth, there are three principal things to be done. They must be inspired with self-respect, their hope must be stimulated and their intelligence must be cultivated, and especially so with the negro, for his self-respect is feeble, his hope faint, and his intelligence slight; he must economically, morally, and socially be born again, and self-respect, hope and intelligence are the trinity that will work out his elevation, and they are also the rule of three to work out our own regeneration.[8]

The Negro should be welcomed back to the polls and the churches and be educated in mixed schools. Blair had more to say on the subject of mixed schools:

The necessity for the abandonment of separate schools is dual—physical and moral. The physical necessity is this: With our sparse population separate schools cannot supply a clientage numerous enough to secure good teachers, upon whom the efficiency of the public schools is absolutely dependent. . . .

The moral necessity is this: Separate schools are a public proclamation to all African or mixed blood that they are an inferior caste, fundamentally inferior and totally unfit to mingle on terms of equality with the superior caste. . . . Hence it follows that separate schools brand the stigma of degradation upon one-half of the population, irrespective of character and culture, and crushes their hope and self-respect, without which they can never become useful and valuable citizens . . . when we make our implement of elevation, namely our public schools, simply a branding iron for stamping the letter "D," degraded, upon the foreheads of millions of black fellow-citizens, we deliberately tear up by the roots all our other efforts for their amelioration.[9]

[8] Lewis H. Blair, *The Prosperity of the South Dependent upon the Elevation of the Negro* (Richmond, 1889), 47. (See also the 1964 edition, edited by C. Vann Woodward and published by Little, Brown and Company under the title, *A Southern Prophecy*—Ed.)
[9] *Ibid*, 98-99.

Blair's was not a lone voice raised in behalf of an oppressed race. Bishop T. U. Dudley of the Protestant Episcopal Church was taking much the same position in Kentucky, basing his arguments upon the Golden Rule and the concept of the brotherhood of man and the fatherhood of God.[10] Agrarian leaders, making their bid for power against the Bourbons, also held out hope to the Negro, but not for long. As they came to terms with their Bourbon opponents and worked out an agreement for disfranchisement of the Negro, some of them became the Negro's most vitriolic enemy.

The new Southern equalitarianism which has been growing within the last two decades of the twentieth century is made up for the most part of the educated young, born in the new century. Two, three, and four generations removed from slavery, they have been able to free themselves from the bitterness and emotionalism which uprooted the system and to look objectively upon the findings of science, for, as Blair had said in 1889, "the clearer one sees and the more enlightened he is, the freer he is from prejudice."[11] This neo-equalitarian group is rapidly leaving the ranks of the paternalists by denying the basic assumptions of Negro retardation and placing less and less stress on the responsibilities of the whites to the blacks and more and more responsibility on Negroes for themselves.

Benevolent paternalism. The benevolent paternalists sprang from the planter aristocracy of the slavery regime. Long before the close of the ante bellum period they had come to an attitude of *noblesse oblige.* They argued that the Negro was a backward, perhaps even a childlike, race of men who had cheerfully adapted themselves to slavery. Slavery had Christianized them and lifted them out of barbarism. They had cleared the land and cultivated the fields of the South, and

[10] T. U. Dudley, "How Shall We help the Negro?" *Century Magazine,* XXX (1885), 279.
[11] Blair, *Prosperity of the South,* 55.

the white man owed the Negro an everlasting debt of gratitude.

The Negro, however, was still a backward race, and because
of this condition needed the protection of whites. It was
always the responsibility of the strong, so ran the benevolent
paternalist's argument, to bear the burden of the weak. The
strong race by virtue of its superior intelligence, culture, and
wealth was the natural protector of the Negro. The white
man must not only protect good Negroes from the trickery of
bad ones, but the white race as a whole must protect the black
race as a whole from the machinations of bad white men
such as federal agents or Northern missionaries who preached
social equality, or even from bad Southern white men who
took advantage of the Negro's weakness.

Because slavery at its best in the South was a patriarchal
system and the entire master's family looked upon their
particular set of slaves as their black family, the benevolent
paternalists tended to identify themselves with the Negroes
after emancipation as they had before. Just as a father always
knows what is best for his child, so did the white man know
what was best for the Negro. With a clairvoyance given only
to Southern white paternalists, the white man also knew
what the Negro thought, what he wanted, and what he needed. This assumption came to be a basic attitude of the
whites as a whole toward the Negroes as a whole.

It was obviously unnecessary for the Negro to vote, to participate in government, or to be consulted in advance about
matters concerning his own welfare. From this position it was
easy for even the most benevolent of paternalists to argue
that the Negro had not been wronged by the segregation acts
of the 1880's and 1890's, by the grandfather clauses, or by
the "permanent taint" acts of the twentieth century.

The question of social distance did not trouble the benevolent paternalists. During slavery this social class of whites
had frequent personal contact with Negroes, and they did

not fear contamination by the emancipated Negro. As Lewis
H. Blair of Richmond wrote in 1889:

> Most of us above thirty years of age had our mammy, and gen-
> erally she was the first to receive us from the doctor's hands and
> was the first to proclaim, with heart bursting with pride, the ar-
> rival of a fine baby. Up to the age of ten we saw as much, perhaps
> more, of the mammy than of the mother, and we loved her quite
> as well. . . .
> And when we became youths and played with negro boys, went
> fishing and hunting with them, gathered berries and nuts together,
> climbed the same trees; . . . and when we became older, young
> men and maidens, and had colored body-servants and colored
> maids, who were constantly at our elbow, and who knew all our
> love affairs, &c., became we then demoralized? No; and why? For
> the simple reason that we were higher, and the higher are rarely,
> if ever, demoralized by the lower.[12]

For this reason spokesmen for the old planter class could in
all calmness take the position, at a time when a Tom Watson
or a Ben Tillman was demanding complete segregation, that
the Negro should worship in the same churches, ride in the
same conveyances, and attend the same schools as whites.
Bishop Dudley, for example, urged his church to retain its
Negro members and actively seek to bring back those who had
wandered away. Pride of race, he declared,

> is but a pretext to excuse the conduct which, in our heart of hearts,
> we know to proceed from the old root of bitterness—the feeling
> of caste which demands that the liberated slave shall be forever
> a menial.
> I charge the Christian white men of the South to mark that
> the effect of this separation, on which we have insisted, has helped
> to drive these people into a corresponding exclusiveness, and is
> constantly diminishing the influence of our Christian thinkers upon
> their belief and their practice.[13]

[12] *Ibid*, 105.
[13] Dudley, "How Shall We Help the Negro?" 279. (At the time
Dudley was writing (1885), Tom Watson was not advocating "complete
segregation," as noted above. Watson did not arrive at this position
until about 1910—Ed.)

The bitterness of the times to which Bishop Dudley referred, together with the impact of Victorian romanticism,
tended to blunt the personal attachment of the white paternalist for the Negro. It came now to be said that the second
generation of Negroes from slavery were not the equal of
their parents and, therefore, were not as deserving of the
consideration due the former slave. The writings of Thomas
Nelson Page reflect the new attitude of the sons and grand-
sons of the planter aristocracy. The rising generation of
Negroes, he wrote in 1904, "are not as good workers,
or as good citizens, as the generation which preceded
them, and use the education so given them, where they
use it at all, in ways which are not beneficial to themselves and are injurious to the whites."[14] Other writers of
the romantic school usually attributed any "bad conduct" of
the Negro during freedom to the errors taught by Northern
missionaries or agents of the Freedmen's Bureau, excused
him, and held out the hope to Southern whites that patience
and time would ultimately bring back the good relations of
"yester year." W. M. Cox of Mississippi, quoted at an education conference in 1904, illustrates the tolerant spirit of
the rapidly diminishing group of benevolent paternalists:

When I consider all the circumstances of the case, the negro's
weakness, his utter lack of preparation for freedom and citizenship,
and the multitudinous temptations to disorder and wrongdoing
which have assailed him, the wonder to me is, not that he has done
so ill, but that he has done so well. No other race in the world
would have borne itself with so much patience, docility and sub-
missiveness. It is true that many grave crimes have been committed
by negroes, and these have sorely taxed the patience of the white
people of the South. I do not blink at their enormity, and I know
that they must be sternly repressed and terribly avenged. But I insist that the entire race is not chargeable with these exceptionable
crimes, and that the overwhelming majority of the race are peace-

[14] Thomas Nelson Page, *The Negro: The Southerner's Problem* (New
York, 1904), 303.

able, inoffensive and submissive to whatever the superior race sees fit to put upon them. Their crimes are not the fruit of the little learning their schools afford them. They are the results of brutish instincts and propensities which they have not been taught to regulate and restrain.[15]

Cox has stated here the conceptual framework of what may be called the "classical position" of upper-class Southerners. Novelists, autobiographers, and Southern historians have revealed these assumptions in their writings, either as stated or hidden value premises, until the rise of the school of objectivity and the impact of cynicism following World War I dictated a re-evaluation of the situation.

A continuing process of re-evaluation of benevolent paternalism had constantly been under way. A planter who lost heavily during the Civil War and had difficulty making a new start easily shed his attitude of *noblesse oblige* and applied instead hard, Malthusian principles to his black labor force. As agricultural depressions and money panics came and economic crisis followed economic crisis, only those of generations of social prestige and wealth were able to cling to their "refined sentimentalities." This group of paternalists, smallest in all periods of American history, has been most subject to loss of followers and has had most difficulty in finding new recruits. Today there is but a handful left, mostly the grandparents and great-grandparents of the children of 1957.

Separate and equal. An offshoot from the benevolent paternalists claimed that the Negro was a retarded race which could be elevated considerably by the right kind of education. The kind of education needed was industrial. Thomas Nelson Page, whose early writings labeled him as a benevolent paternalist, came through the bitter agrarian-Bourbon political battles of the nineties less friendly to the Negro than before. In 1904 he concluded that the Negro race, "under certain

---

[15] Galloway, *The South and the Negro,* 14-15.

conditions of intellectual environment, of careful training, and of sympathetic encouragement from the stronger races," might "individually attain a fair, and in uncommon instances a considerable degree, of mental development."[16] Negroes needed a different kind of education than did whites. That was one reason it would be impossible to educate them in any but separate schools. ". . . the Negro must be taught the great elementary truths of morality and duty," Page wrote. The more than "$110,000,000 contributed out of the property of the Southern whites," which the South had spent on the education of the Negro up to 1904, was "a complete failure," he declared.

He was but repeating the controversy which had been waging against the classical schools set up by Northern philanthropy during the early days of Reconstruction. The George Peabody Fund, the John F. Slater Fund, the Jeanes Fund, and later the Julius Rosenwald Fund were all attacked not only on the grounds of Northern interference with the Negro but also because it was said that the agents of these funds were giving the Negro the kind of education that "made him unfit for work."[17] The fallacious teachings of equality fostered by these agents and the Northern white faculties of the private Negro colleges in the South had "deluded" the Negro into exchanging his skill as a craftsman, learned during slavery, for "book learning" which was of no possible use to him.[18]

In this time of tension a Virginia-born and educated Negro, Booker T. Washington, came forward as the advocate of industrial education for Negroes. As described by a United States Bureau of Education survey of Negro education in 1916, Washington "had so happy a gift of conciliation as to win the friendship and admiration of the southern white

[16] Page, *The Negro*, 250.
[17] See Frazier, *The Negro in the United States,* 457-62.
[18] Page, *The Negro*, 127.

people whenever the opportunity could be found, and to gain from them a moral support that was worth more than money to his work."[19] Booker T. Washington himself described the situation thus:

For nearly twenty years after the war, except in a few instances, the value of the industrial training given by the plantations was over-looked. Negro men and women were educated in literature, in mathematics and in the sciences, with little thought of what had been taking place during the preceding 250 years, except, perhaps, as something to be escaped, to be got as far away from as possible. As a generation began to pass, those who had been trained as mechanics in slavery began to disappear by death. . . . Many were trained in Latin, but few as engineers and blacksmiths. . . . For this reason they had no interest in farming and did not return to it. And yet 85 percent of the Negro population of the Southern states lives and for a considerable time will continue to live in the country districts.[20]

Booker T. Washington became the Negro spokesman for racial peace, a man whom the white paternalists trusted and with whom they were willing to deal; a man also whom the "New Negroes," those educated and themselves several generations from slavery, began to regard as one who had led his race into a new kind of economic and intellectual bondage.[21]

When Washington urged the Negro to "put down his bucket where he was" and become a good manual laborer, he spoke the language of the mass of Southern white men, for the majority of white men had always thought the black race was destined by the will of God to be "hewers of wood and drawers of water." This ante bellum assumption had been re-

[19] *Negro Education* (U. S. Bureau of Education *Bulletin,* No. 38 [Washington, 1917]), 258.

[20] Booker T. Washington and others, *The Negro Problem: A Series of Articles by Representative American Negroes of Today* (New York, 1903), 12-13.

[21] Frazier, *The Negro in the United States,* 523; Robert L. Jack, *History of the National Association for the Advancement of Colored People* (Boston, 1943).

inforced by the implications of the theory of racial instincts which appeared in Charles Darwin's concept of evolution. "Race pride," "race instincts," "instinctive brutish behavior," were scientific terms easily available to justify subjugation of black citizens. This concept became the new cornerstone of degradation. It was the irrefutable justification of segregation. Charles Francis Adams, addressing a Richmond, Virginia, audience in 1908, pointed out the vast change in American thinking on the Negro since 1865. The change had come about because of "a different conception of the facts" which had been produced by Darwin's profound works. The Negro was no longer "God's image carved in ebony, only partially developed under unfavorable fortuitous circumstances," but a race lower on the scale of evolution, "of widely different interests, attainments and ideals."[22]

This assumption took for granted the physical and cultural inferiority of the Negro. The Biblical concept of brotherhood and equality now became, in the light of evolution, the concept of brotherhood and inequality. "It points to heights of human attainment where further development is possible only along spiritual lines, by the exercise of altruism and brotherhood, and so says, 'be patient and helpful,' " wrote a Northern theologian.[23] Bishop Atticus Haygood of the Southern Methodist Church, who in the early years of Reconstruction had wanted the Southern white man to keep a friendly, neighborly contact with the freedmen, came now to justify segregation as something demanded by race instincts, which if frustrated might result in violence:

This [race] instinct will never be satisfied till it realizes itself in complete separation. Whether we of the white race approve or disapprove matters little. . . . We may, all of us, as well adjust our

[22] Charles Francis Adams, *"The Solid South," and the Afro-American Race Problem* (Boston, 1908), 16-18.
[23] Percy Stickney Grant, *Socialism and Christianity* (New York, 1910), 138.

plans to the determined and inevitable movements of this instinct —that does not reason, but that moves steadily and resistlessly to accomplish its ends. It is a very grave question to be considered by all who have responsibility in this matter: Whether over-repression of race-instincts may not mar their normal evolution—may not introduce elements unfriendly to helpful growth—may not result in explosions? I have seen a heavy stone wall overturned by a root that was once a tiny white fiber. Instinct is like the life-force that expresses itself in life or death.[24]

Here was a convenient theory, based, it was believed, solidly upon objective science which relieved both the North and the South of the burden of applying Christian ethics to the lower caste. It was possible to interpret the Golden Rule in terms of segregation and to say that the Negro race was entirely responsible for separation. To abolish segregation would, therefore, be flouting both "natural law" and God's will.[25]

Edwin A. Alderman, at that time president of Tulane University, explained to the American Economic Association in an address in 1903 the position of those in the South who were willing to give the Negro an opportunity to rise within the framework of separate but equal accommodations. He said:

. . . the best Southern people not only do not hate the negro, but come nearer to having affection for him than any other people. They are too wise not to realize that posterity will judge them according to the wisdom they use in this great concern. They are too just not to know that there is but one thing to do with a human being, and that thing is to give him a chance, and that it is a solemn duty of the white man to see that the negro gets his chance in everything save "social equality" and political control.

. . . This does not mean that the lower should be prevented from rising, but that it should not be permitted to break down the higher.

---

[24] Atticus Haygood, *Our Brother in Black: His Freedom and His Future* (Nashville, 1881), 235-36.

[25] It is interesting to note the number of times this point is made in open letters to the press since the Supreme Court ruling in the School Segregation Cases. See, for example, the letter of Mrs. S. F. White in Asheville (N.C.) *Citizen-Times*, September 18, 1955.

. . . Social equality or political control would mean deterioration of the advanced group, and the South is serving the Nation when it says it shall not be so.[26]

Separate and permanently unequal. The segregationists of the paternalistic school were divided in their thinking as to just how far behind the Negro race was and how long, if ever, it would take it to catch up with the white race. Debates waged, North and South, in the Americas and in Europe, on whether it was possible for a retarded race to skip some of the steps toward advancement. Or, it was asked, must a backward race repeat the historical experience of the superior race in order to progress to a higher level and thus be forever behind? The Southern position on white supremacy seemed to imply permanent inferiority, but whenever the question was presented to Negro audiences, the colored man was usually given to understand that his race might eventually by hard work and self-denial win civil and economic equality—but never social equality.

The two categories of Southern paternalistic thinking most unfavorable to the Negro assumed the permanent inferiority of the race. Those who thought in this fashion constituted, perhaps, the majority of Southern whites. They were composed of the lower middle and the upper lower white classes. They were the ones who had fewest contacts with Negroes on any basis except economic competition. New planters in the deep South, a few from the old planter class, the new rich, foremen both in agriculture and industry, carpenters and bricklayers, others from the semiskilled trades made up the large group of white Southerners who thought the Negro permanently inferior.

Edgar Gardner Murphy, an Episcopal clergyman of Montgomery, Alabama, expressing the views of this group, wrote that the Negro was "a backward and essentially unassimilable

[26] Quoted in Edgar Gardner Murphy, *Problems of the Present South* (New York, 1904), 274n.

people" whom the "conciousness of kind," a phrase which he had borrowed from the Columbia University sociologist Franklin H. Giddings, would forever set apart from the whites.[27] Yet it was possible for the Negro "to enter a larger heritage than is open to any like number of his race in any quarter of the world," because of his contact with Southern whites. Murphy said further:

> . . . the negro question is not primarily a question of the negro among negroes, but a question of the negro surrounded by another and a stronger people. The negro is in a white environment; the white man is largely the market for his labor and the opportunity for his progress, as well as the social and political model of his imitative spirit. Where we find the negro in relation to the trained and educated representatives of the stronger race we find few of the evidences of racial friction.[28]

But the Negro had no sense of race pride or integrity, and when thrown in contact with whites readily mixed with them. To those in the North who would point out that the "natural antipathy toward the Negro" should prevent such crossing of the color line, Murphy would reply with shame: ". . . the racial integrity of the Caucasian is threatened, most seriously and not by the negro but by the degraded white man."[29] For this reason segregation must be maintained by stringent laws to lessen in every way the possible contacts of degraded whites with the backward race. The Negro must forever be kept in his place for his own protection, and in this way the debauched white man must be restrained. Murphy explained further:

> Thus understood, I think the educated opinion of the South has no war with the progress of the negro. It has feared the consequences of that progress only when they have seemed to encroach upon the life of the stronger race. It is willing that the negro, within his own social world, shall become as great, as true, as really

[27] *Ibid*, 183.   [28] *Ibid*, 281.
[29] *Ibid*, 272.

free, as nobly gifted as he has capacity to be. It has fixed its barriers —in no enmity of temper but in the interest of itself and its civilization, and not without regard to the ultimate welfare of the negro.[30]

The majority of Southern whites were convinced that the progress of the Negro within the confines of his own race would be limited, because the colored man was an African, "the least endowed of all the races of mankind." Despite more than 250 years of slavery, during which the white man had patiently tried to teach the Negro the ways of civilization, he was still basically an African, and, since the restraints of slavery had been removed, he was becoming "more and more like the African original."[31]

Permanently unequal under paternal supervision. It was but a step from such an argument as this to the conclusion that only under a system of paternal compulsion could the Negro be tolerated in Southern society. The propensity of the Negro to "take a social ell when extended a political inch" was sufficient indication that he must be kept strictly within his own race. Every instance of his "getting out of place" must be terribly avenged, but all "good Negroes" who knew their place and kept it should be protected.

Thomas Carlyle's *The Nigger Question,* written after emancipation in the West Indies, had widely popularized the concept of retrogression and furnished those who would exploit Negro labor with a convenient justification. The anonymous author of "The Negro and the Negrophilists," published in the *Blackwood's Edinburgh Magazine* of May 1866, stated the argument for retrogression. With Negroes, it was held, "liberty and the grave speedily become one and the same bless-

[30] *Ibid,* 274-75.
[31] Northern missionaries who had in 1865 attributed the undesirable traits of the Negro to slavery began, as a result of accepting the theory of race instincts, to place less emphasis on slavery and more upon "barbarism." See American Missionary Association, *Annual Reports,* 1867-1910, *passim.*

ing." Economic laws, "typhus and smallpox, aggravated by
filth and famine, make short work of the black man, and re-
lieve overburdened charity of a task, which charity may have
the will, but has not the means or the power, to perform."[32]

The census of 1870 left still open the question of the high
death rate of the Negro when in freedom, for, having been
taken in a time of general unrest, it was conceded that the
returns were inaccurate and inconclusive. When, however,
the census of 1880 showed a large increase of Negroes, in
some areas a doubling of the population in a decade, the
news aroused consternation and produced a quick revision of
concepts. While many abandoned the theory of the extermination of the Negroes through natural causes, they did not
give up the theory of retrogression. The fact of a rapidly increasing Negro population made the predictions of the theory
seem even more alarming, for an essential premise was the
deterioration of the Negro when removed from the direct supervision of the dominant race.

Philip Alexander Bruce, with ancestry in the old planter
aristocracy of Virginia, was one of the first Southerners to
make a serious study of the problem from this point of
view.[33] His conclusion was that ultimately, and at no distant
date, the Negro would "revert to the African original." Such
a condition was complicated by the high fertility rate of
Negroes. "The probability is that," he wrote, "in a few generations, formal and legal marriages will be much less frequent than they now are, and the promiscuous intercourse
between the sexes will grow more open and unreserved." The
"unlimited increase" of blacks "virtually means that a period
will come when there will be a sharp contest between blacks

[32] "The Negro and the Negrophilists," *Blackwood's Edinburgh Magazine,* XCIX (May 1866), 596.

[33] Philip A. Bruce, *The Plantation Negro as a Freeman* (New York,
1889), 246. Bruce later modified his views in his *The Rise of the New
South* (Philadelphia, 1905), 468-72.

and whites for the possession of a large part of the Southern States." The whites might kill off the blacks or they might migrate in disgust and leave the blacks in barbaric enjoyment of the South. The only real solution, he thought, was in immediate and complete deportation. But since the Negro was useful to the Southern states as an agricultural laborer, a stopgap remedy might be found. Education fostered either by the public school system, with emphasis on industrial education, or by the white evangelical denominations, sponsored by Northern philanthropy, might elevate the blacks, but he predicted that "in the course of the next ten decades American institutions would be subjected to a severer strain than they have yet endured."[34]

In accordance with Malthusian concepts, Bruce believed that a barbaric race might be elevated to a higher cultural level only when supervised by a civilized race under a paternal system of compulsion. Whenever he found whites to be in a considerable majority, he discovered retrogression to be going on at a slower rate. He assumed, however, that the Negro's personality traits would forever prevent the black man's becoming an acceptable part of American society. He enumerated these traits as being "intellectual blindness, moral obtuseness, and a thoughtless indulgence of every appetite." For these reasons, the compulsion by which the white man must direct the black should be stern, constant, and kindly, but never indulgent.[35]

Alfred Holt Stone, planter in the Yazoo-Mississippi Delta, whose magazine articles on the status of the Southern Negro were written in the early years of the twentieth century, based his philosophy on the theories of the permanency of type and the need for compulsion. He declared that the status of the Negro had been fixed several thousand years ago.

[34] Bruce, *The Plantation Negro as a Freeman,* 246, 256.
[35] *Ibid,* 246-56.

. . . the Negro is one of the oldest races of which we have any
knowledge, and . . . its very failure to develop itself in its own
habitat, while the Caucasian, Mongolian, and others have gone forward, is in itself proof of inferiority . . . if we blot out the
achievement of the American Negro who has passed through slavery,
what has the race left to boast of? And if but we go one step
farther, and from the achievement of the "American Negro" obliterate all that the American mulatto has accomplished, what ground
indeed would be left to those whose sentiment and sympathy have
apparently rendered them so forgetful of scientific truth?[36]

From this pseudoscientific approach, Stone justified the pre-
vailing opinion that the South would tolerate the Negro so
long as his services were cheap and he was willing to keep
his place.

Stone belonged to the school of paternalists who were most
hostile to the Negro—the Simon Legrees of freedom—but who
were usually kind to their own house servants and labor
foremen. A Eugene Talmadge of Georgia would exploit the
issues of "black domination" and the "bestiality" of the Negro
to arouse the fears of the lower class whites so that he might
manipulate them to his political advantage, but he would also
help send his cook's son to college. Convinced of the permanent inferiority of the Negro as a race, these most danger-
ously aggressive of Southern paternalists, few in number but
politically powerful, would use the fear of ignorant whites
as a weapon of control over the lower classes of both races.

The erosion of paternalism. After 1914 Southern paternalism began to erode rapidly. The effect of two world wars,
with their accompanying philosophies of the mission of the
United States in behalf of democracy and individual freedom,
had an impact upon the plight of the Negro. Although any
time of crisis has been an occasion for the uneasy dominant
group to maltreat the Negro, the long-range effect of both
wars has been to improve the Negro's status.

[36] Alfred Holt Stone, *Studies in the American Race Problem* (New
York, 1908), 428-29.

The first world war started the movement of the rural Negro out of the South to the city, and the second war greatly accelerated the pace, until today not a single state among the seventeen segregation states now has a Negro population of more than 50 per cent, although there are still counties in the so-called black belt with a majority of Negroes. It had been argued during the debates over the extension of slavery that it would lessen the tensions of the whites to spread the Negro population more evenly. After the Civil War, Carl Schurz had wanted the freedmen drained off into New England and the Middle West because he thought the degradation of the Negro was partly dependent upon the ratio of blacks to whites. The greater ease with which the border states with their smaller population of Negroes have begun desegregation in the public schools would indicate that the spread theory has some merit.

The prosperity of the war years has also had its effect on paternalistic attitudes. As the Negro has come within the benefits of minimum wage laws and has grown more prosperous, his white employers have rapidly lost their attitudes of economic paternalism. The Negro's eagerness to get an education and the large numbers now attending college are producing a greater mass sophistication which, while angering Southern whites who feel most threatened economically by Negroes, nevertheless, increases the respect of whites for the capacity of the Negro.[37]

The question of the Negro's capacity has itself been under scrutiny, and new answers have come forth. In 1906 William Graham Sumner, an economist and sociologist of Yale University, published his *Folkways,* which was to have a profound effect upon social thought. Using the classical economic theory of John Stuart Mill, he developed the concept of the mores. "It is not possible," he wrote, "to change them by any

[37] Guion Grifis Johnson, "The Impact of War upon the Negro," *Journal of Negro Education,* X (1941), 596-611.

artifice or device, to a great extent or suddenly, in any essential element: it is possible only to modify them by slow and long-continued effort if the ritual is changed by minute variations."[38] It was not possible, he contended, for long-established mores to be uprooted by social revolution or legislation. It was, therefore, not blind, racial instincts which caused prejudice against the Negro, but the mores. He said: "In our Southern states, before the Civil War, whites and blacks had formed habits of action and feelings towards each other."[39] Since emancipation these traditional and customary ways had reasserted themselves. Change would come at snail's pace, but come it would.

About the same time a fellow sociologist at Columbia University, Franklin H. Giddings, was also developing a new concept, the consciousness of kind, useful in explaining Southern behavior toward the Negro, but far less effective than the concept of racial instincts in proving the permanent inferiority of the Negro.[40] A decade later, Georgia-born and Northern-educated William F. Ogburn presented the concept of cultural lag which might be used to explain the retardation of the Negro.[41]

Professor Ogburn's fellow sociologist at the University of Chicago, Robert E. Park, who had spent nine years at Tuskegee Institute, was also developing theories on race relations which were to have a profound effect on American thought. "Race consciousness, like the racial reserves, antipathies, and tabus," he wrote, ". . . is invariably, as far as observation goes, an acquired trait, quite as much as the taste for olives or the mania for collecting stamps."[42] Race prejudice, there-

---

[38] William G. Sumner, *Folkways* (Boston, 1906), 5.
[39] *Ibid*, 77.
[40] Franklin H. Giddings, *Principles of Sociology* (New York, 1896).
[41] William F. Ogburn, *Social Change* (New York, 1922), pt. 4.
[42] Robert E. Park, "The Bases of Race Prejudice," *Annals of the American Academy of Political and Social Science,* CXL (November 1928), 16.

fore, was a phenomenon of status. The white man in America had assigned a low status to the Negro because of his degredation in slavery. Every change in status involves a change in social organization. Disrupture of social organization made the white man afraid and uneasy. Conflict was the natural result, and conflict would continue until some sort of accommodation of the contending forces had been achieved. "The Negro is rising in America," Professor Park said, "and the measure of the antagonism he encounters is, in some very real sense, the measure of his progress."[43]

Anthropologists and psychologists contributed their share to the destruction of the assumption of permanent inferiority. Franz Boas, Columbia University anthropologist, published in 1911 an epoch-making volume, *The Mind of Primitive Man,* which pointed up the ability of man to develop a system of human behavior suitable to the environment in which he found himself. This assumption dealt a body blow to the classical theory of superior and inferior races. From this time on, scholars have held that the only significant test to be applied to groups is how well their behavior patterns and value systems serve them in their environment and how flexible they are in meeting change.

The term "race" came now to be examined more minutely and to be discarded by some as a useless concept. It was pointed out that there is no such thing as a pure race, and that all the so-called races of mankind are the results of intermixtures.[44] Melville J. Herskovits, anthropologist of Northwestern University came forward with new studies on African culture, pointing out that, when America understands and appreciates the values of African culture, Negroes will be properly recognized as a group of people with a long and

[43] *Ibid.,* 13.
[44] See Ralph Linton, *The Study of Man* (New York, 1936), ch. ii; M. F. Ashley-Montagu, *Man's Most Dangerous Myth: The Fallacy of Race* (New York, 1942), 14.

honorable past flowing far back into the stream of history.[45]
Otto Klineberg, Columbia University psychologist, was also
saying that it is impossible to attribute certain mental traits
to large groups of people or to claim permanent retardation
for some and permanent superiority for others on the basis of
skin color or other physical features.[46]

In 1950 eight world-famous social scientists signed a declaration which has become the currently accepted thesis of
scholars in this decade: "The prospect of a continuing inferior status is essentially unacceptable to any group of people.
For this and other reasons, neither colonial exploitation nor
oppression of minorities within a nation is in the long run
compatible with world peace. As social scientists we know
of no evidence that any ethnic group is inherently inferior."[47]

Psychiatrists now describe the "peculiar traits of the Negro"
not as the behavior of an inferior type of people but as
"marks of oppression." Dr. Abram Kardiner and Dr. Lionel
Ovesey, in presenting their psychosocial study of the American Negro in 1951, described the work as having been "conceived and written on the premise that group characteristics
are adaptive in nature and therefore not inborn, but acquired.
. . . Hence, the book does not describe Negro racial characteristics; it describes the personality he acquired while being
obliged to adapt to extremely difficult social conditions."[48]

A year earlier, the concluding point of the UNESCO
"Statement on Race," made on July 18, 1950, had declared:

[45] Melville J. Herskovits, *The Myth of the Negro Past* (New York,
1941).

[46] Otto Klineberg, *Negro Intelligence and Selective Migration* (New
York, 1935) ; Otto Klineberg, *Race Differences* (New York, 1935) ; Otto
Klineberg (ed.), *Characteristics of the American Negro* (New York,
1944).

[47] Hadley Cantril (ed.), *Tensions That Cause Wars* (Urbana, 1950),
190.

[48] Abram Kardiner and Lionel Ovesey, *The Mark of Oppression*
(New York, 1951), v.

21. Lastly, biological studies lend support to the ethic of universal brotherhood; for man is born with drives toward cooperation, and unless those drives are satisfied man and nations alike fall ill. Man is born a social being who can reach his fullest development only through interaction with his fellows. The denial at any point of this social bond between man and man brings with it disintegration. In this sense, every man is his brother's keeper. For every man is a piece of the continent, a part of the main, because he is involved in mankind.[49]

Within this frame of reference, the United States Supreme Court delivered its decision of May 17, 1954:

Segregation of white and colored children in public schools has a detrimental effect upon the colored children. The impact is greater when it has the sanction of the law; for the policy of separating the races is usually interpreted as denoting the inferiority of the Negro group. A sense of inferiority affects the motivation of a child to learn. Segregation with the sanction of law, therefore, has a tendency to retard the educational and mental development of Negro children and to deprive them of some of the benefits they would receive in a racially integrated school system.

Whatever may have been the extent of psychological knowledge at the time of Plessy v. Ferguson, this finding is amply supported by modern authority. Any language in Plessy v. Ferguson contrary to this finding is rejected.[50]

The legal walls supporting segregation had been crumbling gradually since about 1935. In that year the University of Maryland Law School had been opened to Negroes by a federal district court decision *(Pearson* v. *Murray)* based upon the doctrine of separate-but-equal. The argument had been that the equal protection clause of the Fourteenth Amendment had been violated because Maryland had a law school for whites but none for Negroes.[51] In case after case coming before the court within the next thirteen years Jim Crow laws and racism were steadily undermined.

[49] Ashley Montagu, *Statement on Race* (New York, 1951), 17-18.
[50] *Brown v. Board of Education of Topeka,* 347 U. S. 483, 74 Sup. Ct. 686, 98 L. Ed. 873 (May 17, 1954).
[51] 169 Md. 478 (1835).

In 1943, for example, in the case of *Hirabayashi* v. *United States,* the court used strong language against race as a criterion of civil liberties, saying: "Distinctions between citizens solely because of their ancestry are by their very nature odious to a free people whose institutions are founded upon the doctrine of equality."[52] It was no surprise to students who had been following the unfolding of the new concepts of individual liberties that the Sweatt Case against the University of Texas in 1946 and the McLaurin Case against the University of Oklahoma in 1948 carried the interpretation of the Fourteenth Amendment to a point from which segregation in elementary schools could be attacked.[53] This attack came in the decision of the School Segregation Cases in 1954. In rapid succession there followed other decisions denying the right of a state, within certain limits, to segregate on the basis of race in public recreation areas and public transportation facilities.

The majority of Southern white men, however, have been unaware of the Supreme Court's gradual departure from the old doctrines of *Plessy* v. *Ferguson.* The decision in the School Segregation Cases threw the South into a virtual state of shock, and each succeeding reversal of the old doctrine has deepened the emotional reaction. The ante bellum arguments in behalf of slavery and the adaptation after emancipation of these arguments in defense of a biracial social structure have been dusted off and proclaimed from the governor's chair, the pulpit, the press, and the college lecture room. It has been said that if the South had been apprised over the years that this change was in process and had been told that the change must soon be faced in its totality, Southern whites would have been prepared for the school desegregation decision and could have accepted the situation with greater emotional maturity. Others have pointed out that the expanding concept of the free individual has never been accepted in the

[52] 320 U. S. 81 (1943).
[53] 339 U. S. 629, 70 Sup. Ct. 848 (1950); 339 U. S. 637 (1950).

South and only partly in other regions of the United States,[54] and that no educational process for change could have softened the South's reaction.

Whatever the basic considerations, all media of communication in the South point to a recrudescence of paternalistic attitudes toward the Negro, albeit a somewhat angry and bitter recrudescence. Southern whites, especially those in the deep South and those with membership in the some eighty-four organizations which have been formed to preserve the public schools from desegregation, are confident that they know what the Negro thinks, what he wants, what he needs, and what is best for him.[55] The argument against mixing in the schools stresses again the concept of superior and inferior races and the obligation of the superior to give the inferior equal but separate facilities so that the Negro may have the opportunity to rise within his own social system. In this way, God's plan will be carried out, for He separated the races and it is a violation of His will for blacks and whites to be mixed in educational facilities.[56]

Instead of the Freedmen's Bureau and Northern missionaries, the scapegoats are now the National Association for the Advancement of Colored People and the Communists. In February 1956, for example, the Alabama Senate passed a resolution unanimously calling for investigation of Communist activity in connection with the NAACP, and United States Senator James O. Eastland of Mississippi declared: "The court has responded to a radical pro-Communist political movement in this country."[57]

About this time, Dr. W. C. George, professor of histology

[54] "Our Own Mote," New York *Times,* March 4, 1956.

[55] See, for example, the Greenville (S.C.) *News,* quoted in *Southern School News,* I (June 8, 1955), 9: "The more responsible Negro parents will want their children to go to schools taught by members of their own race."

[56] See Herman Talmadge, *You and Segregation* (Birmingham, n.d.); *Southern School News,* II (December 1955), 2.

[57] *Southern School News,* March 1956, 16.

in the Medical School of the University of North Carolina and president of the prosegregation North Carolina Patriots, Inc., declared in a public meeting in Raleigh that, while he has great affection for his Negro friends, he feels constrained to point out that: (1) the Negro is a permanently inferior race, (2) desegregation in the public schools will lead to amalgamation, (3) amalgamation will cause the deterioration of the white race, and (4) the deterioration of the white race will destroy American civilization.[58] About a week later, an open letter in the Greensboro (N.C.) *Daily News* repeated the refrain which may be found almost any day in the Southern press: "I shall fight for liberal treatment, broader opportunities and better education of the Negro; but I shall oppose with all my might all attempts to establish conditions conducive to the elimination of the white and Negro races—in short, integration of our public schools."[59]

Almost a year earlier, the president-elect of the United States Chamber of Commerce, Boyd Campbell of Jackson, Mississippi, addressing the Southern Association of Chamber of Commerce Executives, called for an enlightened leadership in the South to deal with the problems of racial desegregation in the schools.[60] "Once Southern leaders admit that the Supreme Court's ruling won't be reversed, we can get along with our work," Campbell said. He predicted that desegregation will come slowly because, he thought, "educational integration must be followed closely by social and cultural integration."

In 1956 Paul Green, North Carolina's Pulitzer Prize-winning playwright, rephrased this thought at a conference on world affairs in Chapel Hill. The Southerner's role in world affairs, he said, was to complete the task started almost a hundred years ago of incorporating the colored citizen into

[58] See Raleigh *News and Observer,* February 28, 1956; interview with W. C. George, in Greensboro (N.C.) *Daily News,* November 19, 1954.
[59] Greensboro *Daily News,* March 4, 1956.
[60] *Ibid,* March 22, 1955.

the body politic. Economic forces which were at work indus-
trializing the South were surely spelling an end to the old
paternalism toward the Negro. The moral and spiritual
strength of the Southern people must now be applied to
usher in the new day in the New South.

Weeks later, a religious body of great prestige, the Protestant Episcopal Church, announced guiding principles to help
rid it of racial barriers throughout the country: "Any attitude or act in the House of God which sets brethren of different races apart from one another is sinful."[61]

In the political and legal struggles of the post-Civil War
South, leaders constantly pointed out that the Reconstruction
Amendments were sleeping thunder which might be hurled
against the "domestic tranquillity" of the South at any moment by a Congress or a Supreme Court favorable to the
Negro. It was held then that the Fourteenth and Fifteenth
amendments negated the major assumption of Negro inferiority and that the preservation of this assumption was basic to
the preservation of a segregated social order. As the years wore
on after 1865, the paternalistic rationale of biracialism began
to crumble.

In the third decade of the twentieth century a philanthropic foundation, created out of the wealth accumulated in
America by a penniless Scottish immigrant, Andrew Carnegie,
concluded that it was time to make an appraisal of the Negro
in America. A Swedish economist, Gunnar Myrdal, was
brought to this country for that purpose, and the substance
of his findings and those of the large staff of American scholars, both white and Negro, whom he gathered about him
was that America is faced with a dilemma.[62] Within the
framework of an equalitarian constitution, America by law
and custom denies equality to more than 15,000,000 citizens
because of race.

Processes had already long been under way to solve this

[61] *Ibid,* February 24, 1956.
[62] Gunnar Myrdal, *An American Dilemma* (2 vols., New York, 1944).

dilemma. The year the Myrdal study was published, 1944, the Supreme Court delivered a death blow to the white-primary system.[63] The concept of inferiority, nevertheless, still prevails in the minds of both white and colored citizens[64] The second emancipation, as most Negro writers like to call the Supreme Court decision in the School Segregation Cases,[65] may now begin to nibble away at the value premises of this assumption just as the forces at work in society after 1865 finally undermined the paternalistic rationale of segregation.

[63] *Smith v. Allwright,* 321 U. S. 649 (1944).

[64] See Charles S. Johnson, *Patterns of Negro Segregation* (New York, 1943), ch. xii; Helen Leland Witmer and Ruth Kotinsky (eds.), *Personality in the Making: The Fact-Finding Report of the Midcentury White House Conference on Children and Youth* (New York, 1952), 135-38; Max Deutscher and Isidor Chein, "The Psychological Effects of Enforced Segregation: A Survey of Social Science Opinion," *Journal of Psychology,* (October 1948), 259-87.

[65] Zora Neale Hurston, Negro novelist and playwright, in " 'White Mare' Doctrine False," reprinted in Asheville (N.C.) *Times,* August 30, 1955, however, called the decision in the School Segregation Cases "an insult to her race."

JOHN HOPE FRANKLIN*

Jim Crow Goes to School:
The Genesis of Legal
Segregation in the South

A survey of the history of the United States in the nineteenth century gives one the distinct impression that Jim
Crow is the creature of a so-called free society. In the North,
where freedom came relatively early, Jim Crow had an early
birth and was nurtured, oddly enough, even by those who
were committed to a loosely defined principle of universal
freedom. The separation or exclusion of Negroes from the
militia of several Northern states, their segregation in the
schools of such states as Massachusetts and Ohio, and the
clear-cut policy of excluding them altogether from certain
other free states are cases in point. Such practices reflect at
times a view, widely held even among those who were op-

* From *The South Atlantic Quarterly*, LVIII (Spring 1959),
225-35. Reprinted by permission of the publisher.

posed to slavery, that Negroes were inferior and deserved special, separate treatment. At other times these practices betrayed an uneasiness among the white population that could be dispelled only by setting up adequate means of control that invariably involved separate arrangements of one sort or another. It is not an accident, therefore, that Jim Crow was practiced first in the very sections of the country that had eliminated slavery.

At the same time, the Southern slave states gave little thought to the problem of keeping the races separate. The entire situation was in the hands of white slaveholders who could relax or apply the controls as they pleased, without endangering or permanently altering the fundamental relationships in the social system. Thus slave children and white children could be cared for in the same nursery and taught their first lessons together either by a white mistress or by a Negro nurse, who frequently had a major responsibility in transmitting the rudiments of the culture to the young of both races.

There was, under such circumstances, no thought or concern over Jim Crow; for this could not be a problem in a social order where the role of each member was rather carefully defined. Thus, too, Negroes and whites could consort together with impunity and produce a mulatto progeny that ran into the hundreds of thousands by 1860 without risking infracting the laws or even the customs of Jim Crow. They simply did not exist; and with the machinery for achieving and holding respectability securely in the hands of the whites, the ground rules, such as existed, were in their hands to manipulate according to their own whims or satisfaction.

At the end of the Civil War it was inevitable that Jim Crow would ultimately be embraced by those who sought ways to perpetuate in the new era the kinds of controls they had maintained during slavery. Its feasibility as a means of social, political, and economic control in a multiracial society had already been demonstrated. It mattered not that the North had begun to abandon *some* of its Jim Crow practices. There was still wide acceptance of them, even in the old abolitionist strongholds. And it was these *old* Northern practices rather than new equalitarian ones that the South preferred to emulate. If the South was to remain a white man's country, as most Southern whites hoped and believed, then strict control of the Negro was desirable, nay, imperative. This was particularly true in the field of education.

In the ante-bellum South widepread illiteracy and the neglect of education were outstanding characteristics of the culture of the region. The aristocratic attitude that it was not necessary to educate the masses, the reluctance of the people to tax themselves for educational purposes, and the marked individualism of the people, born of isolation and the imperfect state of their social and political institutions, were among the factors responsible for this condition. Southerners saw little relation between education and life. Consequently, the view prevailed that those who could afford education could indulge themselves in securing it; and those who could not afford it lost little, if anything. This attitude was aptly summed up fifteen years after the close of the war by Virginia's Governor F. W. M. Holliday who said that public schools were a "luxury . . . to be paid for like any other luxury, by the people who wish their benefits."

When the economic and social structure of the old South toppled at the end of the Civil War, the ex-Confederates immediately began to erect a new structure based on the old philosophy. Perhaps the war had smashed the Southern world, but it had left the Southern mind and will entirely unshaken. During the war, white Southerners had become more self-conscious than they had been before, more convinced that their way of life had superior validity, and more determined to hold fast to their own, to maintain their divergencies, and to remain what they had been and were. The smoke of battle had hardly cleared when the vanquished leaders, enjoying the autonomy inherent in presidential reconstruction, began to fashion their new world upon the model of the old, which they constantly held before them.

In considering an educational policy for the freedmen in the new order the ex-Confederates faced a real dilemma. Many were alarmed over the prospect of living among a huge mass of free, irresponsible, and ignorant Negroes. Perhaps Negroes should, therefore, be instructed in reading, writing, arithmetic, and the ways of Christian living. But many others were convinced that any intellectual elevation of the Negroes would merely make them difficult to control. Taking their cue from the views and policies of the ante-bellum period, they expressed vigorous opposition to "spoiling" Negroes by educating them. There were those, too, who strenuously objected to taxing themselves for the education of anyone, and certainly not Negroes! Finally, some remained under the influence of those Southern "scientists" and men of letters who had been insisting for a generation that Negroes were simply not capable of being educated.

While these and other considerations were present, it appears that the South was "in general, opposed to the education of the Negro." On Independence Day, 1865, the editor of the Charleston *Daily Courier* put it bluntly when he said, "The sole aim should be to educate every white child in the Commonwealth." A member of the Louisiana legislature said he was "not in favor of positively imposing upon any legislature the unqualified and imperative duty of educating any but the superior race of man—the White race." When he appeared before the Joint Committee on Reconstruction, James D. B. DeBow said that Southerners "generally laugh at the idea of the Negro learning. They have become accustomed to the idea that the Negroes are pretty stupid."

Opposition to the education of the Negro was widespread. In 1866 the Florida superintendent of education said that the white people of that state cherished a "deadly hatred to the education and elevation of the freedmen. . . ." In many places teachers in Negro schools were ostracized, and schools could operate only under the protection of federal bayonets. Within a year after the close of the war a reign of terror broke out in Georgia directed against Negro schools. In La Grange a mob burned a building where Negroes were taught, and in Columbus "some of the ladies of the town, 'of the highest standing in society,' were reported to have seriously planned to hang the Yankee teachers."

The dire poverty of the former Confederate states prevented the launching of elaborate programs of public education even where there was a desire to do so. In few instances did the whites regard it necessary to include Negroes in their modest plans. Even if they were of the opinion that Negroes should be educated, they could leave the task to the Freedmen's Bureau and other charitable and religious groups. Thus some states either ignored the question of Negro education or specifically excluded Negroes from public education. In 1866 the Georgia legislature enacted laws providing for a "thoroughgoing" system of free public education for any free white inhabitant between the ages of six and twenty-one. Texas wrote a similar provision into its fundamental law; the constitution of 1866 declared that the public school fund would be "exclusively for the education of all the white scholastics" of the state. It did provide, however, that when the legislature levied taxes for educational purposes the taxes collected from Negroes would be used for the maintenance of a system of public schools for "Africans and their children." Early in the following years Arkansas established a system of free public education limited to whites.

Some towns with control over their own schools seriously affected the education of Negroes by their policies. At the end of the war the city of Mobile, Alabama, merely assumed that its free schools were for whites and, consequently, excluded Negroes. Then, in 1867, the Board of School Commissioners appointed a committee "to inquire whether our system of public instruction can be extended to the colored children of Mobile." In the following year the board extended its facilities and resources to Negro children in the primary grades. In Virginia, the city of Norfolk had a flourishing system of public education for whites for several years before it got around to setting up schools for Negroes in 1870.

In 1862 the Congress of the United States provided for the education of Negroes in the District of Columbia by segregating Negro taxes for the support of Negro public schools. It thus set a precedent that at least one Southern state followed rather closely: Florida in 1866 established a system of separate Negro schools to be financed by a tax of one dollar on all male persons of color between the ages of twenty-one and forty-five and fifty cents per month for each pupil. There is no indication that Negroes were relieved from the responsibility of paying taxes to support white schools.

A more vigorous prosecution of the idea of universal education was one of the results of the inauguration of radical reconstruction in the ex-Confederate states in 1867. Negro spokesmen called for free public education for the newly enfranchised freedmen. Leaders from the North, the so-called carpetbaggers, believed that an expanded educational program in the South would do much to improve the cultural and political life of the region. Augmenting this group were those white Southerners who had become committed before the war to the idea of universal education.

Universal education, even among carpetbaggers and Negroes, did not necessarily mean racially integrated schools. Most Freedmen's Bureau schools were segregated, in the sense that most of them were Negro schools. And the existent public schools were segregated, in the sense that most of them were white schools, with a gesture here and there toward Negroes. But there was some reluctance to be explicit about segregated schools in the face of the equal protection provisions of the Fourteenth Amendment.

Alabama is an example of this cognizance of the possible implications of the Fourteenth Amendment for Southern school systems. The legislators had no taste for mixed schools, but they seemed to realize that it would be indiscreet to forbid them. Consequently in August, 1868, the Alabama Board of Education enacted a law that provided that "in no case shall it be lawful to unite in one school both colored and white children, unless it be by the unanimous consent of the parents and guardians of such children." It seems needless to add that this act established no integrated schools. Rather, it paved the way for a Jim Crow policy in public education in Alabama.

More typical on the question of mixed schools during the radical period was Mississippi's law, which was extremely vague on the subject. In the constitutional convention of 1868 there was some advocacy of racially integrated schools. No positive action was taken, however; and in the constitution that was ratified the following year there is no reference to segregation in the article on education. Nor was any color distinction made in the Georgia, North Carolina, Virginia, and Texas constitutions of 1868.

In Arkansas there never seemed to be any doubt about the wisdom or validity of separate schools, even during the halcyon days of the Radicals. The constitution of 1868 was silent on the racial question in public schools, but later in the same year the assembly took a position that ruled out any possibility of integrated schools. It instructed the state board of education to "make the necessary provisions for establishing separate schools for white and colored children. . . ." Tennessee had likewise segregated its schools from the beginning of Reconstruction.

Only two states were unequivocal in their legal provisions for integrated schools. In its constitution of 1868 Louisiana declared, "There shall be no separate schools or institutions of learning established exclusively for any race in the State. . . ." In 1871 the state forbade any racial discrimination in admission to schools for the blind, and in 1875 a law provided that there should be no discrimination in admission, management, or discipline of the new agricultural and mechanical college. Meanwhile, South Carolina had gone almost as far in its constitution of 1868, which declared that all public schools, colleges or universities supported in whole or in part by the public school fund "shall be free and open to all without regard to race or color."

It would not be too much to say that attempts to integrate schools were generally unsuccessful either in the states where the provisions were sufficiently vague to countenance them or where they were expressedly authorized by law. The initial hostility of white Southerners to schools of any kind had been the most effective weapon against mixed schools. If Negro schools were burned, if white teachers of Negroes were ostracized, threatened, whipped, and chased from the community, any kind of schools for Negroes had little chance of succeeding. Mixed schools had no chance whatever. Even the friends of Negro education and many of those who frowned on separation were forced to the unpleasant but inescapable conclusion that the only real chance for success in the education of Negroes lay in the establishment and maintenance of separate schools.

For one reason or another many of the responsible leaders during the radical regime called for separate schools. Among these was Governor W. W. Holden of North Carolina, who hoped that the separate school would "equally enjoy the fostering care of the state." Another was Governor Robert K. Scott of South Carolina, who declared that while "God hath made of one blood all nations of men, yet the statesmen in legislating for a political society that embraces two distinct . . . races . . . must . . . take cognizance of existing prejudices among both." Such views contributed substantially to the establishment and perpetuation of separate schools.

While some Negroes resigned themselves to segregated schools as the only practicable solution to the problem, others were not so conciliatory. Most of the Negroes in the Mississippi constitutional convention of 1868 were in favor of mixed schools, which they viewed as the only means of securing equal advantages with the whites. On the other hand, meeting in convention in Nashville in 1879, a group of Negroes declared that "separate schools are highly detrimental to the interests of both races, and that such schools foster race prejudice. . . ." Negro members of Congress fought vigorously, if unsuccessfully, to keep the integrated schools provision in the Civil Rights Bill of 1875 because they were convinced that there could be no equality in education in segregated schools.

Meanwhile, white Southerners who were opposed to mixed schools or to the education of Negroes altogether never relented in their fight. When equal educational opportunities were merely implied in legislation, its supporters were attacked as "imported amalgamationists." In Louisiana, where an attempt was made to establish mixed schools, the editor of the New Orleans *Times* predicted that such effort to annihilate "those great laws of distinction in race implanted by the Creator" would, perhaps, serve to destroy the school system. In South Carolina, at the state university, many white students and professors withdrew when Negroes were admitted, and the agitation against its integration all but wrecked the institution.

Here and there a few publicly supported mixed schools existed, and in one quarter there was even enthusiastic support on the part of some white Southerners. As late as 1875 ex-Confederate General P. G. T. Beauregard came out for mixed schools in Louisiana on the ground that Southerners could win over Negroes by giving them the political and

civil equality guaranteed them by the national and state constitutions. In 1874, supporting a national civil rights bill that
included a provision for integrated schools, Representative
C. B. Darroll of the same state praised its mixed schools. He
declared that not only did white and Negro Republicans support it, "but many of the oldest and best of white citizens . . .
have publicly in mass meetings and addresses heartily approved of all the features of the civil rights bill, including
free schools to all."

Most of the mixed schools in the South, however, were the
colleges, academies, and tributary grammar schools established and maintained largely by Northern philanthropic and
religious societies. But mixed schools, public and private, were
doomed from the outset. Their precarious position was constantly assailed by the majority of white Southerners who, by
1874, were powerful enough to have a good deal to do with
preventing the inclusion of a provision for integrated schools
in the proposed federal civil rights bill.

The advocates of Jim Crow in education found vigorous
and enthusiastic support in the Peabody Fund. From its establishment in 1867, this Northern philanthropic agency
founded by a Southern-born business man had opposed mixed
schools in the South. In 1869-70 it had refused to contribute
to the public schools of Louisiana because they were not segregated. The director of the fund, Barnas Sears, told the Louisiana Superintendent of Education that as long as the schools
were so organized as to cause the greater part of the white
population to be unwilling to send their children to them,
the fund could not contribute to them; and he diverted the
fund's resources to the support of white private schools. In
1874 Sears went to Washington to fight the "mixed schools"
provision of the civil rights bill. When the provision was
dropped from the bill late in the year, the fund and its officials took their share of the credit for the victory.

The involvement of Jim Crow in public education in the

South steadily increased from the time the guns were silenced at Appomattox. At times it was fostered by the ex-Confederates during their period of home rule. At other times it was pushed by one group or another during the radical period: the Southern white irreconcilables, the Negroes who wanted an education more than they wanted integration, those radicals who saw in Southern Jim Crow schools an extension of the practices in many Northern communities, and such foundations as the Peabody Fund which disposed of its funds in a manner designed to control policy.

When redemption came, the white Southerner, returning to the control of his government after an absence ranging from a few months to eight or nine years, began in earnest to put Jim Crow permanently into the public schools. This usually merely involved confirming in law a practice that had already become accepted. As the years passed, the ex-Confederate states became bolder in their insistence upon establishing Jim Crow schools in law. More and more, the early examples of Florida, Tennessee, and Arkansas in segregating became the accepted pattern. Georgia had made no color distinction in her formal legislation during the brief period of radical reconstruction; but when home rule was re-established in 1870 one of the first steps the legislature took was the enactment of a law requiring school officials to provide for the "instruction of the white and colored youth . . . in separate schools." The law stated that the trustees of the school districts were to provide the same facilities for each race. This requirement was modified in 1872 when equal facilities were required "as far as practicable."

North Carolina was "redeemed" in 1870, but as early as November, 1868, the legislature had regularized and legalized the practice of Jim Crow in the schools. In 1876 Jim Crow education was written into the state constitution. In 1876 Alabama, now redeemed, deserted her equivocation of 1868 and wrote into her constitution that "separate schools shall

be provided for the children of citizens of African descent."
Since 1866 the constitutions and laws of Texas had been
silent on the question of segregation; in 1873 the legislature
took the first step toward legalizing Jim Crow by requiring
the trustees of school districts to provide school houses "separating the children and so arranging the schools . . . that good
order, peace, and harmony may be maintained in the schools."
Three years later the state more unequivocally provided that
"the two races shall always be taught in separate public free
schools."

South Carolina and Louisiana, where the battle for integrated schools was most vigorously fought, surrendered to Jim
Crow legislation in 1877. Since South Carolina did not repeal
its constitutional ban on segregated schools until 1895, the
state's dual system of public schools actually operated illegally between 1877 and 1895. Louisiana violated its own constitution for even longer, since it did not expunge its constitutional requirement for integrated schools until 1898. Jim
Crow had become so powerful and the possibility of federal
intervention had become so slight that the leadership in these
two states thought nothing of violating the state constitutions.

In 1878 Mississippi required separate schools by law, and
Jim Crow education was written into the constitution in
1890. Although Virginia did not enact its separate school law
until 1882, its public schools had always been separate. A
decade earlier, when W. H. Ruffner, the state superintendent,
made his first annual report, he had proudly reported that
there were 706 Negro schools among the 2,900 schools in
the state.

Thus did Jim Crow become a part of the public school
systems of all the ex-Confederate states. It was seized upon as
an important instrument of control as the whites sought
an acceptable subordinate relationship with their former
slaves. By the end of Reconstruction Jim Crow in the schools
had become an important means of social control and a device

for perpetuating the ignorance of a great mass of blacks. Ignorance would, of course, make them unworthy to participate in the political life of the country. This view of the redeemers was supported by their calling attention to the corruption, waste, and inefficiency during the "years of darkness." They would overcome these deficiencies by retrenchment and improvement; and they would make permanent the time-honored relationship of the races by keeping them segregated. Somehow, retrenchment seemed to go well with segregation, particularly among a people to whom taxation for the support of education was repugnant.

Once the schools were clearly separated on the basis of race it became much easier for the redeemers to retrench without seriously affecting the schools for their own children. In some states expenditures for public education fell off as much as 20 per cent in the years following the overthrow of Reconstruction. While many white Southerners were not averse to slashing educational expenditures across the board, they went as far as possible in cutting expenditures for Negro schools *before* touching the white schools. To be sure, white schools were crippled all over the South, but it was the Negro schools that were all but destroyed at the hands of the enemies of education and of the Negro.

The way in which inequity in the treatment of Negro schools was not only perpetuated but magnified can be seen in what happened to the per capita expenditure for teachers' salaries in some Southern states. In 1871, the year after redemption in North Carolina, it was $.41 for whites and $.26 for Negroes. By 1910 it was $3.26 for whites and $1.38 for Negroes. In Alabama in 1875, the year after redemption it was $1.30 for whites and $1.46 for Negroes. By 1910 it was $6.19 for whites and $1.01 for Negroes. The material effects of Jim Crow could nowhere be more dramatically illustrated.

Once Jim Crow was firmly established in the public schools of the South, the inequities persisted and increased; and the conditions most destructive to the educative process in a democracy were created. White children were taught, if not directly then indirectly by their superior advantages, that they belonged to some kind of a master race. Even the rather dull minded among them, moreover, could see that they lived lives that contradicted the basic democratic tenets of equality and justice. For the Negro children the task was an almost impossible one: to endure the badge of inferiority imposed on them by segregation, to learn enough in inferior Jim Crow schools to survive in a highly complex and hostile world, and, at the same time, keep faith in democracy. For both Negro and white children, one of the most effective lessons taught in Jim Crow schools was that even in institutions dedicated to training the mind a greater premium was placed on color than on brains. True education in the South was languishing. Only Jim Crow was flourishing and making steady gains in the generation after the Civil War.

CLARENCE A. BACOTE*

Negro Proscriptions, Protests, and Proposed Solutions in Georgia, 1880-1908

Following Reconstruction in Georgia, the Negro was not only the victim of political disfranchisement and educational discrimination, but also suffered humiliation in the form of "Jim Crow" laws, lynching, and the convict lease system. These forms of racial proscription brought forth numerous protests from Negroes but to no avail; hence, convinced of the futility of striving for first-class citizenship in such an environment, some Negro leaders proposed three avenues of escape, namely: (1) back to Africa, (2) exodus to the North, and (3) colonization in the frontier West. By these means, they hoped, Negroes might be able to acquire those rights and privileges guaranteed by the United States Constitution.

* From *The Journal of Southern History*, XXV (November 1959), 471-98. Reprinted by permission of the publisher.

"It is paradoxical," says Woodward, "that the barriers of racial discrimination mounted in direct ratio to the tide of political democracy among the whites."[1] Antagonism between the poor whites and Negroes dated back to the ante bellum period and continued after the Civil War, but it was intensified as the two groups became competitors in the labor market. Knowing that they were despised by both the upper-class whites and the freedmen, the poor whites struggled to maintain a floor below which no whites would fall and which at the same time would serve as a ceiling to the rise of Negroes.[2]

Meanwhile, the upper-class whites, who did not wish to see the Southern social and economic structure fractured by a coalition of the poor whites and Negroes, aided and abetted this racial friction by stressing to the poor whites the importance of maintaining white supremacy. Thus white supremacy was the principal theme, and the average white voter was blind to the fact that "Negro domination" was a fantastically false appeal of politicians who had finally succeeded in enslaving the white voter through propaganda. To strengthen the allegiance of the poor whites to the existing social and economic arrangements, the ruling class proceeded in a limited way to establish schools and factories for them. The result was a widening of the educational and economic gap between the poor whites and Negroes.[3]

In 1870, as a result of a bill introduced in the Georgia legislature by two Negro members, James Porter of Chatham County in the House and George Wallace in the Senate,[4] an

[1] C. Vann Woodward, *Origins of the New South* (Baton Rouge, 1951), 211-12.

[2] Gunnar Myrdal, *An American Dilemma: The Negro Problem and Modern Democracy* (2 vols., New York, 1944), I, 582.

[3] W. J. Cash, *The Mind of the South* (Garden City, N. Y., 1957), 178-83.

[4] *Journal of the House of Representatives of the State of Georgia, at the Annual Session of the General Assembly Convened at Atlanta, January 10, 1870* (Atlanta, 1870), Part I, 309; *Journal of the Senate of the State of Georgia, at the Annual Session of the General Assembly, Atlanta, January 10, 1870* (Atlanta 1870), Part II, 261, Part III, 508.

act was passed which stated that "all common carriers of pass-
engers for hire in the State of Georgia shall furnish like and
equal accommodations for all persons without distinction of
race, color, or previous condition."[5] But by 1890, the growing
antagonism between the poor whites and Negroes was reflected on the state level when the Alliancemen gained control of
the Georgia legislature by electing 160 of the 219 members.[6]
While the Alliancemen advocated a liberal platform,[7] at the
same time they enacted several laws which were definitely designed to emphasize the inferior status of the Negro; the most
vicious of these was the Jim Crow law.

When Representative S. W. Johnson of Appling County
introduced a bill in the Georgia House on July 20, 1891, requiring the railroads to furnish separate coaches for whites
and Negroes with equal accommodations for both races, Representative Lectured Crawford, a Negro from McIntosh
County, told the House that

> The railroads would not give equal accommodations if this act
> were to become law, and as long as I buy a first class ticket I have
> a right to such accommodations, whether I am considered below
> the other race or not . . . The railroads sell us first class tickets
> and then put us into cars where white men come in and smoke, use
> all kinds of indecent language, drink whiskey out of water cups,
> and they call this first class passage.[8]

While this bill was under discussion in the House, the

[5] *Acts and Resolutions of the General Assembly of the State of Georgia, 1870* (Atlanta, 1871), 390.

[6] Rebecca Latimer Felton, *My Memoirs of Georgia Politics* (Atlanta, 1911), 646.

[7] The platform proposed (1) increasing the powers of the railway commission to prevent discrimination, (2) abolishing the convict lease system, (3) tax revision, (4) public school improvements, and (5) primary and election reforms. Alex M. Arnett, *The Populist Movement in Georgia* (New York, 1922), 105-06.

[8] *Journal of the House of Representatives of the State of Georgia at the Adjourned Session of the General Assembly, at Atlanta, Wednesday, July 8, 1891* (Atlanta, 1891), 176; Atlanta *Constitution*, July 21, 1891.

Georgia Colored Alliancemen were holding their state meeting in Atlanta. A committee to memorialize the legislature was appointed, with J. W. Carter as chairman, to ask for better laws, not race legislation, but "such laws as will better the condition of the colored race, and promote their happiness and advance the cause of education."[9] On July 23, the members of this committee visited the legislature and took seats in the gallery. Representative J. M. Holzendorf, Negro member from Camden County, obtained permission from the House to allow a representative from the Negro Alliance to address them for ten minutes. Just before their spokesman, J. W. Carter, began to speak, the Alliance members were invited to take seats on the floor of the House. In his plea against the bill, Carter said in part:

> The white people . . . have sold themselves to the negroes . . . .
> You ask them to vote for you, and when you ask the negro to vote
> for you, you are due him a return of the compliment. We negroes
> are voting for you now. Some of these days we expect you to vote
> for us.

After complimenting the Alliance legislature on its successful campaign, Carter turned to the social relationship of the races.

> We don't want social equality. All the negro wants is protection.
> You white people attend to your business and let us alone . . . .
> The politicians and the lawyers say you must keep us negroes down.
> But that is not right . . . . If you have a sow that has a lot of pigs,
> some white ones and some black ones, you don't kill the black
> ones, do you? No sir. You think just as much of the black pigs as
> you do the white ones . . . . If this old state of ours should be
> threatened, these negroes—your mothers in black—would be the first
> to offer themselves in her defense.[10]

It was unusual for a Negro visitor to be extended an invitation to address the legislature from the floor, but the speech was well received. Many of the members congratu-

---

[9] Atlanta *Constitution*, July 23, 1891.   [10] *Ibid.*, July 24, 1891.

lated Carter for his keen logic. However, despite Crawford's protest and Carter's appeal for justice, the Jim Crow bill was passed by both houses and was signed by Governor Northen on October 21, 1891. The law required the railroads to provide equal accommodations in separate cars for whites and Negroes but this did not apply to sleeping cars. In addition, the law authorized street car conductors to separate the races as far as possible.[11]

This Jim Crow law drew nationwide attention. The Chicago *Appeal* declared that

> A state cursed with such a legislative body almost deserves commiseration . . . . The state of 'Wisdom, Justice, and Moderation' is thus set back in this enlightened age by the recent wretched legislation which was a Farmer's Alliance body.[12]

Negroes themselves were disappointed in this group, whose platform seemed to incorporate ideas of justice and fair play. In a lengthy editorial, the Savannah *Tribune* observed:

> The past twelve months have been more prolific of legislation in the Southern States directly antagonistic to the Negro than any similar period since the days of reconstruction.
>
> . . . . in the states dominated by the Farmer's Alliance, and in those legislatures where their influence has been strongest and most commanding, has this tendency to reactionary legislation been most active and pronounced . . . . These exhibitions of prejudice . . . are simply an expression of hostility to the Negro injected by the white farmers of the South into the great currents of passing political opinion. They represent the feeling of the agricultural class always more strongly wedded to old ideas and less susceptible to the newer teachings of an enlarged and progressive humanity. They have their origin in an order dominated from its incipiency by a feeling of enmity to the Negro.[13]

[11] *Acts and Resolutions of the General Assembly of the State of Georgia, 1890-1891* (Atlanta, 1891), I, 157-58. In order to preserve white supremacy at its lowest level, the Alliance legislature passed an act forbidding white and colored prisoners being chained together while at work. *Ibid.*, 211-12.

[12] Quoted in Savannah *Tribune*, November 28, 1891.

[13] *Ibid.*, October 17, 1891.

Negroes pleaded with Governor Northen to force the railroads to provide equal accommodations for both races, and the Negro Press Association of Georgia drew up resolutions advocating such accommodations.[14] These pleas were ignored; consequently, Negroes were herded into crowded coaches without ice water, towels, or soap, and men and women were forced to use the same lavatory facilities.[15]

Since the railroads refused to provide better facilities for Negroes, the latter were advised to stop patronizing railroad excursions and save their money. In most instances these excursions were frequented by the worst element of Negroes, which did the race much harm.[16] The Reverend J. W. Carter, pastor of the Boulevard A. M. E. Zion Church in Atlanta, said "the colored people keep plenty of money ahead in the railroad treasury from the excursion business to take care of and repair all the Jim Crow cars, where the Negroes and dogs ride together . . . . Enough money is spent in one season by Negro excursions to buy one-fourth of the Indian territory." When Negroes returned home from such excursions, continued the Reverend Mr. Carter, they usually found themselves with insufficient money to pay their rent, to buy food, and to provide for their children.[17]

Jim Crow trains were followed by Jim Crow street cars in various cities in Georgia. For years Negroes were privileged to occupy any seat in the street cars, but beginning with Atlanta in the early part of the 1890's, all Georgia cities gradually enacted ordinances providing for Jim Crow seating arrangements on public transportation. This action by the Atlanta city council prompted Negroes to initiate a movement to boycott the street cars. "The time has come," declared a group of Negro women in Atlanta, "when such ac-

14 *Ibid.*, November 15, December 31, 1892.

15 Atlanta *Independent*, September 5, 1908.

16 A Plea Against Excursions," *Voice of the Negro, II* (August 1905), 530-31.

17 Atlanta *Independent*, January 19, 1907.

tions are necessary to secure our rights. What's the use of giving any man or corporation our patronage when it is not appreciated."[18] To Negroes, the Jim Crow policy was absurd. "It is no more contaminating . . . for colored persons to ride in the same car with white persons than for them to cook for them and do other domestic duties."[19]

Savannah did not establish Jim Crow street cars until 1906, although efforts had been made earlier without success. When such a proposal was made in 1902, President Baldwin, of the Savannah Electric Railway, told a reporter for the Savannah *Morning News* that

> It is really not a question of the separation of the races, but of the cleanly from the uncleanly. Now, I do not mind sitting by a decent clean negro on a street car, and I believe there are few people who do. Uncleanly persons of either race are objectionable, however, so that it may be seen that it is really not a question of segregation of races.
>
> Whenever the effort to separate the races has been made it has resulted unsatisfactorily . . . . People recognize its inconveniences and difficulties, and they are soon ready to revert to the old system of getting a seat wherever you can.
>
> It is difficult to make the people take the places set apart for them by law. A policeman would have to ride on every car to enforce a measure for the separation of the races. They had to do it in Jacksonville. The white people are worse, too, than the negroes. A negro will sit where he is told, as a rule, but a white man will kick. Let a white passenger find all seats in the section reserved for his race taken and he will move down to the negro section, if there are vacancies there. He will probably think the law all right, but that it wasn't intended for him.[20]

[18] Savannah *Tribune*, November 5, 1892, August 29, 1896. Albert Thornton, president of the Union Street Railway Company of Atlanta, admitted that "the negro is the best patron of the street car. If he has a nickel and is going anywhere he will ride; while the white man will walk . . ." Atlanta *Constitution*, March 1, 1891.

[19] Savannah *Tribune*, May 22, 1893.

[20] Savannah *Morning News*, quoted in Savannah *Tribune*, July 12, 1902.

These views of the officials and the better element of Savannah prevented passage of the Jim Crow ordinance by
the city council at that time. Shortly after this, a second Jim
Crow bill was introduced in the council but was defeated,
and the councilman who sponsored the measure failed to win
re-election.[21] However, by 1906 the minds of white people
had been inflamed against the Negro by the race-baiting
tactics of Hoke Smith in the gubernatorial race of that year.
Furthermore, many poor whites were moving into the city
from the rural areas, bringing with them their deep-seated
prejudices against the Negro.[22] Thus the time seemed propi-
tious for a Jim Crow street car law, and such a measure was
proposed a third time in the city council. At first the ordinance was withdrawn, but a resolution was passed suggesting
that the city police be authorized to enforce the state segregation law. This was adopted immediately, and the street car
company complied.[23]

Negroes were incensed and immediately laid plans to boycott the street cars. Hackmen and street wagons were pressed
into service to carry Negroes at a reduced rate. The pastor of
the Second Baptist Church, the Reverend J. J. Durham,
advised his members to stay off the cars. A group of enter-
prising Negroes organized the United Transport Company
which planned to invest in vehicles to meet the emergency.
Negroes were advised to walk because walking was healthy.
If they lived a long distance from their destination, they were
advised to start earlier, "thereby increasing your health and
your wealth."[24] Those who defied the request were castigated
as traitors to the race—especially the preachers. "For a few
paltry dollars they will sell their manhood rights and en-
deavor to ruin those who are weak enough to follow them."[25]

[21] Savannah *Tribune*, September 1, 1906.   [22] *Ibid.*
[23] *Ibid.*, September 15, 1906.
[24] *Ibid.*, September 22, 29, October 6, 1906, March 9, 1907.
[25] *Ibid.*, June 8, 1907.

Despite this defection among the Negroes, the boycott was not a complete failure, for President Baldwin of the Savannah Electric Railway told the city council that the Jim Crow law had cost his company fifty thousand dollars in revenue.[26]

Lynching, which added to the social degradation of the Negro, was another weapon used by the Southern whites to keep the Negro in his place. Between 1888 and 1903 there were 241 Negroes lynched in Georgia, which made the state second only to Mississippi with 294 for the same period.[27] Despite the pleas of Negroes to the federal government, urging that legislation be enacted for their protection against this barbarous practice, nothing was done. The Republican party was as lukewarm in this respect as the Democrats.[28] Although there was an anti-lynching law passed during the administration of President Benjamin Harrison, it was inspired by the protests of the Italian government against the lynching of eleven Italians in New Orleans and was designed to protect foreign nationals rather than the Negro. In his last message to Congress, on December 6, 1892, Harrison made the first presidential recommendation to Congress to adopt measures for curbing this evil practice. Since only three months remained in his term, no action was taken. It remained for the only Negro congressman at the time, George White, of North Carolina, to introduce on January 20, 1900, "the first bill to make lynching of American citizens a federal crime," but it died in the Judiciary Committee.[29]

Lynchings were so prevalent in Georgia that Negroes became convinced that few of the victims were actually guilty. In fact, it was proposed that Negroes should set aside Memorial Day, May 30, for the purpose of paying respect to the

[26] *Ibid.*, March 9, 1907.
[27] Ellis P. Oberholtzer, *A History of the United States Since the Civil War* (5 vols., New York, 1917-1937), V, 716.
[28] Rayford W. Logan, *The Negro in American Life and Thought: The Nadir, 1877-1901* (New York, 1954), 76.
[29] *Ibid.*, 77, 91.

innocent victims of mob violence, and ministers were urged to enlist the support of their congregations for such a movement.[30] Although rape was the most publicized reason given for lynchings, actually only about one fourth of them were attributed to that crime. But because Negroes were occasionally guilty of rape, the prejudices of the whites toward them were intensified. On the other hand, while countless Negro women were forced to submit to the lust of white men, Southern "justice" made no provision for this. As the Savannah *Tribune* observed, "The very men who are abridging our rights are the ones who are ruining our daughters."[31]

In the gubernatorial race of 1892, Governor Northen, with the majority of Negro voters supporting him, was re-elected over his Populist opponent, W. L. Peek, and this despite the fact that the bosses of the state Republican organization endorsed the Populist candidate.[32] Most Negroes, like Bishop Henry McNeal Turner of the African Methodist Episcopal Church, felt that Northen deserved the Negro vote because of the courage of his convictions. Furthermore, many Negroes were suspicious of the Populist party, feeling that its members represented the uneducated class in the state and were responsible for the proscriptive legislation passed by the Alliance legislature of 1890-1891.[33] The governor became very popular among Negroes by recommending in his inaugural address that a more stringent law to prevent lynching should be passed. By his proposal a sheriff who was negligent in protecting a prisoner in his custody would be subject to a

[30] W. E. B. Du Bois, *Some Notes on Negro Crime, Particularly in Georgia, Atlanta University Publications, No. 9* (1904), 60; Savannah *Tribune,* May 7, 1892.

[31] Savannah *Tribune,* May 21, 1892.

[32] Atlanta *Journal,* September 27, 1892. Northen, who ran on the Alliance platform in 1890, was the Democratic candidate for re-election in 1892.

[33] *Ibid.,* September 30, 1892; *Bulletin of Atlanta University,* November 1892, 4.

fine and imprisonment and suspension or dismissal from office.[34]

This position induced the Negro Press Association of Georgia at its meeting in Atlanta on June 20, 1893, to adopt a resolution endorsing the governor's stand as well as the support given him by the better element of whites. The meeting also expressed its appreciation to the Atlanta *Constitution*, Augusta *Chronicle*, and other papers for the interest they manifested in the general welfare of the Negro.[35] When the legislature passed a law incorporating many of the recommendations of Governor Northen, Bishop Turner issued a call for Negro mass meetings to be held on Emancipation Day, January 1, 1894, to give thanks for the new law against lynching. From now on, said Bishop Turner, Georgia would serve as a model for the other states; no state in the Union was blessed with such an honorable body of men to represent them in government. "Prosperity shall enthrone her future."[36]

These were noble words from the acknowledged spiritual leader of the Negroes in Georgia. The lawless element of the white population, however, did not heed them, for lynchings continued unabated. In his message to the legislature on October 23, 1895, Governor W. Y. Atkinson deplored the lynchings and asked the Assembly to enact a law which would empower him to remove from office a law officer who permitted a mob to take a man from his custody. In addition, he proposed that the administrator of the victim should have the right to recover from the county the full value of his life. His message was courageous:

What excuse can be given for this conduct when our race has control of the Legislature and the courts, furnishing both the judges and the jurors? No white man should insist upon the in-

[34] Atlanta *Journal*, October 27, 1892.
[35] Savannah *Tribune*, July 1, 1893.
[36] Atlanta *Journal*, December 23, 1893.

fliction of punishment in a case where he is unwilling to entrust the trial to the most intelligent and upright of his race.[37]

The mounting number of lynchings brought forth impassioned protest from Negro leaders. Bishop Turner was so provoked by the callousness of the Republican party toward lynchings in the South that he announced his intention to support William Jennings Bryan for President in 1900 as opposed to William McKinley. He claimed that he was neither a Democrat nor a Republican but a Prohibitionist who would vote for Bryan.

. . . five times before I would vote for William McKinley . . . because we have tried McKinley for four years and he is of no benefit to the black man, except in giving some of them just a few offices, but the great bulk of my race receive no more recognition at his hands than a man who has been dead twenty years.

. . . I am willing as a negro to try some other white man. . . . Grover Cleveland turned out to be one of the ablest and best presidents that ever graced the nation . . . . Ohio has given us three presidents, and if any of them was ever any account, so far as the negro is concerned, I have yet to learn about it.

Turner declared that the vital question concerned discrimination, proscription, disfranchisement, and lynchings, the last having increased almost fourfold since McKinley had been President. Bryan, he thought would take the necessary measures to curb them.[38]

However, with the disfranchisement movement burgeoning at the turn of the century, many white supremacists attributed lynchings to politics. Mrs. Rebecca Felton, the widow of the leader of the Independent movement in Georgia during the 1880's, declared that "when you take the Negro into your embrace on election day to control his vote . . . so long will lynching prevail." She proudly proclaimed that the white

[37] *Message of the Governor of Georgia to the General Assembly, October 25, 1895* (Atlanta, 1895), 19-20.
[38] Atlanta *Journal, September 6, 1900.* For other protests, see Savannah *Tribune,* January 7, May 25, 1899.

women of the South had to be protected from Negroes, even if it was necessary to lynch one thousand weekly.[39] In explaining a lynching that occurred in Newnan, Governor Candler said that the trouble could be laid to one factor, politics.[40] Ex-governor Northen, who was elected in 1890 and 1892 with the aid of Negro votes, told the Congregational Club at Tremont Temple in Boston on May 23, 1899, that the politics learned by Negroes during Reconstruction were responsible for all the ills that beset the South. Furthermore, he accused the Negro of being ungrateful in that he voted against his best friends in most elections. As long as these conditions prevailed, concluded Northen, lynchings and outrages would continue in Georgia.[41]

Probably the worst lynching outrage occurred when two Negroes convicted of murdering four members of the Hodges family were burned at the stake in Statesboro, Georgia, on August 16, 1904, a crime so heinous that even the Charleston (S.C.) *News and Courier* exclaimed that "the eyes of the country and the civilized world are fixed on Georgia. What will she do?"[42] Referring to this incident in a speech at Spartanburg, South Carolina, Senator John Sharp Williams of Mississippi declared that the Statesboro lynching cost the Democrats the support of a quarter of million votes throughout the country in the national election of 1904. "The very affair itself," said Williams, "is a confession on the white man's part of his incapacity for self-government under his own laws . . . . I feel it my duty to say to a southern audience that things like the Statesboro affair must stop."[43] This state-

---

[39] Atlanta *Journal*, November 15, 1898.

[40] *Ibid.*, April 24, 1899. As a rejoinder, the Savannah *Tribune*, August 5, 1899, stated: "Our governor may be true after all . . . when he says that the placing of the ballot in the hands of the Negro is the cause of so much lynching. The lynching record in this state . . . shows they are trying to get rid of the Negro voters."

[41] Atlanta *Journal*, May 23, 1899.   [42] *Ibid.*, August 17, 19, 1904.

[43] *Ibid.*, December 3, 1904.

ment, coming from one "who was a little more polished than other demagogues,"[44] was a serious indictment against those who advocated Negro disfranchisement but favored preserving the white vote, even though the whites were not educated, because of their "inherited" qualities.

To say that all white citizens in Georgia approved of the open defiance of law and order would be misleading. There was a small minority that voiced its protest, but to an ever diminishing audience. One of these individuals was Superior Court Judge Richard B. Russell of Winder, father of United States Senator Richard B. Russell, Jr. As a judge he proved himself one who desired to see justice prevail regardless of the parties involved. This attitude was demonstrated in 1904 when he ordered the grand jury of Franklin County to bring the lynchers of one John Ware, a Negro, to trial. He denounced lynching as a relic of barbarism, and declared that when mob rule replaced authority "you have created something that is subversive of every principle of good government."[45]

Further degradation of the Negro in Georgia was caused by the peonage-like convict lease system established by the state to secure cheap labor. This practice was in keeping with the economy program adopted by the Bourbon Democrats, since it relieved the state of supporting the penitentiary and, in theory, was to provide revenue. To provide an abundant supply of convict labor, the criminal code was revised to make petty offenders subject to very little sympathy from the courts. The legislature was generous in granting to vested interests, planters, and politicians, long term leases extending from ten to thirty years, from which concessions they reaped immense profits.[46]

[44] Logan, *Negro in American Life,* 90.
[45] Atlanta *Journal,* September 28, 1904.
[46] Woodward, *Origins of the New South,* 212-13. One of the big lessees was Joseph E. Brown who owned the Dade coal mines. He, along

When the "Prison Reform Bill" was presented to the Georgia House in 1876, Representative James Blue, Negro member from Glynn County, made an impassioned plea for justice to the Negroes. He opened his speech by declaring that he was vitally interested in this question since his people composed three fourths of the convicts, and that therefore he opposed the practice of farming them out in squads. Citing numerous cases of inhuman treatment, he begged the legislature to make the necessary reforms so that when the prisoners had served their sentences, they "would not go back into the world cripples and invalids in health or outlaws in morals," but come out as reformed men ready to take their places in society once more. The speech was so well received that it had much effect in securing the passage of the reform bill in the House by an overwhelming vote. Later, the governor, on April 14, 1876, proclaimed "an act to regulate the leasing of convicts by the Governor, authorizing him to make contracts in relation thereto and for other purposes."[47]

Despite the passage of the bill, abuses continued to be practiced in the convict camps, and a serious debate ensued in the legislature on this issue in 1881. Representative T. W. Milner, a white man, feeling that present safeguards were inadequate, introduced a bill "to provide for the better inspection and control of the convicts of the state." He cited the case of a young white convict in Dougherty County "with a Negro guard on one side, and a Negro guard on the other side, and a Negro guard behind . . . whipping him," and asked that the system be abolished,[48] although his motives seemed to have been based on different grounds than those which were to be expressed by the Negro legislators.

---

with the other lessees like General John B. Gordon, paid the state twenty dollars annually for each convict, or less than seven cents a day. Arnett, *Populist Movement,* 27-28.

[47] Quoted in Macon *Telegraph and Messenger,* March 4, 1876; *ibid.,* April 22, 1876.

[48] Atlanta *Constitution,* August 10, 1881.

Two of the five Negro members of the House spoke against the convict lease system. One was Representative Ishmael Lonnon of Dougherty County, who said:

I am not opposed to leases but to the system. It ought to be abolished, not for awhile, but it ought to be such forever in the indistinguishable ruin of death. Convicts are so terrified that they are afraid to tell how badly they are treated.[49]

The other Negro member to speak against the system was Representative John McIntosh of Liberty County, an 1877 graduate of Atlanta University. He stated that, as a representative of one half the population of Georgia, he was seeking justice for his people, and referring directly to the convict lease system, asserted: "I am not afraid of men but when I have seen convicts in charge of guards, these guards looked so ferocious that I felt a horror for them." While he favored the abolishment of the system, he doubted that it would come about and so wished some action would be taken to alleviate the situation created by it. Making a humble plea to the white legislators for justice, he declared:

Men talk seriously about regulating railroads, and yet smile when we ask them to talk about the system of punishing criminals . . . . The colored people of the South will be as true to you in freedom as they were in slavery . . . . They were true to you then at home and often on the field of battle, and they will be true to you yet if you will protect them . . . . The colored people come to you and in the name of pity ask you to do something to improve the system.[50]

---

[49] *Ibid.* Lonnon was dark-complexioned and had a soft tenor voice. He was about five feet three inches tall and weighed about one hundred and sixty pounds. He operated a blacksmith shop in Albany. Although he lacked formal education, he could read and write. Interview with George A. Towns, professor emeritus of Atlanta University, June 2, 1951.

[50] Atlanta *Constitution,* August 10, 1881. Other Negro leaders registered bitter complaints against this iniquitous system, but to no avail. At Negro conventions resolutions were adopted condemning the practice as well as demanding that Negroes be included on jury lists. *Ibid.,* April 1, September 19, 1888; Du Bois, *Some Notes on Negro Crime,* 66.

But powerful groups in the state, headed by corporations, influential planters, and politicians, opposed any change. The Atlanta *Constitution,* which was the spokesman for the Bourbon oligarchy, declared that the system was satisfactory, that the issue was raised by scheming politicians to mislead the Negroes.[51] The real fact was, however, that Negroes found themselves the chief victims of this infamous system. The very circumstance that the better element of white people shirked jury duty made the lot of the Negro more precarious, and lacking the power of the ballot, he was subject to the whims of judges and other court officials elected by white voters.[52]

Some state superior court judges used this system to enhance their political fortunes. In order to curry favor with the Democratic bosses of the state, who by and large were the corporations, the planters, and prominent politicians, these judges in meting out punishment to Negroes would sentence them to long terms on the chain gang, which benefited the lessees. The Democratic bosses in turn would show their appreciation by supporting the judges for Congress.[53] Judge John W. Maddox of Rome was alleged to have defeated Congressman Everett from the Seventh Congressional District in 1892 largely by this method. A Negro, Sam Jackson of Rome, was fined $1,000 or a term on the chain gang for gambling, while John M. Vandiver, a white man who later became postmaster of Rome, was fined $10 for the same offense.[54] Judge Charles L. Bartlett of Macon was notorious for sending Negroes to the chain gang for trivial offenses. He sentenced one Negro to fifteen years on the chain gang for stealing some milk, and a twelve-year-old Negro boy to

[51] Atlanta *Constitution,* September 7, 1881.
[52] Du Bois, *Some Notes on Negro Crime,* 65.
[53] Felton, *Memoirs of Georgia Politics,* 655, 658-59.
[54] Rebecca Latimer Felton, *Country Life in Georgia in the Days of My Youth* (Atlanta, 1919), 196.

twelve years of hard labor on the chain gang for taking a horse to ride a few miles and back.[55]

Such miscarriages of justice resulted in the fact that Negroes constituted about nine tenths of the prisoners in the convict camps. Since the income from crime rather than the rehabilitation of the criminal was the primary objective, the future of the Negro prisoner was beyond redemption. In 1895, a prison inspector reported to Governor Atkinson that he had visited thirty-four chain gangs in twenty-three counties and found 795 convicts, of whom 19 were Negro women and only 27 white men. No provision was made for separating the sexes either at work or in sleeping quarters, which increased sexual immorality.[56] From 1879 to 1899 the number of Negro convicts in Georgia increased from 1,109 to 1,953 while for the same period the number of whites increased from 121 to 248.[57]

Although it was obvious that the Negro was the victim of various forms of proscription, some Negro leaders were the first to profess that the Negro was not altogether blameless. The Reverend L. B. Maxwell,[58] Atlanta University and Hartford Theological Seminary graduate and pastor of the First Congregational Church (Negro) of Savannah, in a sermon delivered to his congregation in July 1896, declared that

> More than a quarter of a century has passed since the black man first entered the political arena and yet it is true that he holds

[55] Felton, *Memoirs of Georgia Politics*, 658-59.

[56] Atlanta *Journal*, November 12, 1895. In the Maddox camp in northeast Georgia about twelve children were born of Negro mothers and white fathers. Savannah *Tribune*, April 28, 1894.

[57] *Second Annual Report of the Prison Commission of Georgia from October 1, 1898 to October 1, 1899* (Atlanta, 1899), 5-6. In this number were included three white women and sixty-eight Negro women convicts.

[58] The Reverend Mr. Maxwell finished Atlanta University in the class of 1886, and at the commencement exercises he spoke on "A Man is a Man for That." After he had finished, Governor Colquitt of Georgia walked over and shook his hand and congratulated him on his excellent speech. For a number of years he was the international Sunday School lecturer for Negroes of the Congregational Church. He died in 1902. Savannah *Tribune*, March 22, 1902.

today a place of influence very little advanced of what he did in
the beginning . . . . The common reasons given have been race prejudice and bad leadership, but tonight I beg to take exception to
the wholesale acceptance of these reasons . . . . The greatest obstacle
has been neither race prejudice nor bad leaders, but something
which . . . is far more harmful, it is that curse of narrow, selfish,
concentrated individualism which hinders race concentration, race
combination and race cooperation.[59]

All of the various proscriptions stimulated Negroes to think
seriously of fundamental solutions to the race problem in
America. The most crude and reactionary elements of the
community appeared to be taking over, and the traditional
Southern liberals, always few in number, seemed almost non-
existent at the time. When the latter did insist on speaking
out in behalf of the Negro, they found themselves subject to
threats and abuse from members of their own race. A typical
example was that involving the editor of the Hawkinsville
(Ga.) *Dispatch,* who received a letter from one of the white
citizens of the county dated July 13, 1891, and threatening
him or any other white person who might defend any Negro
in his rights. The citizen wrote:

Mr. Editor if the foling article appears in your Paper Five Dolers
will appear in the (PO) addressed to you But if it don't appear 25
of your subscribers will sure to stop and we will stop all the rest
We can Your White Brothers.

Notice, We hereby forewarn any and all Persons from taking
up for the nigroes in any shape form or fashion We the undersign
will declare any white man that Takes Sides With any nigroes
against a white person no matter how lodown he or She is just so
they are White We are White men organized For the Perpose of
protecting the White Race and we are going to carry out or Plans
at the Pearl of our Lives Dark Nights and cool heads Will our
work quitly Mr. Editor if this fail to appear in the next issue of
Your Paper Will Consider you in favor of civil wrights and We
Will deal you properly Many Sitersons.[60]

In view of this growing tension, several suggestions for the

[59] *Ibid.*, August 1, 1896.
[60] Quoted in Savannah *Tribune*, September 12, 1891.

improvement of race relations were offered by Negroes. One was for the white press to cease publishing anti-Negro articles. It was pointed out that Southern papers made deliberate efforts to portray Negroes in the most unfavorable light, such as referring to them as "big burly brutes," and branding them as the "aggressors" whenever there was a misunderstanding with the whites.[61]

Some Negroes, however, believed it impossible to reason with the Southern whites, that the Negro had extended the olive branch for twenty-five years and the net result was Southern hate and barbarism. Therefore, rather than remain in an environment offering little hope for the future, the Negro should seek greener pastures if he was to realize the privileges that went along with first-class citizenship.[62]

The first of such plans of escape was the "Back-to-Africa" movement. Foremost advocate of this idea in Georgia, if not in the United States, was Bishop Henry McNeal Turner, of the African Methodist Episcopal Church. The Bishop not only was well acquainted with the Negro and his ills in all parts of the United States, but had actually lived and travelled in Africa. He was convinced that the Negro in America had no future above that of an inferior being. If he had any doubts before 1883, said the Bishop, the United States Supreme Court, when it killed the Civil Rights Act of 1875, completely removed these doubts. He emphasized that this decision was written by a Republican justice and every member of the court was a Northerner except one, Associate Justice John Marshall Harlan of Kentucky, who ironically enough, cast the only dissenting vote.[63] Turner was so disappointed in the

---

[61] *Ibid.*, December 10, 1898.   [62] *Ibid.*, February 11, 1893.

[63] Atlanta *Journal*, August 12, 1893. Turner further stated that this decision was even more revolting than the Dred Scott decision since Chief Justice Taney "only voiced the condition of things as they existed in the days of slavery, while Justice Bradley issued a decree on behalf of the supreme court that nullified the plain acts of congress and the expressed provisions of the constitution of the United States."

Republican party that he deserted its banner for that of the Prohibitionists and even supported the Democratic candidates for the presidency in 1900 and 1908. He and others made vigorous attempts to secure appropriations from Congress in support of voluntary colonization of American Negroes in Africa where they could enjoy first-class citizenship. "The Negro . . . is an outlawed inhabitant of the country," said Turner, "for a people divested of their civil rights can hope for nothing but degradation and contempt."[64]

In 1892 the popularity of the "Back-to-Africa" movement reached its crest among a few of the more credulous Negroes in Georgia. This enthusiasm was partly caused by the Jim Crow law that recently had been passed by the state legislature, as well as by the election of Grover Cleveland for his second term as President. On the Sunday following this election a few Negro ministers predicted a dark future for their race. At Big Bethel Church, one of the largest in Atlanta, a minister advised his listeners "to leave Georgia and go to their own country, Africa, where they would have equal rights and help govern and have street cars of their own." At the annual Republican picnic in Blackshear, I. J. White, a Negro, exclaimed "We would rather be eaten by wild Negroes than to be lynched by white men in the South." Some Negroes of Polk County sent a memorial to the Georgia House of Representatives requesting permission to go to Africa or some free country.[65] As late as 1903, a group of Negro women sent a petition to the Georgia House requesting the legislature to appropriate $2,000 in order that they might take themselves and their families to Africa. Amid much mirth, the petition was referred to the Committee on Emigration.[66]

These efforts bore no fruit, and few Negroes actually went

[64] Atlanta *Constitution,* July 13, 1891; Atlanta *Journal,* August 12, 1893.
[65] Atlanta *Journal,* November 22, 1892, November 30, 1894; Savannah *Tribune,* May 26, 1894.
[66] Atlanta *Journal,* June 25, 1903.

to Africa. By and large, Negro leaders and the Negro press were opposed to the idea. For example, Representative Lectured Crawford, Negro member of the legislature, declared that the only solution was through education which would reveal to the Negro the folly of such a project.[67] Frederick Douglass, the titular leader of the Negro race at the time, in a speech in Atlanta on May 23, 1892, said "the glory of Africa is in her palm trees and not her men," and that the Negro's home was America.[68] Others thought that it was "dangerous to fly from evils that we know not of." Some suggested that Bishop Turner might demonstrate his sincerity by going to Africa himself instead of remaining in America. It was even hinted that any movement that had as its goal the sending of Negroes to Africa would mean having to take half of the white race, since it was difficult to distinguish almost a third of the Negroes from Caucasians. The Negro Press Association of Georgia advised Negroes to "remain where they are: go to work industriously with renewed vigor," and "cultivate a friendly feeling with their white neighbors."[69]

The crowning blow to the movement, however, was the testimony of Negroes who actually had been to Africa and reported their experiences on their return home. Such was the case of Green B. Parks, who left Atlanta on May 24, 1891, for Monrovia and returned to Atlanta in September of the same year. He told Negroes that Monrovia was a very undesirable place in which to live and denounced the African movement and those who sponsored it. "The only hunting in Liberia," he said, "is to hunt a way to leave."[70]

Testimony of a more realistic nature was that given by C. H. J. Taylor, a Negro lawyer of Atlanta and prominent

[67] Atlanta *Constitution,* November 22, 1890.

[68] *Ibid.,* May 24, 1892.

[69] Savannah *Tribune,* July 18, 1891, September 3, 31, November 12, 1892.

[70] Atlanta *Constitution,* September 15, 1891.

Democratic politician who served as United States minister to Liberia during Cleveland's first administration and as recorder of deeds in Washington, D. C., in his second term.[71] While expressing deep admiration for Bishop Turner as a leader of the Negro race, Taylor questioned his glowing accounts of the great possibilities that awaited the Negro in Liberia. Taylor understood, however, that Turner would naturally be inclined to urge African emigration, since the Bishop was Liberian consul in this country, and it was his duty to promote the development of Liberia. He declared that the conditions in Liberia were so degrading that a law should be passed making it a felony for anyone to encourage the Negro to leave the United States for that country. To convey the idea that by going to Liberia Negroes could become officeholders, statesmen, and financiers was absurd. A Negro policeman in Atlanta, he said, would be envied by a cabinet officer in Liberia. Describing the government while he was a resident of Liberia, he stated:

They have a president . . . cabinet officers in name only . . . a secretary of the treasury, but not a dollar in the treasury . . . a secretary of war with no guns . . . a postmaster general with no postal system. . . . In 1886 the total vote cast for president in the whole republic by all parties was 2,325, of this number of voters, and only Liberians are allowed to vote, 1,333 were officeholders. There were 817 men in the republic's military regiment, 787 of whom were military officers and 30 privates.[72]

While the "Back-to-Africa" movement failed to gain many

[71] Savannah *Tribune,* June 3, 1899. At the time of his death in 1899, Taylor was editor of the Atlanta *Appeal* and dean of Morris Brown College. He was born in Alabama in 1856 but spent most of his boyhood in Savannah. He attended the University of Michigan, where he earned the bachelor's and master's degrees. In 1882 he was an assistant prosecuting attorney in Kansas City, Missouri, receiving his appointment from a Democratic mayor and council. After practicing six years there, he was sent to Liberia by President Cleveland. Atlanta *Constitution,* December 21, 1887.

[72] *Atlanta Journal,* January 29, 1898.

converts, some Negroes suggested that the salvation of the race lay in a mass exodus to the North. Had not the North been responible for their emancipation? Did not many Northern orators frequently emphasize human and civil equality? Did not Northern teachers come South after the Civil War to preach social equality to Negroes and urge that they should be protected in their civil and political rights? Thus it was only natural that many Negroes became obsessed with the idea that only by going North could they realize those privileges that were associated with first-class citizenship.

Much to their disappointment, many Negroes who left the South for the North in the 1880's and 1890's to escape Southern proscription found conditions anything but ideal. Although they were not "Jim Crowed" to the extent that they were in the South, they found it extremely difficult to obtain work, since many of the trade unions excluded them from membership. What advantage was there in being able to ride on nonsegregated trains, attend nonsegregated schools, and enjoy nonsegregated amusements if they did not have the money to avail themselves of these opportunities?[73]

Even in New England few jobs were open to Negroes and great pains were taken to prevent Negroes from competing with whites. E. J. Bruce, a Negro of Savannah who went to Providence, Rhode Island, in the 1870's and secured a job with the largest contracting firm in the state, declared that while Negro civil rights were observed more in the North, the economic opportunities were far more limited than in the South. He cited numerous cases in which Negro mechanics were denied work because the whites threatened to strike

[73] Thomas J. Bell, "Does the Colored Man Have a Chance in the North," *Bulletin of Atlanta University*, January, 1894, 2. Bell was a member of the Atlanta University class of 1891 and served as YMCA secretary in New York, Denver, and Brockton, Massachusetts. "Who's Who Among Atlanta University Graduates and Former Students," *Phylon*, III (Second Quarter, 1942), 166.

if they were hired.[74] The Washington (D.C.) *Bee,* a Negro paper, stated that Negroes in the North, even the educated ones, could work only as waiters, caterers, porters, or barbers; and as far as political activity was concerned, they might have their ego inflated by being appointed as doorkeepers at the Republican national conventions.[75] W. R. Davis, a Negro who left the South to live in New York, declared that while Negroes in 1885 had most of the jobs as waiters in hotels and restaurants, by 1895 only a few remained. Even the Negro bootblack was replaced by the Italian. So many opportunities for work had been denied the Negro man that the responsibility for supporting the family fell upon the women, who were forced to take in washing to keep the family from becoming a burden on the community. The situation was becoming so desperate, Davis said, that the Negro was "almost denied the right to breathe."[76]

As a substitute for the "Back-to-Africa" and "Exodus-to-the-North" projects as means of solving the race problem, another distinguished Georgia Negro, Bishop Lucius H. Holsey of the Colored Methodist Episcopal Church, proposed that the federal government set aside out of the public domain a separate state where Negroes might enjoy first-class citizenship. He declared that "two distinct peoples can never live together in the South in peace, when one is Anglo-Saxon and the other Negro, unless the Negro, as a race or en masse, lives in the submerged realm of serfdom and slavery."[77] To justify his stand, he pointed out the refusal of the South to provide adequate educational facilities for the Negro, and the antagonism ex-

[74] Savannah *Tribune,* May 2, 1903.

[75] Quoted *ibid.,* January 24, 1903.

[76] "Give the Negro Work," New York *Press,* quoted in Atlanta *Journal,* April 10, 1895. For a description of the hardships experienced by Negroes who went to Kansas in 1879, see Logan, *Negro in American Life,* 133-34.

[77] Lucius H. Holsey, "Race Segregation," *The Possibilities of the Negro in Symposium,* ed. by Willis B. Parks, 102, 109.

pressed towards the educated Negro; the denial of political privileges; the Jim Crow policy; the lack of protection for Negroes in rural areas; and the prevalence of mob violence.

Under these conditions, said Bishop Holsey, it was not practical to continue to allow the South to settle this problem, since it was national in scope, involving national honor and national law. Therefore, in order that the Negro might enjoy all the privileges that were guaranteed by the United States Constitution, he requested the federal government to establish a Negro state in part of the Indian territory, New Mexico, or in some other part of the public domain in the West. In this territory white persons would be ineligible for citizenship, except through marriage, and only those white persons who had some official connection with the government would be permitted to reside therein. By having responsibilities of government thrust upon his shoulders, the Negro would become inspired and more willing to help the Anglo-Saxon race to develop a greater civilization in this country.[78]

While the leaders of these movements to provide an escape for the Negroes had good intentions, they failed to convince the Negro masses that their conditions would be improved by leaving the South. A number of Negroes followed "Pop" Singleton to Kansas in 1879 and to several Northern communities, but there was no significant migration northward until World War I. It appears that the Negro masses were resigned to staying in the South, hoping eventually that the tide would turn in their favor. Such a development, they believed, was dependent upon two factors: (1) the ability of the Negro to improve his social, economic, and educational status in order to win the respect of his white neighbors, and (2) the willingness of the whites to cease vilifying the Negro in the white press and at the same time to extend to the Negro his constitutional rights.

[78] *Ibid.*, 104-19.

Not only were Negroes critical of the white press but also of the Northern Negro press for meddling with affairs pertaining to the Negroes in the South. Many of these Northern Negro journals criticized the Southern Negro press for not taking a more militant stand against Southerners who were responsible for repressive measures aimed at the Negroes. This was especially true of the New York *Age,* whose editor, T. Thomas Fortune, became a nationally known figure through his condemnation of the South in his paper. The editor of the Savannah *Tribune* advised Fortune that if he desired to "be so base and outspoken" toward the South, then he should come down to the "seat of battle" and give vent to his feelings.[79]

White people were admonished that the South could not possibly advance unless the Negroes were given the same opportunities as the whites, that it was necessary to encourage Negroes to participate in politics in order that they might have an interest in the community and the community an interest in them. Furthermore, Negroes urged that it was the duty of the parents and teachers of both races to teach their children to respect each other, since the South, unlike the North, had only two races, "both of whom are true American citizens who love themselves, their country and its flag and their neighbors." As the Negro had proven himself to be a faithful worker for over 250 years, the whites were advised not to import foreigners as laborers in the South, for such a policy might result in a tragedy similar to the Haymarket riot in Chicago. "Let the Southern Negro and Southern white man ever remain and stick together, for they understand each other as no one else understands them."[80]

This sentiment was concurred in by many white people who believed that the Southern whites were the true friends of the Negro. Negroes of Atlanta were reminded of this when

[79] Savannah *Tribune,* December 2, 1893.
[80] *Ibid.,* June 5, 1897, February 4, 1893.

an unusual cold spell struck the city in the winter of 1895 and caused considerable hardship for thousands of people. To meet this emergency, the white people formed a relief committee which raised $5,000 to care for the victims, and of this amount, $4,500 went to the relief of Negroes. The Atlanta *Journal* claimed that while many Negroes owned property and were gainfully employed, they contributed only $3.50 to the effort to alleviate the misery among their own people. "If the Negroes will think over this and many similar events," observed the *Journal*, "they will discover who their true friends are and will pay less attention to lying negro preachers and politicians who preach doctrines of hate and revenge."[81]

Furthermore, the unfortunate experiences of Negroes who had gone North and West to escape Southern proscription convinced the Negro masses that the future of the Negro lay in the South where, even though he received lower wages, he was not denied work on account of his color. Because of the perpetuation of the old slave idea that work was only for "niggers and poor whites," Negroes were able to engage in labor activities which were closed to them in the North. Numerous cases were cited in which Negroes worked alongside of whites without incident, where Southern Negro contractors frequently hired whites and Negroes on jobs.[82] Southern white people were urged to "take away mob violence, court injustices . . . and let us have in full the constitutional rights of this country, and the South, if anywhere, . . . is the best for us. We are more united and progressive there than in any other section of the land."[83]

[81] Atlanta *Journal,* March 2, 1895
[82] Bell, "Does the Colored Man Have a Chance," 3.
[83] Savannah *Tribune,* May 2, 1903. Even Bishop Turner admitted that while Northern whites might be more friendly politically toward the Negro, the South afforded him better economic opportunities. He stated that employment was opened to Negroes in almost every field except that of operating railroad locomotives. Atlanta *Constitution,* July 14, 1890.

The Reverend Charles T. Walker, pastor of the Tabernacle Baptist Church in Augusta, and next to Bishop Turner probably the most widely known Negro churchman in the state, declared that it was a mistake for the Negro to leave the South, since prejudice was national and not sectional. He admitted that the North did not disfranchise the Negro nor "Jim Crow" him to the same extent as did the South; but, on the other hand, he noted that the North did not guarantee the same economic security. He advised the Negro to remain in the South, buy land, engage in business, and educate his children, for it was only a matter of time until the best people of the South would come to his aid and defend him in all of his rights.[84]

The Negro editor of the LaGrange (Ga.) *Enterprise,* W. S. Cannon, believed that it was far better to develop friendly relations with the white people of the South, and promised the support of his paper to any movement that would create a spirit of good will between the races, which in the long run would advance the interests of both groups.[85] The point was constantly stressed by many Negroes that the South was the natural home of the Negro and it was his duty to make himself indispensable to the community. "If we cannot vote for president, we can vote five dollar bills in a bank to our credit all day and the cashier will count them . . . . If we cannot govern, we can produce that which the ruling class must have." By doing this, Negro leaders said, the road to political equality, which was the dream of the Negro, would be paved.[86] Furthermore, Negroes were reminded that in certain places in the North Negroes were forced to leave the community in which they lived just because they wanted to earn an honest living. Such was the case in Dent, Ohio. In cities like Boston

[84] New York City *Presbyterian Herald,* quoted in Savannah *Tribune,* December 29, 1900.
[85] Quoted in Atlanta *Journal,* January 9, 1901.
[86] Atlanta *Independent,* March 26, 1904, April 8, 1905.

and Chicago there were signs reading, "No Negro help wanted." In Indiana, upon learning that Negroes were planning to come to the state to work, white men met them at the state line with guns and forced them back. As the Atlanta *Independent* aptly put it: "In the south we make them get a move on them because they won't work, but in the north, they make you move because you want to work."[87]

The economic plight of the Negro in New York by 1908 had become so acute that the Committee for Improving the Industrial Conditions of the Negro in New York, composed of both races and headed by William Jay Schiefflin, addressed a communication to the Negro editors and ministers of the South asking their aid in stemming any further migration of their people to the North. This communication pointed out that due to discrimination against Negroes in the labor field, inferior housing facilities, unfavorable climate, and the increasing crime rate among Negroes as a result of these factors, living conditions in the North were almost intolerable. In their opinion, the solution to the race problem in the South had to be worked out through the co-operation of the better elements of both races, which in the final analysis would prove beneficial to the material and moral growth of the South.[88]

Thus the Negro masses were resigned to stay in the South, hoping eventually that sentiment and conditions would move in their favor. Probably the general attitude of the Negro in Georgia at this time was best expressed by the Reverend C. L. Bonner, pastor of the St. Paul Colored Methodist Episcopal Church of Savannah. At the annual Emancipation Day exercises held in that city on January 1, 1902, the Reverend Mr. Bonner said:

There are men who are more profound in thought, loftier in ideas . . . than I am . . . who think and express their thoughts

[87] *Ibid,* April 8, 1905.
[88] Savannah *Tribune,* May 9, 1908.

differently to me. . . . There is my own Bishop Holsey's doctrine
of segregation, Bishop Turner's emigration, ex-Senator Butler's
expatriation, John Temple Graves' colonization, T. Thomas Fortune's . . . amalgamation, Ben Tillman's extermination. My doctrine is, if you let me coin a word, *"stayhereation"* and when I say
that, I mean stay here as a separate and distinct race, and the God
that has brought us thus far can carry us on.[89]

And "stayhereation" it was, as the vast majority of Negroes,
either by preference or by circumstances over which they had
no control, remained in the South despite segregation, political disfranchisement, mob violence, and other forms of race
proscription. As the twentieth century wore on, the Negro
would find an increasingly hostile environment. Despite his
efforts to improve his economic status, his struggle to educate himself, and his attempts to promote his social betterment, his hopes of attaining first-class citizenship were to be
engulfed by the wave of white supremacy which grew in
volume and intensity after the turn of the century.

[89] *Ibid.*, January 18, 1902. Italics mine.

CHARLES E. WYNES*

Lewis Harvie Blair, Virginia Reformer: The Uplift of the Negro and Southern Prosperity

In January 1889, a new book written by a prominent Richmond, Virginia, businessman began to attract the attention of reviewers and editors from New York to San Francisco. Unfortunately, its title, *The Prosperity of the South Dependent Upon the Elevation of the Negro,* made it little welcome in the so-called New South, of whose power and prosperity Southerners were wont to boast. In the book, Blair put Southerners on the defensive, first by denying the very existence of a prosperous New South, and then by suggesting that any future prosperity in the South would require the introduction of social reforms of a kind abhorent to most white Southerners.

* From *The Virginia Magazine of History and Biography,* LXXII (January 1964), 3-18. Reprinted by permission of the publisher.

What was worse, the book could not be dismissed as Northern propaganda, inasmuch as the author was a member of one of Richmond's most prominent families, a Confederate veteran, and one of the South's best examples of material progress and prosperity. But those who knew Blair had no cause to be surprised. He long had been what Richmond more charitably termed a "radical," when it preferred to call him a heretic — an advocate of mixed schools, a foe of "worship of the past," and a businessman who deplored high tariffs, who saw little or no danger in free silver, and who believed that government should perform more services for society through higher taxes.

Truthfully, it cannot be explained how Blair arrived at his unorthodox and unpopular views. They certainly were not the product of a liberal formal education, because the education he received was quite ordinary and was gained in several private schools in and about Richmond. His home environment had been staunchly Whig in politics and Presbyterian in religion, with the family bread provided by his father's association with a Richmond bank — scarcely the sort of environment likely to produce a liberal, albeit pragmatic, reformer.

Truly a voice crying in the wilderness of Southern economics, Richmond's Blair, unlike Atlanta's Henry W. Grady, saw the South through dark glasses. In appraising Southern society both before and after the Civil War, his conclusions were the antithesis of those of his romantic contemporary, Thomas Nelson Page. Fate had laid a heavy burden of unpopular reform upon Blair, and then, unable to reward him with success in his crusade, had compensated him by allowing him to make a fortune in the very society he criticized so sharply.

Lewis Harvie Blair was born in Richmond on June 21, 1834, the eleventh of thirteen children of Sarah Ann Eyre Heron and John Geddes Blair. Blair's paternal grandparents were the well-known Presbyterian minister, John Durburrow Blair ("Parson Blair"), and his wife, Mary Winston Blair. The Blairs were Scotch-Irish, having emigrated from Ireland to Pennsylvania early in the eighteenth century, and thence to Richmond at the close of the American Revolution. The ancestors of Blair's mother, the Herons, had come from Scotland to Richmond shortly after the Revolutionary War. James Heron, Blair's maternal grandfather, was highly successful in the West Indian trade, and Blair pronounced him to be the only wealthy ancestor he had. An ardent Whig and veteran of the War of 1812, Lewis' father was cashier of the Farmers' Bank of Virginia for many years prior to his death in 1851.[1]

With the passing of Blair senior, Lewis, at age seventeen, was thrown on his own, and thus began his remarkable career. Blair's formal education also ended at that time, although he was an avid reader throughout his life. Of his education, Blair later wrote: "When I left school I could boast little of scholarship because I had not gotten beyond trigonometry and Cicero — neither of which I understood much about — and the rudiments of Greek."[2]

Blair's older brother, William, had just been promoted to the rank of captain in the army and assigned to San Antonio, Texas, as chief commissary of the eighth department. Appoint-

---

[1] Lewis H. Blair, "Autobiography II," 7-13. There are two unpublished autobiographies — a handwritten original in three volumes, written in 1897-1898, and a greatly revised typescript version, done in 1915. Because the two are different in content and tenor, the author of this essay has chosen to identify them as "Autobiography I" (the original), and "Autobiography II" (the revised version), and to cite them separately here. Both of the autobiographies are in the possession of Blair's daughter, Mrs. Pierre Daura, Rockbridge Baths, Virginia. Much of the genealogical data appearing in the autobiographies, as well as a very incomplete and ambiguously general sketch of Blair, is also to be found in *Men of Mark in Virginia*, Lyon G. Tyler, editor (Washington, D. C., 1906-1909), IV, 30-34. See also, Louisa Coleman Gordon Blair, *Blairs of Richmond, Virginia : The Descendants of Reverend John Durburrow Blair and Mary Winston Blair, His Wife* (Richmond, 1933).

[2] Blair, "Autobiography I," vol. I, 18.

ing Lewis his clerk, at the then princely salary of $75 a month, William set out for Texas taking his younger brother with him.

While in Texas, Lewis got to know personally several army officers who became generals during the Civil War — Don Carlos Buell, Albert Sidney Johnston, William F. Smith, James Longstreet, and William E. Jones. Some of these friendships were valuable in the Confederacy. Sixty years later, Blair recalled in a remarkably vivid and accurate account the Texas of 1851-1855.[3]

Returning to Virginia in late 1855, Blair went to work at Binford, Mayo and Blair, a Richmond drygoods firm in which his brother John was one of the principals. Eighteen months later, in 1857, he left Richmond for Detroit, to serve as clerk to Captain William F. Smith, a Texas acquaintance who had just been appointed engineer-superintendent of lighthouses on the Great Lakes. Unmarried, peripatetic, but home-loving, Blair returned to the falls on the James in early 1860.[4]

At home in Richmond, Blair, like most Americans, eagerly followed the events of 1860, culminating in the election of Lincoln and the secession of South Carolina. Shortly afterward, he was unwillingly caught up in the events following the firing on Fort Sumter. A jump ahead of the conscript law of 1862, Blair volunteered for the Confederate artillery. But in doing so he was not prompted by burning patriotism for the Confederate States, nor was he swept up in the hot-blooded emotion of the moment. He volunteered, he said, lest he be drafted and thus not get to pick his branch of the service. And he chose the artillery, he recounted, because he had no flair for the glory of the infantry and because the artillery appeared to be physically the safest.[5]

[3] Blair, Autobiography II," 26-38. See Charles E. Wynes, ed., "Lewis Harvie Blair: Texas Travels, 1851-1855," *Southwestern Historical Quarterly*, LXVI (1962-1963), 262-70.

[4] Blair, "Autobiography II," 48-58.

[5] *Ibid.*, 61.

Seeking no commission in spite of his high placed friendships and the prominence of his family name, Blair entered the army in 1862 as a private. Three years later he left the army, *still a private*. Aside from his lack of motivation, this fact was undoubtedly due in part to his dislike for authority, coupled with a penchant for engaging in camp fights (at age 28-31), which caused him to be well acquainted with the interior of army stockades.[6]

Blair's Confederate service was neither dramatic nor exciting. After some eighteen months in southwestern Virginia, he was detached and assigned to the headquarters of General William E. "Grumble" Jones, commanding general of the Department of Southwest Virginia. When General Jones was killed in the Valley, Blair was returned to the artillery, but he was not long a member of a gun crew. Espied by his former battalion commander, J. Floyd King, Blair became King's adjutant for the remainder of the war. He was with General Jubal Early when he made his famous but futile advance upon Washington, D. C., in July 1864. Later Blair contracted typhoid fever, which kept him out of action until the war ended.[7]

To many Southerners, the years 1861-1865 were the focal point of all Southern history. Events were said to have taken place "before the War," or "after the War." "The War" itself was, of course, the South's finest hour. What then was to be said of a Southerner of good family, who had served the Confederacy honorably, if without distinction, who in 1897-1898 closed the brief memoir on his war experiences with the statement:

And thus ended my martial life; more than three years wasted in the vain effort to maintain that most monstrous institution, African slavery, the real, tho' States Rights were the ostensible cause of the War.[8]

[6] Blair, "Autobiography II," 61-62.   [7] *Ibid.*, 62-64.
[8] Blair, Autobiography I," vol. I, 120.

Returning to a burned-out and destitute Richmond in 1865, Blair floundered about looking for something to do; but soon, with a $20 greenback given to him by his mother, he opened first a wholesale auction business and then a retail store in nearby Amelia County. In 1867, while still in Amelia County, Blair married Alice Wayles Harrison, by whom he was to have seven children — six boys and one girl.

In 1868, having accumulated $7,000, Blair sold his retail business and returned to Richmond to enter the wholesale grocery business. Success followed, and in 1878 Blair became associated with the Stephen Putney Shoe Company of Richmond. He had meanwhile built up one of Richmond's largest real estate businesses.[9]

Uncommon for his day among businessmen, Blair held laissez-faire views on economics and commerce, which led him to condemn high protective tariffs. Beginning in 1884, he became a frequent contributor of letters to the Richmond newspapers, mostly on economic subjects, but especially on the subject of protection. Then in 1886 he marshaled his views in a book, *Unwise Laws: A Consideration of the Operations of a Protective Tariff Upon Industry, Commerce, and Society,* published by G. P. Putnam's Sons, New York. As far as the volume gained circulation (only about 400 copies were sold), comments were generally favorable, even from those who disagreed with the views expressed.[10]

Unwise Laws was soon forgotten, or forgiven; but the sub-

[9] *Ibid.*, 123, 132-33; Blair, "Autobiography II," 65-67.
[10] Blair, "Autobiography I," vol. III, 2-6. Blair quotes from numerous newspaper reviews, and apparently with impartiality as both favorable and unfavorable reviews are cited. Except for the New York *World,* though, none of them are major newspapers. The *World* termed *Unwise Laws* "self flattery," and declared that Blair did not know the meaning of protection. The Richmond *State* called the volume "a masterly exposure of protection." Other reviewing newspapers, favorable and unfavorable, cited, were: Hartford, Conn., *Post;* Newark, N. J., *Advertiser;* Providence, R. I., *Star;* Chicago, Ill., *Standard;* and Brooklyn, N. Y., *Eagle.*

ject of Blair's next book, the prosperity of the South, as he developed it, was not easily tolerated nor was he forgiven for having written it.

The talk of the South by 1885 concentrated on the New South—that is, when it was not on the Old South. But it was one of the ironies of history that the South became conscious of a *New* South before it did of an *Old* South. Indeed, it was the New South which gave rise to the myth of the Old South.[11]

The term "New South" stood for economic reconstruction completed—but in the form of cities, factories, mines, railroads—not cotton plantations restored. It was a part of the creed of the New South to be openly boastful of the successes and achievements of the region. But it was also a part of that creed to brand as heretics any who questioned the existence of a New South or who pointed to the even greater growth of the North since the Civil War.

Denying that there was any such thing as a New South, and pronouncing Southern prosperity a delusion, Blair first put his case in print through the columns of the New York *Independent*. In the summer of 1887, there appeared a series of articles collectively titled, "The Prosperity of the South." It was these articles which grew into the book, *The Prosperity of the South Dependent Upon the Elevation of the Negro*. One of the cardinal points of Blair's arguments—a point which appeared in the *Independent* on June 23, 1887—was that separate schools for each race were impractical in the sparsely settled South. Actually, Blair took a mild stand. Only later, in his book did he pronounce separate schools as inherently unequal, thereby anticipating the United States Supreme Court by sixty-five years. In the *Independent,* he cautiously wrote:

If we desire to progress and prosper we *must* have educated citizens, and to get them we are entirely dependent upon public schools. But

11 C. Vann Woodward, *The Origins of the New South, 1877-1913* (Baton Rouge, 1951), 154-58.

we see that, owing to the sparseness and heterogeneousness of population [black and white] these are impossible as long as we insist upon separate schools. . . .

Where good separate schools—as in cities—are possible, it will then, for the present at least, be wise to continue them; but where they [racially separate, good schools] are manifestly impossible, and when in consequence, the children are growing up in ignorance, it would seem to be the height of folly to insist upon them.[12]

Hardly had Blair's article appeared in the *Independent* when there broke out in Richmond, not discussion of the validity of his assertions, but angry debate over what should be done to the author for writing as he had. The Richmond Democratic Committee, of which Blair was treasurer, was prepared to expel him, when Chairman Charles E. Wingo, sought and got Blair's immediate resignation.[13]

The very next day, June 28, 1887, in a public letter to his friend Wingo, Blair wrote:

I say to my opponents: Prove also your point and defend your position. The day has gone by forever among intelligent, thoughtful peoples, unless perhaps Richmond and the South be an exception, when clamor, however vehement, or predictions, however dreadful, will pass for either sense, wisdom, or statesmanship. . . .

If the South was a little or even a big island in the vast South seas, so cut off by distance that the world could not get to it and it could not get to the world, it might then safely maintain and even encourage all of its many and great prepossessions; but as it is in the world and seeks to be a part of the world it must accommodate itself to the current ideas of the world.[14]

The argument rested here with neither side willing to give ground. Meanwhile, Blair polished and perfected his case, and in January, 1889 the Richmond concern of Everett Waddey printed *The Prosperity of the South Dependent Upon the Elevation of the Negro*. Blair's was no case made by an

[12] Quoted by Blair in a letter to the Richmond *Dispatch*, June 27, 1887.
[13] Blair, "Autobiography I," vol. III, 8.
[14] Richmond *Dispatch*, June 27, 1887.

idealistic moralist. Rather it was a realistic, pragmatic pres-
entation made by a hardheaded, successful businessman. To
Blair, the prosperity of the South was the *end*, with the elevation of the Negro only the *means* to that end. This is not to
demean either his purpose or his humanitarianism. Rather it
is only a statement of Blair's recognition as a businessman
that the surest way to men's understanding and acceptance of
the unpopular was through an appeal to their self-interest.

Seemingly with a heavy heart, Blair commenced his volume
with the statement:

Twenty-odd years ago, when I cast aside the sword and re-entered
the walks of civil life, I fondly imagined a great era of prosperity
for the South. Guided by history and by a knowledge of our people
and our climatic and physical advantages, I saw in anticipation all
her tribulations ended, all her scars healed, and all the ravages of
war forgotten, and I beheld the South greater, richer and mightier
than when she moulded the political policy of the whole country.
But year by year these hopes, chastened by experience, have waned
and faded, until now, instead of beholding the glorious South of
my imagination, I see her sons poorer than when war ceased his
ravages, weaker than when rehabilitated with her original rights,
and with the bitter memories of the past smouldering, if not rank-
ling, in the bosoms of many.[15]

Who said the South was prosperous anyway? Blair asked. And
then answering himself, he scornfully replied that it was the
"so-called Manufacturers' Records which are circulating a
vast amount of misinformation about the growth and prosperity of the South, and misleading multitudes on this
point."[16] These salesmen of the New South, said Blair, were
careful to take visiting Northern businessmen to only a few
selected spots, such as Birmingham and Chattanooga. These
visitors forgot or did not see

[15] Blair, *The Prosperity of the South Dependent Upon the Elevation
of the Negro* (Richmond, 1889), 1. (A new edition, edited by C. Vann
Woodward, and published by Little, Brown and Company under the
title, *A Southern Prophecy*, appeared in 1964 — Ed.)
[16] *Ibid.*, 3.

the hundreds and hundreds of miles of poor country passed through [in palace-like cars], with its fenceless plantations, its unpainted and dilapidated homesteads, its small proportion of cultivated fields and its large proportion of lands returning and returned to a state of nature, its patches instead of its fields of crops, the scarcity of stock of all kinds, and the thriftless and idle groups found at almost every depot.[17]

Turning instead to the United States census reports to show that the South was not prosperous, Blair made a convincing case as he repeatedly showed the tremendous disparity between growth of Southern manufactures, cash savings, and cities, as compared to that of the North. In these areas the South appeared to be in approximately the same position relative to the North as it had been in 1860. Southern progress, on the basis of the South of 1860, there had been, but what of the North? Progress there had been infinitely greater. The South compared its present self only with its former self, not with the North of the present.[18]

Citing the report of the United States comptroller of the currency for December 4, 1886, Blair asked: "What shall we say, then, of the prosperity of the South when it possesses six per cent of [the] banking capital for twenty-six per cent of [the] population?" From Henry V. Poor's *Manual of the Railroads of the United States* for 1886, Blair reported Southern railroad investments as only $1,108,428,000 as compared to $7,230,858,000 for all the other states. Blair used these sources in addition to the official census reports, he said, because the last census had been held nine years ago in 1880, and he knew the South would point out that its *real* growth had occurred since then. It was true, he admitted, that Southern production of pig iron had more than tripled between 1880 and 1887, but meanwhile the Southern percentage of the total United States pig iron production had only doubled, from 5 to 10 per cent.[19]

[17] *Ibid.*, 6.   [18] *Ibid.*, 13-26.   [19] *Ibid.*, 17, 19.

"Patriotism" would say hide all these uncomplimentary facts, but common sense says it is better to look our deficiencies squarely in the face, for we will never overcome our shortcomings until we are convinced of their existence.[20]

Why then was the South not prosperous? The causes were many, but chief among them were "illiteracy, disregard of human life, lack of economy and self-denial, and degradation of the negro."[21] A region's prosperity, Blair maintained, was in proportion to the intelligence and education of its people, particularly of its workers. And in the South, both white and black were deficient on this score. "Thus our prosperity is bound up in the elevation of our laboring population."[22] But a large part of the South's labor force was made up of "depraved and degraded human beings,"—the Negroes. These must first, said Blair, "be inspired with self-respect, their hope must be stimulated and their intelligence must be cultivated."[23] In these things, the Negro could be aided only by the white man, for

If he is to remain forever a "nigger," an object of undisguised contempt, even to the lowest whites, the negro will naturally say to himself, Why strive, why labor, why practice painful self-denial in order to rise, if I am to derive no good from my effort? . . . The South can never become prosperous, with its laboring population bereft of hope.[24]

If the Negro was to rise in dignity and self-respect, the South must obliterate race and color prejudice. "Many glory in prejudice," Blair wrote, "foolishly thinking it a mark of superiority, but prejudice is always a weakness, and when it is extreme it is a badge of dishonor."[25] The Negro must, in short, be treated exactly as the whites, with free access to all public places and business establishments.[26] "For public sentiment to shut the doors of these places in the faces of any

20 *Ibid.*, 20.   21 *Ibid.*, 27.   22 *Ibid.*, 34.
23 *Ibid.*, 47.   24 *Ibid.*, 51-52.   25 *Ibid.*, 54-55.
26 *Ibid.*, 60.

portion of the community, is to degrade and to humiliate it, and is greatly to impair its ability to serve the best interests of society."[27]

Public sentiment, which Blair saw barring most public places to Negroes, was within a few years given the force of law. Segregation in the South then became universal, whereas, when Blair wrote, the situation which he deplored was not nearly so rigid as it became by the early twentieth century.[28]

When it came to the question of public education and segregation, Blair took a more advanced position in his book than he had taken in the *Independent* in 1887. Then, he had advocated abandonment of separate schools for fiscal reasons alone—the sparseness of population in the rural areas of the South made the maintenance of two good public school systems in such areas impossible. In 1889 he added to this argument moral reasons for a single school system.

Separate schools are a public proclamation to all of African or mixed blood that they are an inferior caste, fundamentally inferior and totally unfit to mingle on terms of equality with the superior caste. . . . Hence it follows that separate schools brand the stigma of degradation upon one-half of the population, irrespective of character and culture, and crushes their hope and self-respect, without which they can never become useful and valuable citizens. . . . We can never make men of human beings simply by attending, however carefully, to their physical necessities. . . . We can only make men of them by cultivating and stimulating their higher and nobler natures, their mental and moral parts, and this can never be done while the principle of separate schools remains in force.[29]

Blair saw no danger to the whites or to education itself in the mixing of the races in the schools. In his opinion, "The higher ranks of society elevate or demoralize the lower, but

---

[27] *Ibid.*, 62-63.
[28] On the subject of Virginia segregation practices in the years following the Civil War and down to 1902, see Charles E. Wynes, *Race Relations in Virginia, 1870-1902* (Charlottesville, Va., 1961), 68-83.
[29] Blair, *Prosperity of the South*, 99.

rarely do the virtues or the vices of the lower affect the higher one way or the other."[30] Blair did not, but here he might also have used one of the South's own ante bellum arguments to justify the institution of slavery: contact of the backward, heathen Africans with the superior white planters had Christianized and generally uplifted the former; and those Africans who had the closest contact, often including education by tutor—the house servants—had been lifted highest of all.

White men, Blair thought, would also benefit greatly from this increased association, as they learned that "the difference between man and man is not color, but character and conduct."

One reason, most likely, why the South has always shown, and still shows, so little intellectual development, apart from law and politics, is because the whites have been possessed of the idea that the height of superiority is a white skin, and that they have been content with that kind of eminence.[31]

Closing his argument for equal treatment of all, regardless of race or color, Blair charged: "Oligarchy, caste, vassalage, are the regnant spirit in the greater portion of the South, and no country can prosper under their weight." He concluded: "Until the negro sees and feels that he can of right enter the school attended by his white neighbor, the brand of degradation must eat into and consume his soul."[32]

The dangers of the situation were seen clearly by Blair:

We have raised up an enemy, silent and sullen, at our very doors, who, though he will never conquer, stands ever ready to vex and harass, and to league with those who, for any cause, seek to upturn the present order of affairs.

Inferior as the negroes undeniably are, they have sense enough to see that the whites, as a caste, are their constant and inveterate foes, not that individually they are harsh and cruel, but they know that this kindness springs mainly from the same benevolence that prompts consideration for their horses and cattle, for their cats and dogs. . . . They remember that the whites fought a long and bloody

---

[30] *Ibid.*, 104.   [31] *Ibid.*, 109-10.   [32] *Ibid.*, 117.

war, not desisting until absolutely exhausted, or until they literally had reached the last ditch, to keep them in servitude; that they organized [the] Ku-Klux to render their freedom nugatory; that they violently opposed the Federal amendment granting suffrage; that civil rights were conferred in spite of all their efforts, and that generally they have opposed everything tending to their elevation. . . .[33]

Hence the whites, instead of having six millions of friends and co-workers in prosperity, as they should have if they showed only a willingness to elevate the negro, have that number of secret foes in their midst.[34]

Any book containing these views was bound to gain attention and provoke repercussions. These were not long in coming. Describing the reaction to his book, Blair later wrote: "It brought me both [financial] loss and odium, at least at home in Virginia, tho' it spread my name favorably from Maine to California."[35]

Actually, Virginia newspapers, especially those of Richmond, almost completely ignored the book—perhaps to minimize the dissemination of such heretical views. The Alexandria *Gazette,* while agreeing with Blair that no reliance should be placed in Southern newspaper reports of that region's prosperity, fatalistically pronounced as "poor indeed" the future prospect if it was dependent upon the elevation of the Negro.[36] The New Market *Shenandoah Valley* commended the book, though, and termed Blair "a statesman, a philanthropist and a Christian."[37] Outside the South, the New York *Herald* in an editorial pronounced the book "a valuable contribution to the literature on this puzzling problem." On another page, the *Herald* also ably summarized the gist of the book in a two-column spread headed, "The Negro's Champion; A Rich and Aristocratic Virginia Democrat Demands Education for the Black Man."[38] The Chicago *Tribune* in an

[33] *Ibid.,* 118-19.   [34] *Ibid.,* 120.
[35] Blair, "Autobiography I," vol. III, 6.
[36] Alexandria *Gazette,* May 20, 1889.
[37] New Market *Shenandoah Valley,* May 20, 1889.
[38] New York *Herald,* January 14, 1889, the summary is on 8.

editorial "Southern Championship of the Negro," termed the book "the most remarkable contribution from the South upon the race problem which has yet appeared." (The reader should remember that the major writings of George Washington Cable on the "Negro Question" were already in print, and hence, the editor was not even excepting them.) The *Tribune* declared that, "If there were more Blairs in the South the conditions for the solution of the race problem would soon be placed upon an intelligent and practical basis."[39] Other favorable reviews or editorials appeared in the Minneapolis, Minnesota, *Journal,* the Chicago *Times,* the New York *Sun,* and the Alto *Californian.*[40]

Prosperity of the South gained Blair such fame in the Negro community that he was invited to deliver an address on "The Southern Problem and its Solution" before the African Congress held at the 1893 Chicago World's Fair. Blair prepared the paper, but the economic crisis of that year prevented his leaving Richmond to read it in Chicago, so it was read for him. The theme of this paper, too, was that the Negro must be uplifted if the South ever was to know prosperity. In the paper Blair quoted at length from an editorial in the Charleston, South Carolina, *News and Courier*—before that paper turned its face from the New to the Old South:

We need not shut our eyes or our minds to our condition; it is known to all men and they avoid our soil as they would a desert. We must work a change somehow and soon or it will be worse than a desert.[41]

[39] Chicago *Tribune,* January 17, 1889.

[40] Cited, with quotations, by Blair, in "Autobiography I," vol. III, 11-13. Blair does not give the dates of the issues of these papers, however, so the author has not seen them. Reviews in the Alexandria *Gazette,* the New Market *Shenandoah Valley,* the New York *Herald,* and the Chicago *Tribune,* were, however, read by the author.

[41] Lewis H. Blair, "The Southern Problem and its Solution," *Our Day,* XII (November 1893), 373, as quoted from the Charleston *News and Courier,* June 16, 1892.

His paper was published in full as the lead article in the November 1893 issue of the journal, *Our Day*.[42]

With the fat in the fire, Blair continued his heretical and iconoclastic blasts through the columns of the Richmond newspapers, to their editors' great discomfort. In 1896 we find him writing on Virginia's "past consciousness":

> Our hearts, souls, energies—our all—being thus absorbed in the past, we have nothing, or not enough, left for the present. . . . We look to the set, and not to the risen sun; we live in the past, and not in the present. . . . We must let the [recent] past be like the Revolution [of 1776]—simply an historical memory.[43]

To this letter, the editor of the *Dispatch* heatedly replied on the following day:

> How can we who remember the war, we who live in the sight of Hollywood and Oakwood [cemeteries], we who cannot take a suburban drive without passing over battleground, nor plow a field or dig a post-hole without turning up a shell or a bullet, "let the past be like the Revolution, simply a historical memory." That is asking too much.[44]

To which, Blair calmly replied: "[My] protest is not against a reasonable respect for the past, but against erecting the past into a fetish and worshipping it at the sacrifice of the present."[45] Impatiently terminating the whole imbroglio, the editor replied in the same issue:

> It is doubtful whether in justice to our readers, or to the family and friends of L. H. B. we ought to publish any more of his letters on the past and present; but we make place for another today rather than give him ground to say that he has been denied a fair hearing by the *Dispatch*.[46]

[42] XII, 361-76.
[43] Richmond *Dispatch*, February 12, 1896.
[44] *Ibid.*, February 13,1896.
[45] *Ibid.*, February 20, 1896.
[46] *Ibid.*, February 20, 1896. It should be pointed out, that in all this exchange, Blair had signed his letters with only the initials L. H. B. However, this practice, and the use of Greek or Roman pseudonyms, was

Late the next year, in December 1897, Blair commenced writing his autobiography, which he finished sometime the following year. Totaling 357 handwritten pages, it is written in a simple, direct style, lacking the occasional literary grace found in *Prosperity of the South*. It is simply a man's account of his life down to the time of its composition. There are no observations on the important Virginia figures of the day or on current political or social questions—except the Negro, briefly. Rather it is a straightforward account of Blair's life, and little else. However, assessing the race problem in the South nearly a decade after the appearance of *Prosperity of the South,* he despairingly wrote:

The Prosperity of the South . . . was published more than nine years ago, yet the Negro Problem is further than ever from solution, the South is more than ever bent upon keeping the negro an oppressed and therefore degraded serf and the North is more than ever indifferent to human rights.[47]

While Blair was engaged in his 1896 running feud with the editor of the *Dispatch,* and then with writing the "Autobiography," he was a widower. His wife had died in February 1894. On October 27, 1898, Blair married again. His second wife was his secretary at the Putney Shoe Company, Martha Redd Feild, one of fifteen children of John Shaw and Jean Bland Ruffin Feild, of Meklenberg County, Virginia. She was less than half his age, but she had a "keen sense of humor and the spirit of sociability," according to Blair, which caused them to "live happily ever after."[48] Four daughters were born to this union. Mrs. Blair, possessed of her keen sense of

---

a common one in the last century. Unlike today, editors then did not refuse to print letters not containing the writer's full name and address. However, Blair's prominence, his two published books and his well-known views undoubtedly made the initials L. H. B. no mask for the letters' author. Neither was Blair the sort of man to seek such refuge. In using initials he was simply following a common practice of the day.

[47] Blair, "Autobiography I," vol. III, 14.
[48] Blair, "Autobiography II," 95.

humor till life's end, died on April 26, 1962, at age ninety-five.

Aside from the "Autobiography," there is little record of the last eighteen years of Blair's life. He had retired from business and was undoubtedly still avidly reading and, *unfortunately,* writing. Sometime between 1898 and 1915, Blair completely reversed himself on the position he had taken in *Prosperity of the South.* In an unpublished manuscript, written during this period—a manuscript of 270 handwritten pages—Blair repudiated everything he had said about the intellectual capacity of the Negro and the equal treatment he deserved. He advocated repeal of the Fourteenth and Fifteenth Amendments and segregation of the Negro who as a lower form of man should be made "a ward of the nation."[49]

Declaring that "negroes are by nature . . . children to the day of their death," Blair advocated the establishment of special courts similar to juvenile courts for the trial of Negro offenders.[50]

Some quotations from this manuscript, without further comment, will perhaps serve to make clear Blair's new position on the Negro.

The humblest Caucasian is *ipso facto* the superior of the highest African or half-breed, even tho' this be Booker [T.] Washington, estimable, admirable and wise tho' he be.[51]

The only thing to do is to elevate him not as if [he were] a white man, but as a very different being—a negro . . . in line with his African nature and antecedents.[52]

The only logical position for the negro is absolute subordination to the whites.[53]

Like white Southerners generally, Blair claimed to esteem the Negro—but as an inferior being, dependent upon the su-

[49] This manuscript, bearing no title, the author, has arbitrarily designated, for purposes of identification, "The Prosperity of the South Reconsidered." The above material from this manuscript is from pages 3-7. The manuscript is owned by Mrs. Daura.

[50] *Ibid.,* 10-11.   [52] *Ibid.,* 54.
[51] *Ibid.,* 32.   [53] *Ibid.,* 245.

perior whites. He explained Booker T. Washington's achievements and eminence by the "Caucasian blood [which] flows in his veins," and by his being "surrounded, encouraged, and buttressed by able and wealthy whites."[54]

No man could have reversed his convictions more completely! Replying to a letter from Oswald Garrison Villard, grandson of William Lloyd Garrison and president of the New York *Evening Post,* in which Villard praised *Prosperity of the South,* Blair wrote: "I think I reasoned logically from my premises, but since then, experience and observation have convinced me of the fallacy of my premises."[55] No other explanation apparently was ever given for the reversal of Blair's position on the Negro, and the author has been able to deduce no other sound explanation. There is no record to show whether he read any of the racist literature which appeared early in the twentieth century, and thereby became converted. Possibly, he was influenced by his second wife, who disagreed completely with his liberal views on the Negro. Southern white reaction on the race question—including that of most Southern Progressives—was a hallmark of the early twentieth century. Blair simply did not escape the conventional, for at least once in his life.

After the completion of this pessimistic work on the Negro, Blair commenced revising the "Autobiography." At least twice, he sent revised chapters to his friend, Herbert W. Jackson, president of the Virginia Trust Company, for his comments.[56] As it emerged in final form—349 typewritten pages—the revised "Autobiography" bore almost no resemblance to the original. The chapter headings—twenty-three in the first and twenty in the second—are completely different. Chapters

[54] *Ibid.,* 244.

[55] Quoted in a letter from Mrs. Lewis H. Blair to Charles E. Wynes, October 24, 1960.

[56] Herbert W. Jackson to Blair, April 6 and July 1, 1915. Blair Papers, in the possession of Mrs. Daura.

of the original each embrace a definite year span in Blair's life, which is stated in the chapter title. In the revised, or second version, eleven of the twenty chapters contain the title, "Recollections of . . ."—"a Private," "Richmond Doctors," "Richmond Lawyers," "Sundry Old Citizens," "Younger Men of Prominence," etc. There are also two chapters on Richmond hotels and one on Richmond churches and pastors. In the original, which is admittedly not a "gold mine" either, Blair at least comes through to the reader as a true liberal and man of both thought and action, even if at times impetuous. The revised version is better written, but it is "harmless," and typical of an old man musing, without thought, over the past.

Still, Blair had not become a complete reactionary, as one might suppose from his second work on the subject of the Negro. Nor was he mentally senile in 1915, as one might conclude from what has been said about the revised "Autobiography." Rather, like most old men, he simply liked to reminisce and can thus be forgiven for the lack of real content in the second version of the "Autobiography." Like most Southern Progressives of the early twentieth century, he was utterly reactionary on one subject—the Negro. In 1915 he could still write of his renouncement of Herbert Spencer, whose writings he once had greatly admired. To the elderly Blair, Spencer seemed to put the obligation of the individual to the state before the obligation of the state to the individual. Blair said that he himself inclined toward state paternalism, fostered by taxes upon the individual[57]—certainly not an unfair statement of a part of the philosophy of the Progressive movement. As further evidence that Blair was in camp with the Progressives in 1914, he wrote to Georgia Senator Hoke Smith—who is one of the best examples of a typical Southern Progressive—praising him for the help he had given President Woodrow Wilson

[57] Blair, "Autobiography II," 73-74.

in getting the President's liberal domestic program through Congress.[58]

In spite of all the inconsistencies and reversals of position in his life, Blair was true to two ideals—logic and rebellion against conformity. And he never allowed fidelity to the latter to lead him astray from logic, as witnessed by the repudiation of his earlier conclusions in *Prosperity of the South,* because he became convinced that his initial premises had been wrong.

Tactless, withdrawn, almost austere in the simplicity of his tastes, Blair did not like golf or tennis and never saw a horse race or a ball game. Caring nothing for the theater, clubs, or entertainments in general, his only genuine pleasures were his business, his family, and omnivorous reading. Abstaining from both tobacco and alcohol, Blair almost wistfully admitted that he regretted that he did not indulge in these masculine comforts because of the sociability, or excuse for sociability, which they afforded. A lover of things of beauty, early in life he began collecting eighteenth-century Chinese porcelains and "choice oil paintings," in the selection of which he was guided by a friend, Thomas B. Clarke of New York. On his first wife's fiftieth birthday, he presented her with a large oil painting, "September Noon," by George Inness, America's foremost landscape painter.[59]

On November 26, 1916, aged eighty-two, Blair succumbed to a heart attack at his home, 2327 Monument Avenue, Richmond. For two years, his health had been declining as the physical infirmities of old age caught up with him. He was buried in Hollywood Cemetery.[60]

In his day, Lewis Harvie Blair certainly had given his family, his friends, Richmond, his home state, and indeed

---

[58] Copy of letter from Blair to Senator Hoke Smith, August 29, 1914. Blair Papers.

[59] Blair, "Autobiography II," 71-75, 83.

[60] Richmond *Times-Dispatch,* November 27, 1916.

the whole South, many an uncomfortable moment, as he turned his barbed pen and agile mind to the social and economic ills surrounding him. Now, with his demise, the storm of controversy subsided, and a thorn was removed from the consciences of his contemporaries.

Government clerk, soldier, merchant, manufacturer, and author-reformer, Blair died, as he had lived—and to some extent remains—an enigma to friend and foe alike.

LOUIS R. HARLAN*

The Southern Education Board and the Race Issue in Public Education

When the Southern Education Board was created in 1901 to direct a region-wide public school crusade, it at once encountered a powerful movement which had been accumulating force for a decade. Disfranchisement of Negroes in state after state was accompanied or followed by new segregation laws, discrimination of various sorts, and extralegal violence. Sometimes called the white supremacy movement, this current of extreme racialism enveloped all other movements in the region within its context, tingeing them with its attitudes and deflecting them from their original directions into its own stream. "These new antipathies are not defensive, but assertive and combative," Edgar Gardner Murphy noted at the

* From *The Journal of Southern History*, XXIII (May 1957), 189-202. Reprinted by permission of the publisher.

time; "this popular temper is . . . frankly and ruthlessly destructive."[1] Southern progressivism could not avoid or evade the white supremacy issue, nor could Southern prohibitionism or the Southern education movement.

The Southern Education Board, with eleven Northern and fifteen Southern members in its thirteen-year history, was an intersectional partnership of moderate progressives, moderate in the North on the delicate racial and sectional issues, and progressive in the South in the limited sense that it offered education as a key to regional progress. In challenging racialism by good will, tact and hard work, the Board's efforts were a test of the efficacy of moderate progressivism in a field where the Radicals of Reconstruction had signally failed. The Northerners on the Board were from New York rather than Boston. Robert C. Ogden was manager of John Wanamaker's New York department store. George Foster Peabody, a Wall Street banker, and the young railroad president William H. Baldwin, Jr., had long been associated with Ogden as trustees of Negro industrial schools. These men financed the Board's modest budget, with help from Andrew Carnegie and the General Education Board. Walter Hines Page and Jabez L. M. Curry, Southerners transplanted in the North, served as intersectional diplomats. Booker T. Washington was the agent for Negroes, but did not attend the Board meetings. Most of the Southern members were college presidents. The veteran campaigners Charles D. McIver, Edwin A. Alderman, and Charles W. Dabney had been partners in the earlier North Carolina school crusade. Edgar Gardner Murphy, on the other hand, had attracted the philanthropists' attention by organizing an intersectional conference on Southern race questions at Montgomery, Alabama, May 8-10, 1900.[2] These

---

[1] Edgar Gardner Murphy, *The Basis of Ascendancy* (New York, 1909), 27.

[2] Washington met frequently with the Northerners, and spoke on the same platforms with the Southerners in the North and South, but did not

were the chief policy-makers, though other Southerners were later added.

As Ogden explained the attitude of the philanthropists at a Southern gathering, "While we were originally interested in the South through negro education, our impulses have risen from negro education to the question of the entire burden of educational responsibility that you have throughout this entire section of the country."[3] This change of perspective grew out of sober thought about the significance of the white supremacy movement. As early as 1896 Ogden predicted that the ensuing ten years would cover the Negro's crisis, "and within that period it will be determined whether as a mass his race is to rise or fall in this country. I very much fear the fall."[4] The new philanthropists were not as concerned about Negro civil rights as were the humanitarian radicals of an earlier generation.[5] William H.

---

attend the Board or Conference meetings. Ogden failed in an effort to get Washington on the program of the Conference for Education in the South. Robert C. Ogden to William H. Baldwin, Jr., May 27, 1903; Ogden to Oswald Garrison Villard, March 11, 1905; Ogden to the Rev. Samuel H. Bishop of New York City, March 27, 1906; Robert C. Ogden Papers (Division of Manuscripts, Library of Congress). Unless otherwise indicated the Ogden Papers hereinafter cited are in the Library of Congress. Washington complained of this slight to Baldwin, January 22, 1904, Booker T. Washington Papers (Division of Manuscripts, Library of Congress). Unless cited otherwise the Washington Papers are in the Library of Congress. On Murphy's race conference, see Isabel C. Barrows, "The Montgomery Conference," *Outlook,* LXV (May 19, 1900), 160-62; "The Montgomery Conference," the *American Monthly Review of Reviews,* XXI (June 1900), 655-56; Montgomery *Advertiser,* January 11, 1900; Ogden to Walter Hines Page, April 5, 1900. Walter Hines Page Papers (Houghton Library, Harvard University). A scholarly account of Murphy is Allen J. Going, "The Reverend Edgar Gardner Murphy: His Ideas and Influence," *Historical Magazine of the Protestant Episcopal Church,* XXV, (December 1956), 391-402.

[3] Fourth Conference for Education in the South, *Proceedings* (Winston-Salem, N. C., 1901), 6.

[4] Ogden to George Foster Peabody, June 11, 1896, Ogden Papers.

[5] Ogden could say "Amen" to several stanzas of Rudyard Kipling's "The White Man's Burden," even in the presence of Negroes. Clipping

Baldwin's hard-boiled philanthropy assumed that the Negro "will willingly fill the more menial positions, and do the heavy work, at less wages," leaving to whites "the more expert labor." Baldwin's advice to the Negro was quite specific: "avoid social questions; leave politics alone; continue to be patient; live moral lives; live simply; learn to work . . . know that it is a crime for any teacher, white or black to educate the negro for positions which are not open to him."[6]

Though these philanthropists may have been complacent about an inferior status for Negroes, they were perturbed by the social and economic hindrances placed on Negroes by the dominant whites. After several experiments within the Negro community, they concluded that the key to Negro problems lay within the white community. There had to be a working compromise between the "best North" and the "best South."[7] The "best North," in Ogden's scale of values, was men like himself, conservative business and professional people; the "best South" included educators and a remnant of upper-class paternalists, "a minority powerful to restrain if not always powerful to accomplish."[8]

If race prejudice was due to ignorance and economic competition, the philanthropists reasoned, then through public schools the whites might learn racial tolerance along with skills which would widen their opportunities. An educational movement of constructive character, moving in a path parallel to the insistent white supremacy demands, could so har-

---

from Philadelphia *North American,* June 21, 1901, in George S. Dickerman clipping books (Southern Historical Collection, University of North Carolina).

[6] William H. Baldwin, Jr. "The Present Problem of Negro Education, Industrial Education," *Proceedings* of the Second Capon Springs Conference for Christian Education in the South (Washington, republished by the Southern Education Board, n. d.), 72, 74.

[7] Ogden to Richard Watson Gilder (editor of the *Century*), February 25, 1903, Ogden Papers.

[8] Murphy, *Basis of Ascendancy,* 29. See also Fourth Conference for Education in the South, *Proceedings,* 5-6.

bor strength by avoiding direct clashes as to outdistance and check the rival force.

The regional approach of the Board is significant. A single, pervasive social institution, the public school, was the lever by which it hoped to move the region, to solve all of the other complex problems arising from Southern poverty, ignorance, and racial tension. The Board undoubtedly viewed the South as an underdeveloped region. Its task was to furnish technical assistance and a little money if the South would supply the educational enthusiasm and local leadership. Massive economic aid would have had to be federal aid, because of the sheer size of the school systems, and that was apparently out of the question after the Blair education bill was defeated in Congress in the eighties.

The Southern education movement began in 1901 with a Pullman-train journey of influential and philanthropic Northerners to North Carolina, the first of an annual series of such excursions at Ogden's expense, and a public meeting with its governor, Charles B. Aycock, and other members of the Conference for Education in the South. Just elected on a platform coupling Negro disfranchisement and universal education,[9] Aycock represented the conservative wing of the white supremacy movement. A tacit bargain with him underlay the whole educational movement and dictated its tactical methods. The philanthropists acquiesced in disfranchisement and Jim Crow laws and undertook to promote their views in the North, while Aycock openly pledged that the schools of the disfranchised Negroes would have protection from hostile state legislation through the power and prestige of his high office.[10]

[9] Helen G. Edmonds, *The Negro and Fusion Politics in North Carolina, 1894-1901* (Chapel Hill, 1951), 198-204, is a valuable supplement to earlier accounts of this campaign.

[10] Raleigh *News and Observer,* May 21, 1901, January 9, 1903; Robert D. W. Connor and Clarence Poe, *The Life and Speeches of Charles Brantley Aycock* (New York, 1912), 132-35. Actually Aycock did little

Ogden's guests, on their return to the North, indicated a complete surrender to white supremacy. "We have to get rid of our more or less vague idea that all men are created free and equal," announced editor Lyman Abbott of the *Outlook*.[11] The Rev. Charles H. Parkhurst preached at the Madison Square Presbyterian Church that "we learned to look upon matters more in the way in which the Southern mind regards them." Good Southerners advised the Negro to "keep quiet," said Parkhurst, who had been convinced that "the less the negro talks about his civic rights under the Constitution, particularly the right of suffrage . . . the sooner he will attain to all the rights that justly belong to him."[12] Walter Hines Page of *World's Work* admitted that race friction was getting worse, but thought it could not be "allayed . . . by anything whatsoever except the training of the inefficient and the ignorant." Page stressed a positive approach to the Southern problem. "The statesman-schoolmaster," he affirmed, "is the man to build our hopes on."[13] These spokesmen for the philanthropic capitalist did not so much change Northern opinion as indicate its final capitulation to racialism. Others had already taken the same path to reunion, and racial discrimination was spreading in the North.

Seeking to cushion the shock of racialism and keep public education open as an avenue of Negro advancement, the phil-

---

to protect Negro school funds at the county and district levels, and, according to the state school superintendent, James Y. Joyner, less was spent on Negro rural schools in 1905 than in 1895. He is quoted in Thomas Jesse Jones, *Negro Education: A Study of the Private and Higher Schools for Colored People in the United States* (United States Bureau of Education, *Bulletins*, 1916, Nos. 38 and 39 [2 vols., Washington, 1917]), I, 29.

[11] Clipping from New York *Journal*, May 24, 1901, Dickerman clipping books.

[12] New York *World*, April 29, 1901.

[13] "The Only Way to Allay Race-Friction," editorial in *World's Work*, VI (August 1903), 3720-21.

anthropists offered the Negro charity rather than full-fledged philanthropy. They were willing on the Negro's behalf to renounce some of his claims to equal status and opportunity. Not being Negroes themselves, they were probably not fully aware how disappointing such a compromise was to many Negroes, or how vulnerable the complete loss of political power made the Negroes. And they fatally miscalculated in assuming that the upper-class wing of Southern racialism, because it spoke the language of conservatism, would be their effective partner in protecting Negroes. People who were disturbed by the collapse of the Reconstruction settlement undoubtedly sighed with relief that the Negro was keeping education as a solace and hope, and that all they needed to do to further Negro progress was to ride on Ogden's train to hear Southerners speak at educational conferences. But they were misled in this facile optimism.

The Southern Education Board members agreed that for the first two years, at least, "we would not emphasize the *negro* too much," according to Dabney, who ran the Board's propaganda bureau at Knoxville. "In the excited state of public sentiment," he wrote, "this was considered wisest."[14] The Southern campaigners preached in general terms the education of all the people and fairness to Negroes. But as Alderman stated their position in a Northern magazine, the education "of one untaught white man to the point that knowledge and not prejudice will guide his conduct . . . is worth more to the black man himself than the education of ten Negroes."[15] As Charles B. Aycock simplified the doctrine: "Education of the whites will provide education for the

14 Charles W. Dabney to Charles L. Coon, August 27, 1903, Charles W. Dabney Papers (Southern Historical Collection, University of North Carolina).

15 Quoted in Dumas Malone, *Edwin A. Alderman: A Biography* (New York, 1940), 145-46. Cf. Charles W. Dabney at Carnegie Hall, quoted in Raleigh *News and Observer*, January 11, 1903.

negroes."[16] Exactly how this magic would work was never clear, but its Southern advocates insisted that education for Negroes was also essential. They said nothing about desegregation, and as little as possible about "separate but equal" education, a doctrine then popular only among constitutional lawyers.[17]

The Northerners took Dabney to task in 1903 for ignoring the Negro entirely in the propaganda he spread over the South. In Mississippi, for example, Negro education was not mentioned at a time when James K. Vardaman was trying to destroy the state's Negro school fund. "When I reminded them that a year ago all of them . . . were proclaiming the same principles and policies, I was greeted with silence or explanations," Dabney wrote home. "Recent events have re-excited them about the negro's interests and put them to thinking how they can help to maintain them against the white aggressors."[18] Dabney considered resigning, but the other Southerners patched up the intersectional compromise again.

Spokesmen for Negro schools watched from the sidelines with attitudes fluctuating between suspicion and hope. "The fact that it is controlled by Mr. Ogden & Peabody will make it necessary to devote much thought to Negro as well as white education," Principal Hollis B. Frissell of Hampton assured Booker T. Washington in the first year.[19] But Negro college graduates and some Northern liberals were alienated

[16] Charles B. Aycock interview, clipping from Charlotte *Observer,* April 26, 1901, in Dickerman clipping books.

[17] The Southerners' stand on school segregation was rigid. Edgar Gardner Murphy, *Problems of the Present South* (New York, 1904; 2d ed., 1916), 37. Ogden told the editor of the Richmond *Times-Dispatch* that he opposed desegregation. Ogden to W. Scott Copeland, February 24, 1905, Ogden Papers.

[18] Dabney to Coon, August 27, 1903; Peabody to Dabney, October 7, 1903, Dabney Papers.

[19] Hollis B. Frissell to Washington, November 9, 1901, Washington Papers.

by the fact that the Northern members, who sat on all of the leading philanthropic boards interested in the South, channeled these funds into Negro industrial institutes and white colleges. And Washington himself wrote privately that the Southern educational campaign meant "almost nothing so far as the Negro schools are concerned." He charged that "the Southern members . . . do not put themselves on record in a straight and frank manner as much as they should."[20]

One might expect the General Education Board, with its millions, prestige and relative independence, to balance the caution of the Southern campaigners with its own boldness. But Wallace Buttrick, its executive secretary, was equally cautious and perhaps a bit frightened by the emotional timbre of Southern racialism. After a grass-roots conference in the South with North Carolina county school superintendents, Buttrick decided that equal treatment for Negroes would make whites cold toward philanthropy. "As a matter of absolute justice they ought to participate proportionately with the whites," he said in a confidential report. "But we are confronted 'with a condition and not a theory.' . . . We shall err and invite defeat, if, in the present state of public sentiment, we demand too much from the white people of the South."[21]

Ogden restrained his own sincere impulse to speak up for Negro education partly from loyalty to his vulnerable Southern allies. He was constantly aware of the danger that the whites might divide educational tax funds so that Negro schools would receive only the returns from Negro taxes, and his Southern friends convinced him that if this question were submitted to Southern voters, the demagogues would win.

[20] Washington to Ogden, July 18, 1906, with copies also to Peabody, Buttrick, and Frissell, *ibid.*

[21] Wallace Buttrick, "Educational Conditions and Needs of North Carolina," confidential report to the General Education Board, January 27, 1904, Southern Education Board Miscellaneous Papers (Southern Historical Collection, University of North Carolina).

"For these men to openly attack you," warned Murphy, "would not only be 'unpleasant' but would 'drive to cover' men . . . on whom we—and the negro—*must* depend for fairness and patriotism." "I feel 'like a dog' to have to say these things," Murphy protested, "but I *know* our people."[22] The philanthropists assumed that Southern sensitivity would permit discussion of racial issues only by Southerners. But they might well have risked their timid millions, and the added capital of good will so painstakingly accumulated by intersectional conciliation, in bold leadership on the Negro's behalf in ventures their Southern colleagues could not risk. They decided instead to intensify their original efforts for general popular education.[23] Such action had much to be said for it, but as far as Negro education was concerned it was simply evasion. The real dilemma of the public school campaigns was that white educational sentiment, as it grew, increased the temptation to take the Negro's share of school funds. Educational promoters were tempted to promise taxpayers a fiscal saving through racial discrimination.[24] The philanthropists, seeking Southern allies against the demagogues who exploited lower-class prejudices, actually joined forces with the upper-class conservatives who quietly administered school discrimination.

"Within the saving limits of established principles," said

[22] Murphy to Ogden, April 8, 1904, Ogden Papers. "So many of the officials of the Southern Board are identified with state institutions that it has been difficult to do much without embarrassing them (even the University of Virginia is almost absolutely at the mercy of every passing Legislature). . . ." Murphy to Washington, March 29, 1908, Washington Papers.

[23] Ogden to Peabody, March 23, 1906, in Ogden Papers. Ogden to Page, March 31, 1906, George S. Dickerman Papers (Southern Historical Collection, University of North Carolina).

[24] For example, see R. F. Beasley (Monroe, N. C.) to Eugene C. Brooks (secretary of the North Carolina Educational Campaign Committee, Raleigh), September 9, 1903, James Yadkin Joyner Papers (Southern Historical Collection, University of North Carolina).

Ogden, "I strive to be, in this Southern Education matter,
all things to all men that peace may in the future reign
throughout the length and breadth of our land."[25] He sometimes went to great lengths to promote intersectional harmony. He appeared at the New York Union League Club to
scotch a proposal to reduce Southern congressional representation as a reprisal for disfranchisement.[26] Avoiding visits to
Negro colleges[27] and warning friends against accepting pro-
fessorships there,[28] he advised Negro leaders to employ "con-
cession, moderation and patience."[29] The editors and public
figures who accompanied him southward were counseled to
be as "wise as serpents" and as "gentle as doves."[30] "I pursue
my own course quietly," he wrote a liberal Southerner, "always, however, adapting myself to the standards of the environment in which I may be found."[31] But adaptation to the
environment of Southern racialism weakened the philanthropists' position as guardians of Negro interests.

It was clear by 1906 that racialism continued to dominate

[25] Ogden to Rev. Theodore L. Cuyler, March 30, 1904, copy in
Dabney Papers.

[26] Ogden was denounced for this by Negro leaders. He explained his
motives at length in Ogden to Peabody, April 10, 1903; Ogden to
Thomas Wentworth Higginson, June 25, 1904, Ogden Papers.

[27] Ogden was particularly careful to avoid contact with Berea College.
William G. Frost to George S. Dickerman, April 7, 1906, in miscellaneous
Ogden Papers (Southern Historical Collection, University of North
Carolina); Ogden to Buttrick, April 13, 1906, Ogden Papers (Library
of Congress). Baldwin disagreed with Ogden's cautious policy of refusing
invitations to visit Negro colleges en route to his annual conferences.
Ogden to Baldwin, April 12, 1904, Ogden Papers.

[28] Ogden to Julius D. Dreher (Selwood, S. C.), March 26, 1906,
Ogden Papers.

[29] Ogden to Rev. Teunis S. Hamilton (Howard University), March
23, 1903, Ogden to Helen M. Ludlow (Hampton Institute), June 15,
1905, *ibid*.

[30] Ogden to James E. Russell (Dean of Teachers College, Columbia
University), March 27, 1906; Ogden to Charles D. McIver, January 27,
1903, *ibid*.

[31] Ogden to Dreher, March 26, 1906, *ibid*.

Southern affairs. The Northerners and Murphy held a caucus,[32] and at the next Board meeting Peabody broached the topic of a special campaign for Negro education. The Southern members tried to delay action. "We should avoid anything like a crusade," said Alderman; "guard against going into it with heat." When Peabody replied that it was "about time for a crusade of the right kind," Alderman rejoined: "Southern men have shied from this subject. It has been touching a sore tooth. . . . We want now to influence public sentiment: stop being silent, but be wise; go forward, but with forethought, not so spectacularly as to set back the movement."[33] This discussion made clear the Board's dilemma, that a crusade for Negro education would jeopardize the crusade for white education. Yielding reluctantly to the superior power of the white supremacy movement, the Board continued its strong efforts for a middle path between equalitarianism and racialism, and resigned itself by default to the growth of separate and unequal schools.

Pressed from the South by an opposition led by the *Manufacturers' Record,* organ of industry in the South, Page told a Southern newspaper reporter: "You will find when the wood pile is turned over not a nigger, but an uneducated white boy." "There is a man," he said, "and it is the man we want to reach."[34] Ogden himself yielded to the temptation to describe his movement as "almost exclusively in white interest."[35] Believing that commerce and education could go hand in hand, Ogden was sincerely puzzled by the attacks from the New South. His guests were being called "picturesque junk-

[32] Minutes of informal conference at the Union League Club, New York, April 25, 1906, Albert P. Bourland Papers (Southern Historical Collection, University of North Carolina).

[33] Minutes of Southern Education Board meeting, August 6-8, 1906, Ogden Papers.

[34] Columbia (S. C.) *State,* April 24, 1903.

[35] Ogden to George W. Boyd (passenger agent of Pennsylvania Railroad), February 27, 1904, Ogden Papers.

eters," "Pullman car philanthropists," and "the swell-belly parade."[36] The conciliatory methods may have won over some moderate Southerners, but the language of the opposition press could hardly have been stronger if the movement had been bolder.

The Southern attacks did not conceal the movement's conservatism from the more doctrinaire liberals. Ogden's characteristic methods seemed to Oswald Garrison Villard of the *Nation* "too complacent and too conciliatory; as if there was some lack of the fiery indignation of the reformer."[37] Negro leaders who shared Villard's distrust of the philanthropists and their allies formed in 1906 the militant Niagara Movement, out of which grew the National Association of the Advancement of Colored People, a protest group with a long-range objective of full democratic equality with whites.[38] Warned by Hollis B. Frissell that the new movement stressed "the rights rather than the duties of the colored people," the philanthropists received it with cold silence and expressed private disapproval.[39] Washington, whose leadership was challenged, went further. Maintaining an unmistakably hostile

[36] Charleston (S. C.) *News and Courier,* editorial, March 13, 1905.
[37] "Robert C. Ogden," editorial by Villard, *Nation,* XCVII (August 14, 1913), 139; editorial in New York *Evening Post,* August 7, 1913.
[38] Jack Abramowitz, "Origins of the NAACP," *Social Education,* XV (January 1951), 21-23. See also W. E. Burghardt Du Bois, *Dusk of Dawn: An Essay toward an Autobiography of a Race Concept* (New York, 1940), 89-92; Eric F. Goldman, *Rendezvous with Destiny: A History of Modern American Reform* (New York, 1953), 176-83; Helen M. Chesnutt, *Charles Waddell Chesnutt: Pioneer of the Color Line* (Chapel Hill, 1952), 206; Gunnar Myrdal and assistants, *An American Dilemma: The Negro Problem and Modern Democracy* (2 vols., New York, 1944), II, 819-36.
[39] Frissell to Peabody, October 9, 24, 1906, Hollis B. Frissell letterbooks (Hampton Institute, Virginia); Peabody to William E. Burghardt Du Bois, August 26, 1911; Du Bois to Peabody, August 28, 1911, Ogden Miscellaneous Papers (Division of Manuscripts, Library of Congress); Ogden to Peabody, January 5, 1904; Ogden to Kelly Miller (Howard University), September 28, 1908; Peabody to Ogden, September 1, 1911 (in Samuel C. Mitchell, MS. biography of Ogden), Ogden Papers;

public silence,[40] he privately ordered his assistant, "Telegraph
. . . newspaper men that you can absolutely trust to ignore
[the] Niagra [sic] movement."[41] His efforts at suppression
extended to buying up hostile Negro newspapers.[42]

Washington's own racial policy was failing tragically at the
time he was trying to prevent alternative policies. His own
school and his Southern supporters were under attack.[43]
Southern officials were giving Negro schools a smaller and
smaller proportion of tax funds. The General Education
Board refused to aid Negro high schools,[44] and the Peabody

Du Bois to Peabody, December 28, 1905, quoted in Herbert Aptheker
(ed.), *A Documentary History of the Negro People in the United States*
(New York, 1951), 881-83.

[40] Washington's public remark that "a hungry race cannot live upon
'principles' " was in reference to educational policy rather than public
affairs, but perhaps it reveals his frame of reference. E. Davidson
Washington (ed.), *Selected Speeches of Booker T. Washington* (Garden
City, New York, 1932), 203. On Washington as a racial leader see C.
Vann Woodward, *Origins of the New South, 1887-1913: A History of
the South*, vol. IX (Baton Rouge, 1951), 350-68; Oliver C. Cox, "The
Leadership of Booker T. Washington," *Social Forces*, XXX (October,
1951), 91-97; Samuel R. Spencer, Jr., *Booker T. Washington and the
Negro's Place in American Life* (Boston, 1955), 87-143. After his
generous article, "A University Education for Negroes," *Independent*,
LXVIII (March 24, 1910), 613-18, Washington wrote to Robert R.
Moton on March 24, 1910: "This matter of explaining and defending
these so-called higher institutions makes me tired." Washington Papers.

[41] Washington to Emmett J. Scott, telegram from New York, July 17
[1905 or 1906?]; Washington to Scott, July 27, 1905, Washington
Papers. The spelling error was probably that of a Southern white
telegrapher.

[42] Abramowitz, "Origins of the NAACP," 23; August Meier, "Booker
T. Washington and the Negro Press: With Special Reference to the
Colored American Magazine," *Journal of Negro History*, XXXVIII
(January 1953), 67-90, based on research in the Washington Papers.

[43] Washington to Dabney, February 10, 1903; Washington to Peabody,
July 18, 27, 1907; W. N. Sheats (former state superintendent, Gaines-
ville, Florida) to Buttrick, May 25, 1904, copy sent to Baldwin and
thence to Washington, Washington Papers; Ogden to Frederic L. Moore
(Washington, D. C.), February 9, 1903, Ogden Papers.

[44] Washington to Buttrick, July 23, 1909; Washington to Ogden,

Fund was dissolved without giving Negro schools a proportionate share of the principal.[45] Even in education, the traditional touchstone of Negro advancement, the conservative Negro leader had little to conserve, as he made clear at a gathering of Southern professors in 1915. "We are trying," he said, "to instil into the Negro mind that if education does not make the Negro humble, simple, and of service to the community, then it will not be encouraged."[46]

Perhaps the Southern Education Board can better be judged on the basis of general trends in the South than on its discreet utterances. There really was a Southern educational awakening between 1900 and the first World War. Annual expenditures for education quadrupled, kept well ahead of the rise in property values, and acted as a springboard for further increases in the next decade. Though other improvements did not always keep pace with physical expansion, and though the lag behind non-Southern schools continued, Southern whites had better schools and more books, necessities of life in a state of civilization.[47] The Southern Education Board

October 18, 1909; Buttrick to Washington, June 18, 1910, Washington Papers; Walter H. Page to Buttrick, February 23, 1910, Buttrick to Page, February 26, 1910, Walter Hines Page Papers (Houghton Library, Harvard University). And [Abraham Flexner and Frank P. Bachman], *The General Education Board: An Account of Its Activities, 1902-1914* (New York, 1915), 155-57, 203, 209, shows that that foundation disbursed $3,052,625 to Southern white colleges, $555,781.13 to Negro industrial institutes, and $140,000 to Negro colleges in the twelve-year period.

[45] Washington to Samuel A. Green, January 21, 1904, January 21, 1913, September 15, 1914, Peabody Education Fund Papers (George Peabody College for Teachers).

[46] [William M. Hunley, secretary], *Minutes of the University Commission on Southern Race Questions* (n p., n. d.), 29. Washington spoke at the fifth meeting, May 5-7, 1915, at Montgomery, Alabama, and Tuskegee Institute.

[47] The expenditures for thirteen Southern states (Virginia, North Carolina, South Carolina, Florida, Georgia, Kentucky, Tennessee, Alabama, Mississippi, Louisiana, Texas, Arkansas, and Oklahoma) were $20,833,135 in 1900 and $82,772,095 in 1915. The amount for

played an important part in the work which brought about this public school expansion.

On the other hand, the Board's efforts seem to have had almost no effect on the Negro schools. Nor did the Board brake or deflect the course of racialism. "Passionate and rapidly developing enthusiasm for white education is bearing sharply and adversely upon the opportunities of the negro," the sensitive Murphy noted. "There is not only no chance to help the situation of the negro educationally, but it is steadily growing worse, and their schools, upon every sort of pretext, are being hampered and impoverished where they are not actually abandoned."[48] Marked financial discrimination against the already conveniently segregated Negro schools apparently developed from a conjunction of motives: increased white desire for education, white racial hostility, and efforts of taxpayers to limit taxation. It is misleading to think of the dual system of education as a financial burden when the two systems were grossly unequal. Discrimination against Negro schools represented a fiscal saving and was a basis for compromise between taxpayer and tax-layer. The educational campaigns themselves drove the wedge of inequality between the two systems. Discrimination varied from place to place, but it was almost universal, flagrant, and increasing. In South Carolina, for example, in 1900 the white child of school age received about $5.75 for every dollar expended per Negro child, whereas in 1915 the ratio was about $12.37 to

---

Oklahoma as a territory is included in the 1900 total. United States Bureau of Education, *Report of the Commissioner of Education for the Year 1899-1900* (2 vols., Washington, 1901), I, lxxvii; United States Bureau of Education, *Report of the Commissioner of Education for the Year Ended June 30, 1917* (2 vols., Washington, 1917), II, 53. The latter volume contains educational statistics for 1914-1915, because Congress failed to appropriate to the bureau a sufficient sum for earlier publication.

[48] Murphy to Buttrick, November 14, 1907, Southern Education Board Papers (Southern Historical Collection, University of North Carolina).

one dollar.[49] By other measurements such as school property, transportation, attendance, pupils per teacher, and high school opportunities, the contrast was even more striking.

Educational reform within the context of racialism partook of racialism, whatever may be the long-range effect of expanded education on white attitudes. Discrimination in education was a cancerous growth out of reform. The Southern Education Board's sympathetic and gentle approach to the race issue in Southern public education lacked moral firmness and was therefore weakened by compromise.

[49] United States Bureau of Education, *Report of the Commissioner of Education for the Year 1899-1900,* II, 2503; *ibid., 1917,* II, 17; *Thirty-Second Annual Report of the State Superintendent of Education of the State of South Carolina, 1900* (Columbia, 1901), 253; *Forty-Seventh Annual Report of the State Superintendent of Education of the State of South Carolina, 1915* (Columbia, 1916), 310.

PHILIP DURHAM*
EVERETT L. JONES

Negro Cowboys

Among the cowboys who went up the trails from Texas
during the years following the Civil War, more than five
thousand Negroes played a part and did a job—doing no more
and no less than cowboys of other races and nationalities.
They crossed the Red River and the Cimarron, the Pecos and
the Platte, and they rode the streets of all the early cowtowns.
They fought Indians and other cowboys, and some of them
were buried on Boot Hill or in unmarked graves along the
trail.

While the trail drives lasted, Negroes had a conspicuous
place in the life of the cattleman's West. They fought with
guns and bullwhips on the streets of Dodge City, and they

* From *The American West*, I (Fall 1964), 26-31, 87. Reprinted by
permission of the authors. See by the same authors, *The Negro Cowboys*.
New York: Dodd, Mead and Company, 1965.

roamed the streets of Cheyenne. They carried gold through outlaw country, and they took part in bloody range wars. If one got drunk, he could crash through a plate-glass window, shoot up a saloon, or land in jail. If he turned outlaw, he usually died young.

Negro cowboys hunched in their saddles during blizzards and thunderstorms, fought grass fires and turned stampedes, hunted wild mustangs and rode wild horses. Wolves threatened their cattle, and rattlesnakes crawled into their blankets. Like all other cowboys, they led hard and dangerous lives.

Typical of the accounts of Negro cowboys is the story told to J. Frank Dobie by an old Texas trail driver who described a death in the Panhandle:

We had a negro cowboy named George who was not very well clad because he liked to pike at monte too well to buy clothes. We all had colds and coughs till it was like a bunch of Texas pot hounds baying a 'possum when we tried to sleep. One bitter night I was near George on herd and tried to get him to go to the chuck wagon and turn his horse loose, but he was too game for that. His teeth were chattering as he said to me, "I can stand it if the rest of you all can." Presently I saw him lean over his saddle horn, coughing, and he looked like he was losing his breath. By the time I got to him he was off his horse, as dead as a mackerel and stiff as a poker. He had simply frozen to death sitting on that horse.

It may be doubted that a modern post-mortem would have shown death by freezing, but certainly many cowboys died of exposure, drowning, or Indian arrows. Hundreds more narrowly escaped death.

For instance, on long trail drives every river was a potential killer when it was in flood. Cowboys, if they could swim at all, were rarely strong swimmers; and the treacherous currents of high, muddy rivers were made even more dangerous by struggling cattle and horses, floating branches and debris, and hidden rocks and snags. Not everyone was so lucky as the Negro cowboy who had a narrow escape in a crossing of the flooding Canadian River. Near the middle his horse sank under him, leaving him near drowning. But another cowboy saw the danger, swam his horse to the rescue, and told the Negro to grab the horse's tail. Once ashore, the rescued man thanked his benefactor and vowed that the horse's tail had been just like "the hand of Providence."

Such were the routine adventures of the trails when thousands of cowboys and millions of cattle drove north after the end of the Civil War. Two great markets lay to the northwest and northeast. Northwest were hungry miners, soldiers, and reservation Indians, as well as northern range ranchers eager to buy breeding and feeder stock. Northeast were railheads opening to a beef-hungry East and Midwest. Neither market was easy to reach, but Texas cattlemen tried for both.

To reach these markets they pioneered dozens of main trails and hundreds of feeder trails, but the great movement of cattle is most easily followed if one looks at the three principal routes they developed: the Chisholm Trail, the Goodnight-Loving Trail, and the Western Trail.

The Chisholm Trail, first opened in 1867, passed Fort Worth and headed north, crossed the Red River, moved through sparsely settled areas of the Indian Territory (now Oklahoma), and entered mid-Kansas south of the new shipping point of Abilene. The Goodnight-Loving Trail, pioneered at about the same time, started west from Tom Greene County in Texas, followed the route of the old Butterfield Overland Mail to the Pecos River, and then turned north to New Mexico and Colorado. The Western Trail, opened a few years later, ran north through the edge of the Indian Territory to western Kansas and Dodge City.

As they established these trails, the Texas cattlemen perfected the organization of their drives. They early agreed that the ideal number of cattle for a single drive was about 2,500. With a herd that size, an average crew operated with about eleven men: the trail boss, a wrangler, a cook, and eight cowboys. The boss pointed the way and ran the whole operation. The wrangler took charge of all the crew's horses, while the cook handled the chuck wagon and fed the men. Working as a team, the cowboys drove the cattle—two riding point near the lead steers, four riding swing along the sides, and two riding drag behind the stragglers. At night the cowboys took turns keeping watch over the resting herd.

The trail boss was usually a white man, although on occasion he might be the Negro boss of an all-Negro crew. The wrangler was either white Texan, Negro, or Mexican. The cook was often a Negro, normally one who had become too old or too heavy for constant riding. Among the eight cowboys, two or three were usually Negroes.

A few simple listings from the records and memoirs of old Texas trail drivers illustrate the composition of typical crews:

C. W. Ackerman rode up the trail with seven white men and one Negro; R. F. Galbreath rode with four white men and three Negroes; G. W. Mills trailed with six white cowboys, two Negro cowboys, and a Negro cook—none over twenty-three; William G. Butler drove to Abilene with two Negroes, Levi and William Perryman; Charlie Siringo rode point with "Negro Gabe"; and Jim Ellison went up the trail with all Negro hands.

Whenever cowboys on a drive were identified (usually they were not named or described unless they were spectacularly good or bad), two or three Negroes were likely to be among them.

A Negro cowboy, George Glenn, is the only man remembered from the crew that R. B. Johnson took from Colorado County, Texas, to Abilene in 1870. Shortly after reaching Abilene, Johnson died, his body was embalmed, and he was buried in Kansas. The following September the body was disinterred, and George Glenn took his old boss home. Because there were no railroads leading from Kansas to Texas, Glenn loaded the body in a Studebaker wagon and drove it back, making a trip that took forty-two days, sleeping every night in the wagon by the coffin.

Another Negro cowboy named Dick was described in an old cowhand's memoirs only because Dick was treated in crude frontier fashion for a rattlesnake bite. He rode into the chuck wagon sucking his thumb, his hand and arm badly swollen. One of the other cowboys immediately drew a knife and gashed—"almost hashed"—the thumb around the fang marks. He then opened a pistol cartridge, poured powder over the wound, and lighted it with a match. Dick appears to have survived both the bite and the treatment.

Almost all of the best-known pioneer cattlemen employed some Negroes. The nearly legendary Shanghai Pierce, for instance, always went on cattle-buying expeditions accompanied by a Negro cowboy who carried his gold. Ab Blocker, one of the most active of the early trail drivers, employed large numbers of Negro hands; and one of them became famous as a roper of fabulous skill. Colonel Goodnight and Oliver Loving pioneered their trail from Texas to Colorado with the help of many Negro cowboys. One of these, Bose Ikard, the colonel said, "His behavior was very good in a fight, and he was probably the most devoted man to me that I ever had. I have trusted him further than any living man. He was my detective, banker, and everything else in Colorado, New Mexico, and the other wild country I was in." When Bose Ikard died in 1929, the colonel erected a marker with the following inscription: "Bose Ikard: Served with me four years on the Goodnight-Loving Trail, never shirked a duty or disobeyed an order, rode with me in many stampedes, participated in three engagements with Comanches, splendid behavior." Other Negro cowboys worked with almost all the outfits that employed Charlie Siringo, an early cowboy writer, who wrote that Negroes saved his life on several occasions.

While many Negroes herded cattle, others drove chuck wagons and cooked for the trail crews. The cook was an important man, essential to the well-being of the outfit and the success of the drive. He was usually respected in that although he might be called "the old woman," he mighι also have several notches on his gun. He frequently carried the only banjo or fiddle that relieved the monotony of quiet nights on the plains. Thus one old-timer and western historian reported that he always had a special interest in trail cooks after the day he watched Gordon Davis, Ab Blocker's Negro cook, ride into Dodge City mounted on his left wheel ox, fiddle in hand, playing "Buffalo Girls Can't You Come Out Tonight?"

While reminiscing with J. Frank Dobie, John Young remembered a cook who was a treasure:

The one man in our outfit that I recall most often and most vividly was Sam, the negro cook. He always had a cheerful word or a cheerful song, and he seemed to have an affection for every one of us. When we camped in the vicinity of brush, every cowboy before coming in would rope a chunk of wood and snake it up to the chuck wagon. That wood always made Sam grinning happy whether he needed it or not.

Carrying 225 pounds at thirty-five years of age, Sam was too heavy and too old for the active life of a cowboy, but he was still a good rider; frequently one of the crew got him to ride and gentle an unruly horse. He was also part of the general hell-raising of a happy camp. One day, for instance, a cowboy looked at Sam's great bulk and joked that Sam was too big for a man but too small for a horse. Sam answered that *"he was a horse* and that he would give a dollar to any man in the outfit who could ride him without spurs." That night the crew camped in a sandy place, and the game began. Sam stripped, wearing only a bandanna around his neck for his riders to hold onto. One after another the cowboys took off their boots and mounted his back. One after another they were thrown into the soft sand by the human "horse" who could anticipate and bewilder the reactions of his riders. No one earned a dollar that night.

A good trail cook was so important to the success of a drive that the cowboys protected him on most occasions. One such Negro cook came up the trail with a Texas outfit to Abilene in 1870. In that year the city began building a stone jail, but before the construction went very far, cowboys had pulled down its walls. After that the town trustees hired a strong guard, and under its protection workmen completed the structure.

The Texas outfit camped on Mud Creek, and the cook rode into town to drown with heavy draughts of Abilene whiskey his memories of smoking fires and hungry cowboys. After he got drunk, he began shooting up the town—not doing much damage, but making a lot of noise. The town marshal came running, and as one story has it, "managed by some unaccountable good luck" to arrest the cook and throw him into jail. There the cook stayed until his hungry trail crew learned where he was, upon which they mounted, rode into town, drove the marshal into hiding, shot the lock off the jail door, and freed the cook. Then "they galloped past the office of Theodore Henry, chairman of the town trustees, and shot it full of holes." Finally, having rescued one of their own men and expressed their contempt for the town's government, they rode back to camp. Thus a Negro posted two records: He was the first man thrown into the new jail and the first man to break out.

Besides working as cooks and wranglers, Negroes also worked as ranchers and horsebreakers throughout the old West. Accounts of them are many and varied. One reports that a Negro trail cook in Montana died violently when he attacked a white cowboy with a butcher knife. Another tells of a Negro rancher in Kansas who grew tired of being hazed by a group of white cowboys. When one of them roped him and started to pull him off his horse, the Negro drew his gun and killed his tormentor. A Negro horsebreaker in South Dakota won admiration for his skill in breaking horses — one of his admirers who imitated his methods being Theodore Roosevelt. A Negro range boss in New Mexico was so well

liked by all the cattlemen and cowboys in his part of the
country that when he got married he and his bride found
nineteen cookstoves among their many wedding presents. In
Arizona a Negro cowboy volunteered to go two rounds with
the great John L. Sullivan—but lasted for less than a minute.
Like the white cowboys, Negroes usually made news and got
their names in the paper only when they disturbed the peace.
Thousands of others did their jobs and drew their pay without making even local history.

A few settled down and made places for themselves in the
hearts and memories of ranching communities. One such man
was Willis Peoples, who built up a small ranch south of
Meade, Kansas, near the Neutral Strip. When the ranchers
in his neighborhood began losing cattle to a wolf called Old
Two Toes—so called because he had once lost part of a front
paw in a trap—they offered bounties for his destruction. They
even called in professional wolfers to stalk the lobo. But all
these efforts failed. Old Two Toes continued to pull down
fullgrown cows and even to cut up nearly wild range bulls.
When he took to mate a bitch wolf, the damage tripled.

Finally, Willis Peoples drove into town and made the other
ranchers a proposition. If they would leave the wolves alone
for a month and keep him supplied with food and fresh
horses, he would destroy Old Two Toes. A few men laughed,
but those who knew Peoples were glad to agree.

The Negro rancher camped on the trail of the two wolves,
and for two weeks he never allowed them a moment's rest.
By this time the bitch had had enough and deserted her
mate. A few days later Peoples began to detect a weakening
in Old Two Toes, and he sensed an increasing advantage.
The tired wolf was now less careful in hiding his tracks and
in doubling back. Late one day he finally crawled up an
arroyo and lay down under a bank of clay. There Peoples
came upon him and shot him from a distance of fifty feet.

The next evening he drove his wagon into Meade and

dropped Old Two Toes into the street. The townspeople gathered to congratulate him and to gaze at the wolf—a dead animal seven feet long. One of them asked why Peoples had known from the outset that he could capture the wolf, especially when so many others had failed. The answer was simple. Peoples said that he knew that any man with his mind made up was a majority. His mind, he added, had been made up, and that was "how it was."

Another Negro cowboy who helped to settle the West was Big Jim Simpson, who first came up the trail from Texas with a white and Negro crew driving a herd of longhorns. Instead of returning to Texas after the herd was delivered, Jim Simpson and Joe Proctor, another Negro cowboy, stayed in Wyoming and worked for the Flying E ranch. Both were good hands, but Jim Simpson was more. Soon he was known as "about the best roper on the range." When he became older and heavier he turned to driving a chuck wagon and cooking.

As a ranch and roundup cook his reputation grew, and many cowboys praised him as one who really "knew how to wrastle Dutch ovens, pots and pans." Because he also knew the range and its ways, he became a friend and adviser for younger cowboys. When one of them became sick from drinking alkali water, Jim would send him off the next morning with a can of tomatoes and with instructions to drink nothing but tomato juice. If one of them had more serious problems, Jim could explain the strange behavior of men—and cattle— and women. Cowboys listened respectfully and repaid him by dragging in his wood and taking care not to raise dust around his camp.

Although Jim knew his trade, building cooking fires which were steady and even, rarely blackening his pots and pans, he had the inevitable problems of any cook on the high Wyoming ranges. Floyd Bard, a white cowboy who rode with Simpson, remembered one cold morning during a late season roundup. A heavy snow fell during the night and everybody was cold. As Bard said:

It didn't take us long to get dressed and to start running foot races to warm up a bit. Simpson over under the fly of his wagon was having a lot of trouble trying to cook some breakfast. The wind was blowing out the fire about as fast as he could build it. It was ten o'clock before we had breakfast.

During the winters, Jim was welcomed at the homes and ranches of his many friends. He spent two winters at the George Harper ranch, helping a busy mother who had lost a hand from blood poisoning but still had to care for four small children. During many long evenings he played the fiddle for "kitchen dances," so called because the kitchen of a small ranch house was frequently the only room available.

Once, at least, Jim Simpson appeared in a situation that could have been a scene in an old Western movie in which shy cowboys kiss only their horses. He was working at the Flying E, a ranch that was "a bachelor stronghold" filled with bashful men. They could battle blizzards or rustlers, but they were afraid of good women. As a result, when a newly married school teacher arrived at the ranch, all the cowboys scattered. According to the account in the *Annals of Wyoming*, "when the new bride stopped in to get warm while on the way to Buffalo, the assembled cowboys gave one glance and disappeared like magic, leaving Jim Simpson, colored round-up cook, fiddler and expert roper, to entertain her."

Jim Simpson, like Willis Peoples, was one of the scores of Negro cowboys who rode out of Texas to settle permanently in some other part of the West. But they were the exceptions. For every Simpson or Peoples there were a hundred Negro cowboys who delivered their trail herds and then rode back to Texas.

One of these was Bronco Sam who stopped briefly in Cheyenne when he and his crew halted a slow drive to give their cattle a rest. According to Bill Walker, a white cowboy who rode with him, Sam was a "genuine black buckaroo" who was afraid of nothing and who could ride anything.

Sam and Walker and the rest of the crew rode into Cheyenne to see the sights. As Walker remembered:

Cheyenne had only one real street then, about three blocks long, but it was sure a great street of its size. It had a clothing store with a plate-glass front, and that store front was the only mirror that a lot of those cowboys had ever looked into. That burg had plenty of ladies, too, as well as saloons and poker joints, and they all got plumb fat and prosperous as soon as our bunch hit town.

Three days later the bunch was back with the herd, nearly broke, still a little drunk, probably a little hung over, and somewhat resentful of the bartenders, gamblers, and "ladies" who had efficiently emptied their pockets. So they planned one last fling—something to make Cheyenne remember them.

Because Sam was a great rider, the crew decided to rope the biggest longhorn in the herd, saddle it, and have the Negro bronc buster ride it through Cheyenne's main street. Bronco Sam, who was no more sober than the rest, thought it a great idea. They roped and saddled the steer and Sam mounted it. Riding toward Cheyenne, they whooped and hollered and swung knotted ropes to drive the bucking steer. By the time the show got into town, Sam's mount was frantic and maddened, and when it saw itself reflected in the plate-glass window of the clothing store it was ready for a charge. Charge it did—through the window, down the aisles, over the counters, around the shelves—with the clerks diving into corners for protection. Then it plunged back out through the empty frame.

According to Walker, "Sam was still in the saddle, the steer's horns decorated with pants, coats, underwear, and other odds and ends of gearin'." The steer was still jumping as the cowboys closed in to drive him back toward the herd, and Sam was shouting that he had brought out a suit of clothes for everybody in the crew. He and all the others had sobered up by the time they had unsaddled the steer and turned it back into the herd. They rode back into town, faced the angry storekeeper, paid the damages, and went back to the dusty routine of driving cattle.

Somehow Sam and nearly all the other Negro cowboys got lost when the trail drives ended and the dust settled. Comparatively few of them stayed permanently on the northern ranges of Wyoming, Montana, Nebraska, or the Dakotas, and so today many residents of those states do not know the part that Negroes played in the opening of the cattle country. Old cowboys remembered the Negroes, but cowboys wrote little, and much of what they did write has only recently been collected or published.

Most Americans know the old West as it was described by Owen Wister, Zane Grey, and the hundreds of later Western story writers. From that West, a land of myth and legend the real Negro cowboys have been fenced out. Western stories are peopled by tall, lean, tanned—but lily white under the shirt—heroes who ride through purple-sage country made dangerous by dirty villains, red Indians, and swarthy "greasers," only occasionally being helped by "good Indians" and "proud Spanish-Americans." Even the Chinese survive in fiction, if only as pigtailed caricatures who speak a conventionalized "no tickee, no washee" pidgin English as they shuffle about the ranch houses. Although the stereotypes are sometimes grotesque, all but one of the races and nationalities of the real West appear in novels, movies and television programs.

All but the Negro cowboys, who have been forgotten.

ROBERT MOATS MILLER*

Southern White Protestantism and the Negro, 1865-1965

When Agnellus, the ninth-century Bishop of Ravenna, undertook to write a complete series of lives of his predecessors, he was undaunted by the lack of source materials on one of his subjects and composed the life himself, "with the help of God and the prayers of his brethren." I, too, would solicit the prayers or at least the compassion of my scholarly brethren, not because of a dearth of source materials, but because in a presumptuous moment I agreed to write a short essay on Southern white Protestantism and the Negro, 1865-1965. It would be a difficult assignment to fulfill in several volumes; it is an impossible one to honor in several pages.

* This essay was written especially for inclusion in this volume and is published here for the first time.

About all that can be attempted are a few generalizations, and very tentative, subjective ones at that.

To begin with, this essay rests on the conviction that the story of Southern white Protestantism is not entirely or even primarily a chapter in the history of race relations. If tomorrow through the bestowal of grace all men became perfectly color blind, if racial pride were suddenly and totally expelled from all hearts, the Church would not then become expendable. Christians know that public worship is their bounden duty and solemn obligation, and also their richest privilege, and as in the past they would gather on holy ground, turn their broken and contrite hearts upward, and await in the expectation of being found. They would continue to come together in the awful presence of the Eternal to adore Him, confess their sins and seek forgiveness, affirm their faith, and dedicate their lives. As in the past corrupt and haunted men would hunger to hear the Word of God preached and to partake in Holy Communion of the Body and Blood of His son in order to be cleansed, healed, and made whole again.

However, in a thousand recent articles and conversations dealing with the Church in the South the only apparent concern is what the Church can do or what the Church has done in the area of race relations. I should like to suggest that the Church, though corrupted by denominational arrogance, social snobbery, and racial pride, by its very being has brought men and women, Negro and white, into existential confrontation with the Father of all. This is not an inconsiderable thing.

Secondly, this essay assumes as self-evident the historical fact that the sin of racial pride is the sin of the Christian Church in America — indeed in the Western world — and not simply the sin of those churches in which the scoffing spirit of the times has called the Bible Belt. Is it really necessary to explicate this point? Can we not agree that it is the consensus of recent scholarship that racism was an article of faith with almost all modern Europeans and their descendents in North America, and that almost until our generation it was a faith seemingly supported by much scientific and scholarly opinion? Parenthetically, it is simply not true, despite all the assertions to the contrary nowadays, that the record of the Roman Catholic Church's treatment of the Negro in the United States is cleaner than that of the Protestant denominations.

Thirdly, may a man whose skin happens to be white make the incredibly brazened conjecture that demoniac as has been the exploitation of the black citizen since emancipation, things might have been worse; that is, the painfully slow road toward integration was ultimately followed, the fork toward colonization, deportation, apartheid, even genocide was shunned, though perhaps by the narrowest of margins. "All men are created equal" is the democratic dogma which coincides with the Christian dogma that "He hath created of one blood all men to dwell on the face of the earth." The conscience of white America has never quite been able to be totally faithless to these twin dogmas. It does not suffice to say that the Church in America has permitted, even sanctioned, first body breaking slavery and then soul-searing segregation. This is a hard truth but not the whole truth. It is comparable to judging the Medieval Church solely in terms of the Inquisition. The fate of the black man in America has been utterly agonizing, but what would be his condition today if no white man had heard the judgment: if a man says he loves God and hateth his brother, he is a liar.

Tangentially, it is my hunch that historians and sociologists have exaggerated the pervasiveness of piety below the Potomac. On every hand we read and hear of the intense religiosity of the Southern people. We are assured that Dixie has been and is the bastion of evangelical Protestantism. In no section of the nation did the clergy enjoy such prestige, the churches such power. In no section were revivals so endemic, worship so fervid, the Book so pondered, ecclesiastical censure so feared, denominational membership so high or so prized. "The South is by a long way the most simply and sincerely religious country that I was ever in," observed an English traveler. True enough. But it is one thing to assert the tremendous authority of the Church in the South relative to other sections, or even other lands, and quite another to conclude therefore that the Church possessed the transcendent power to redeem Southern society. It is really unhistorical to speak of the "Christian South." In no era — not even Innocent's Thirteenth Century or Cromwell's England or Winthrop's New England — has it been possible for the Church totally to transfigure culture. We must acknowledge at the onset that the "Protestant South" has always been more Southern than Protestant, more secular than sacred. Parenthetically, despite impressive proportional church membership statistics, it is well to recall the great numbers of unchurched, especially among the poor and illiterate, the urban and mill village proletariat, the hard-scrabble 'croppers, and among the isolated socially, physically and disinherited. Reinhold Niebuhr wrote: "If there were a drunken orgy somewhere, I would bet ten to one a church member was not in it. That is long odds, but on the whole I would assume a church member was not in it. But if there were a lynching I would bet ten to one a church member was in it." Perhaps for once Niebuhr's justly famous skepticism betrayed him. I am inclined to bet (giving about two to one odds) that those participants in the drunken orgy would be on hand in predominant numbers at the lynching — and yet drunk. To be sure, church members did lynch Negroes just as they did join the Klan, but as a generalization it is my guess that the majority of the acts of terror, intimidation, and torture were the work of the Southern underworld, the beaten men of a once cruelly beaten section, in fact, the unchurched.

Yet ultimately it is the white Christians of the South whose hands are most darkly stained with the blood of "persons of color;" it is from their lips that protestations of innocence vomit most obscenely. The unchurched believe they have only death to fear, but Christians know that for their radical disobedience of the Law of Love, they have God to fear. It is for this reason that judgment falls most heavily on them. Nothing that has been said thus far can expiate the searing truth that the Church in the South was and largely is a segregated and segregating institution.

Almost without exception, the published and unpublished studies (and many of the best remain unpublished) of historians, sociologists, journalists, and, indeed, churchmen have indicted Southern Protestantism for its capitulation to Southern racism. Moreover, the critique by Negroes is sharper than a serpent's tooth. "If the treatment of the Negro by the Christian church is called 'divine,'" wrote W. E. B. Du Bois, "this is an attack on the conception of God more blasphemous than any which the church has always been so ready and eager to punish." Asserted James Baldwin: "It is not too much to say that whoever wishes to become a truly moral human being [and let us not ask whether or not this is possible] must first divorce himself from all the prohibitions, crimes and hypocrisies of the Christian Church. If the concept of God has any validity or any use, it can only be to make us larger, freer and more loving. If God cannot do this, then it is time we got rid of him." These statements may strike us as too strident to be altogether convincing. In that case, let us listen to the words of the fraternal delegate from the Colored Methodist Episcopal Church addressing the first General Conference of Southern Methodism in the twentieth century: "We, as well-raised children, delight to look on the greatness of our parent." He asked only one boon: "And that is, wherever, whether in town or city, you are strong and we are striving to house our people, please give us attention, and remember it is your little black child out of doors and asks for help." There followed "hearty applause" and "the most unbounded good humor" and a prayer that "our sable brethren" be "strong workers for truth and righteousness." One hardly knows whether to weep for the emasculated "sable speaker" or for the applauding friendly emasculators.

Prior to the Civil War all of the major Protestant denominations in the South contained slave members, though if they worshipped with whites they were segregated within the sanctuary or if their numbers warranted a separate service or even congregation, the shepherd was usually white. (Only occasionaly were Negro preachers permitted to exhort their brethren.) To be sure, some masters honored as a sacred trust the Christianization of their bondsmen, and from early colonial days the churches genuinely sought to save slave souls. Yet it is sad rather than cynical to observe that sermons were not preached from the text "the truth shall make you free," but from "slaves be obedient to your masters." The salvation of the black man's soul and the continued enslavement of his body were rarely seen in tension. An old slave recalled the preaching of his white minister: "He just say, 'Serve your masters; don't steal your master's turkey; don't steal your master's chicken; don't steal your master's hog; don't steal your master's meat; do whatsoever your master tells you to do'."

If in the ante bellum South the Protestant churches were integrated in only the most cribbed and un-Christian sense, the post bellum period witnessed such a total regrouping into all-white and all-Negro denominations that 11:00 Sunday morning became in fact the most segregated hour in the week. Thus, Negro Methodists withdrew to affiliate with the existing African Methodist Episcopal Church and the African Methodist Episcopal Zion Church or the newly formed (1870) Colored Methodist Episcopal Church. Thus, in the thirty years following Appomattox the segregation of Southern Baptists into racially discrete denominations was virtually completed. Thus, Negro withdrawals from the Southern Presbyterian Church were so overwhelming that between the years 1861 and 1916 the colored membership declined from 31,000 to 1,322. And the few Negro Episcopalians, while not forming an independent body, were frequently set apart in their own parishes. A number of distinguished historians have interpreted this vast exodus as evidence that Negroes really "prefer" to be with their own kind. Writes C. Vann Woodward: "Withdrawal of Negroes from the churches . . . was voluntary. It was a means used by Negroes to gain control over some of their most important institutions." There was, of course, an element of voluntary choice involved, but this should not obscure the ultimate fact that we are dealing with Christians who were rejected and then expelled by other Christians who claimed to be the darlings of Christ. How wounded were the Negroes who found it necessary to organize their own churches if they were to worship in freedom and joy! Perhaps, as Robert W. Spike has speculated, the Negroes took most of both commodities with them when they left, with the result that white-establishment church worship is often cold and sterile.

Even as Southern Christians were separating themselves into racial divisions, Southern society was pressing the black man into a caste system, steel-like in its rigidity — a system by the early 1900's enforced by laws unknown in the 1870's and 1880's; and to this cancerous social arrangement white Protestantism acquiesced. Indeed, this judgment is too generous, for the churches did not merely endure the unendurable; they bestowed positive sanction. The Southern Methodist College of Bishops in 1886 cautioned against racial co-

mingling, warning that there was "no conceivable result that
would compensate for this crime against nature." Theories
of race were as much a part of Southern Baptist thinking, declared Rufus Spain, "as the Virgin Birth or the
Second Coming." The antipathy of race, editorialized
the Nashville *Christian Advocate* in 1906, "is so deep-
seated and so ineradicable that the man, white or black,
who looks forward to its elimination, be the progress of
the negro race what it may, is simply a fool." I have
read in Negro and Communist Party papers accounts of
ministers leading their congregations in hunting down
victims, of colored men being lynched in church yards, of
ladies selling grisly pictures of lynched mutilated bodies in
order to raise church funds; and in the church press such
expressions of hate as, "We will keep the Negro in his place
if we have to dig his grave." However, it is necessary to
emphasize that these manifestations of viciousness (if in fact
authentic) were very rare. Southern white churchmen almost
always referred to the Negro in kindly, paternalistic tones. He
must be protected from mob violence. He should be encouraged to remain in the South, for colonization is a hopeless
dream and migration to the North a cruel experience. Aid
to his schools and churches and hospitals should be freely
given. Hearts must be joined in Christian love. Southern
white churchmen believed — perhaps had to believe — the
myth that a peaceful, just, and harmonious relationship existed between the races. Nature and nature's God had placed
upon the earth the black and the white, the one to serve and
the other to rule. On the one hand, "darkies" should be content, law-abiding, industrious, and cheerful in their subordinate but hardly onerous status. On the other, it was the
white man's duty to be patient, helpful, kindly but firm in
his relations with his child-like, simple, irresponsible, sexual-
ly-wild and often mischievous colored wards. Without segregation, warned the *Religious Herald,* the gates would be

opened for "the mongrelization of the noble Anglo-Saxon race"; such a fate would be a crime against nature, for "The Negro is no more the white man's brother than the owl is the sister of the eagle, or the ass is the brother of the horse." Therefore, as the Episcopal *Southern Churchman* advised, "Let our Christian people set the example of never occupying a seat in the street car reserved for colored people, no matter how crowded that car may be. . . . When certain seats are set aside for colored people in the street cars, they should be guarded and reserved for that purpose just as scrupulously as are the seats kept for the white people." This attitude, as Waldo Beach observed, can more fitly be called perversity of love than hatred. This paternalistic love twists the love revealed in Christ on the Cross, for the neighbor is loved only in so far as he understands the terms of transaction and "keeps his place."

The intensity of the commitment of Southern white Protestants to segregation may be gauged by the fact that Southern and Northern Presbyterians and Southern and Northern Baptists have been unable to reunite, in part because of differences in racial attitudes. This is the conclusion of other scholars. My own researches have convinced me that the major obstacle to Methodist union in 1939 was the place of the Negro in the new church. I remember how I shivered when reading in the files of a Northern minister who favored full equality a letter from a Southern layman: "a bunch of really white men ought to catch you and stick your nose in a damn niggers ass and hold it there until you smuthered to death."

It is now time to speculate as to why Southern white Protestantism practiced segregation in its own churches, schools, seminaries, and hospitals and sanctioned segregation in Southern society as a whole. To begin with, as Woodward poignantly reminds us, "A century ago, Southern whites were given a momentous assignment by history, a role that was not to be required of the dominant whites throughout the

Western World until our own time. This was the imposed obligation of abandoning the racial assumptions of a lifetime and uprooting dogmas deeply embedded in regional culture." This assignment fell to the defeated Confederacy because the history of Negro life in America originated and took form in the South; and as late as 1900 nine-tenths of the Negroes in the United States yet lived in the South. In sum, the South historically has been the American Negro's home, and though he may flee to New York or Detroit he cannot shuck his Southern heritage. Thus, until almost today the burden of black and white living together has been shouldered by Southerners, black and white. If the sin of segregation seems a peculiarly Southern sin it is because of the Negro's massive presence in the South. Parenthetically, only a Yankee Pharisee could take much pride in the record of Northern Protestantism and the Negro. Moreover, it is not simply playing the game of "one-upmanship" to suggest that the treatment California Christians accorded Orientals, or the Northern Christians the "new" immigrants, was less than redemptive.

In the second place, the cry of the Oxford Conference, "Let the Church be the Church," was seldom uttered in the South. To be sure, as Durkheim reminds us, "The religious life is the concentrated expression of the whole collective life." To survive, religion must be institutionalized, and as institutions the churches are as subject to the pressures and mores of society as any other agencies. And precisely because the treasure of faith is perpetuated in earthen vessels, compromise and corruption is inevitable. This is the tragedy of religion: institutionalized it becomes flawed; without the church it dies. The message of the Church, thus, is always superior to its practice. Its central message is the Lord's. But it must live its life in human society. This means that the Church must always be in tension with culture; the hard commandments of Jesus must always knife into the cake of custom. Alas, there emerged in the South what Samuel S. Hill has termed a "culture-Protestantism," wherein the Church tragically took on the protective coloration of its environment. Indeed, Southern Protestantism became subtly enveloped and smothered by Southern society. The identification of Christ and culture was so complete as to melt all tension. The churches were more than domesticated, they were virtually emasculated. As the eunuchs of old, they adorned, without seriously disturbing, their master's establishment. Ultimately, the issue was not one of hypocrisy, but of idolatry, not of cultural lag but of conflicting faith.

This is so, it seems to me, for several reasons. For one thing, many Southern Christians accorded prior loyalty to their parochial church rather than to Christ's ideal of brotherhood. Institutional peace was purchased at the price of ethical faithlessness. The cost of discipleship came too high for many. As one saddened minister expressed it: "I reluctantly have come to a conclusion. It is one that causes me deep grief. It is that many people love their church, but not the Christ and His teachings." This betrayal came especially easy in the South, for in that section, more than any other, the church plant tended to be modest, even "homey"; the membership small in number, perhaps only a score of families; the fellowship warm. Paradoxically, the more a local church is what it ought to be — the center of the most intimate relationship between people — the more difficult in fact is the problem of integration. It is quite one thing for blacks and whites to attend Mass in the anonymity of a great Northern Catholic cathedral; it is quite another for them to come together in a hot little frame meetinghouse, to share a hymnal, exchange gossip on the front steps or later in the week at a sewing bee, and partake of the inevitable fried chicken at the proscriptive "socials." "The actual chumminess of the local congregation," Niebuhr commented, "has invalidated the universal principle at the heart of the gospel. Particular brotherhood, ethnically based, has invalidated the universal brotherhood implicit in the Christian ethic."

For another thing, white Southern Protestantism suffered from an excess of democracy. I once listened in endless fascination to a group of Roman Catholic priests compare, in some bitterness, the tightly disciplined structure of their church with alleged freedom afforded the clergy of the Protestant sects. As an Episcopalian who has studied Methodism in some detail, their naive observation struck me as rather quaint. Nevertheless, the generalization is valid that the Protestant denominations are the lengthened shadows of their people, they are mostly democratically governed and reflect the views of their members. This is one of the glories of the heirs of the Reformation, but it may also be a source of misery to the ministry. Too many Protestant laymen are like Crèvecoeur's "Low Dutchman" who could conceive of "no other idea of a clergyman than that of a hired hand; if he does his work well he will pay him the stipulated sum; if not he will dismiss him, and do without his sermons, and let his church be shut up for years." Recently this has been the fate of scores of ministers who dared to place the South's segregated society under the judgment of the Kingdom of God. We may never know how many other hundreds of men of God in the past century have remained prudently silent because they honored harmony in their parishes (or coveted their jobs) more than they feared God. Parenthetically, the old parson who termed denominational social pronouncements the most harmless form of amusement ever devised by the human mind missed the point, for such pronouncements do strengthen and support the local minister who takes an advanced position.

The number should not be exaggerated of Southern clergymen who knew the true meaning of Paul's anguished cry: *"For necessity is laid upon me.* Woe to me if I do not preach the gospel!"* My guess is that, at least until recently, the ten-

sion between pulpit and pew in white Southern Protestantism
has not been crucial. Long ago E. McNeill Poteat, Jr. observed "that the conflict between progressive preaching and
reactionary hearing" has not been serious in the South. In
the even more distant past Chaucer asked, "If gold rust, what
then will iron do?" But this was hardly a relevant question
in the South because clergy and laity were forged from the
same metal. As often as not, the Southern preacher did not
merely resemble the Southern tobacco farmer or cotton 'crop-
per or textile mill "lint head," he was that man. Estimates
suggest that nearly half of the parsons supplemented their
income by another occupation. Their clerical wages, lower
than in other sections, united them with their flocks in a
common bond of poverty, as their brief pastorates (averag-
ing about two years) united them in a common insecurity
with tenant farmers and migratory workers. More significant
is that ministers shared with their parishioners the tragic
penalties of ignorance. Limited schooling, often not beyond
the elementary level, was a hallmark of the Southern ministry. A cleric with a college degree was rare in urban pulpits
and almost unknown in the vast hinterland. Seminary graduates were perhaps not a hidden remnant, but considering
the suspicion leveled at this tiny minority, they might well
have gone into hiding. In brief, the Southern pulpit was unable to transcend the racial bigotry of the pew in part because the occupants of both were twisted by the same forces
of poverty and ignorance. Yet, it is undeniable that in recent
years there has been a growing cleavage between clergy and
communicants, especially as the percentage of university and
seminary trained ministers mounts.

A final reason for the dangerous melding of church and
society below the Potomac is paradoxical: the singular tri-
umphs of the Southern denominations, particularly the Southern Baptists, in bringing the unchurched into their folds, the
relative and absolute growth of Southern Protestantism in

terms of membership, wealth, and property has fostered a
sense of complacency and prudence. Like individuals grouped
before a camera, the Southern sects seemed to feel that any
movement would spoil the picture. Since by almost every
statistical measurement they have done well, why endanger
success by attempting to do better by the Negro?

There is, of course, more than a casual relationhip between
Southern white Protestantism's sanctioning of segregation and
its theology. This point has been much noted by scholars and
hardly requires elaboration. "Scratch any sectarian skin and
the same orthodox blood flows," declared Poteat. A dogged
insistence on Biblical inerrancy and a wooden literalism has
made it possible for a century of Sunday School teachers to
extend the curse of Ham to every man of color down to
Martin Luther King. A harsh Calvinism curiously combined
with an individualistic Arminianism made irrelevant man's
horizontal relationship with man; all-consuming was the
vertical relationship of the isolated individual with a judg-
mental God. Since life was contingent and this world transi-
tory and since heaven and hell existed for all eternity, the
preparation of the soul was unspeakably paramount to the
reformation of society. And it was believed that one prepared
for eternity through the cultivation of an exclusive piety and
the practice of a legalistic moralism.

It is not very fashionable nowadays to praise the liberal
theology that came to transform the Northern churches early
in the century, but I am convinced that racial brotherhood
was retarded in the South because Southern fundamentalism
was so little penetrated by the insights of Walter Rauschenbusch and the other champions of the so-called "social gospel." The immanence of God, a solidaristic view of society,
the essential goodness of man and the brotherhood of men,
the possibility of peaceful progress, the moral order of the
universe, the insight that men are damned and saved in a
social context, the application of the teachings of a historical

Jesus, the truest revelation in Christ of the nature of God, the visions of the Kingdom of God as the dear truth, the marrow of the gospel (as Rauschenbusch believed), these were the elements of the then new liberal theology that demanded implementation in social action. But they were imperatives unacceptable in most of Dixie. And if today we are in a post-liberal era, it must not be assumed that the so-called neo-orthodoxy of Niebuhr and Tillich is simply a sophisticated updating of fundamentalism.

Though Southern white Protestantism largely rejected first the liberal theology of the social gospelites and then the crisis theology of the Age of Existentialism and remained loyal to a nineteenth century Biblical literalism and individualistic piety, these folk claimed to be followers of Christ, and not even the most ardent white supremacist can make a segregationist out of Jesus. Therefore, almost all liberal scholars have assumed that Southern church people were burdened with a terrible guilt arising from the tension between the precepts of their faith and their practices of segregation. How could the self, it is commonly asserted, fail to be torn asunder by this racking ambivalence? How could the white Christian not be made anxious by the gulf between the American Creed (compounded of the ethics of Jesus and the idealism of Jefferson) and Southern caste? Alas, I have lived long enough to know that how a person ought to feel is not always how he does feel, even unconsciously. Perhaps the Eichmann trial has something to tell us on that score. Guilt feelings result from the violation of group ideals and in the minds of many good people, caste is not such a violation. I am much impressed by the researches of Ernest Q. Campbell into moral discomfort and racial segregation. Professor Campbell's studies led him to this disturbing conclusion:

It seems apparent that the American Creed simply is not transmitted to many people as a set of values pertinent to racial issues. Further, a segregated system provides its own set of counter-norms, a rationale that justifies the system while it helps the actor in the system to compartmentalize or re-interpret the American Creed. But perhaps most important, the Creed is not the only set of perfectly legitimate and acceptable norms relevant to the prediction and implementation of racial change. Certain virtues valued especially in middle and upper class white culture operate to check the pace of social change that the flow of guilt would initiate were these other things not valued. The Myrdalian emphasis leads us to see the support of segregation, or hesitancy to change from it, as a set of rationalizations, as defenses used to protect the person from an otherwise sure awareness that he is wrong. And when one is 'troubled' about race relations, we make of this a 'troubled conscience.' Such does not follow.

Finally, in our effort to understand the intensity of the commitment of white Southern Protestants to segregation, I should like to mention two passing points. First, the Christian Negro is himself guilty of idolatry. His church is his chief joy, in part because it is so distinctly and completely his. He, too, has placed a sinful value on the preservation of his institutional church and the powers, prerogatives, and prestige that a segregated church affords. He, too, cries, "Peace, peace," because the price of protest seemed so painful. The Negro churches are also segregating as well as segregated bodies. For example, the Colored Methodist Episcopal Church at the time of its formation stipulated that no white person could become a member, and when a white man later applied for admission into one of the conferences he was refused. Second, it is necessary to bite the bullet and make the flat assertion that the desegregation of American society — and of Southern Protestantism — has been, is, and will continue to be an excruciatingly painful ordeal; and the consequences have been, are, and will continue to be ambivalent, at least for a long, long time.

My concern in this essay has been with the "spotted actuality" because Southern white Protestantism first must face up to its racial record in shame and contrition. But it would be both unfair and unhistorical to conclude on a cynical or mordant chord. I am absolutely convinced from the evidence available to historians that Southern Christians, white and black, have led in the shattering of racial pride in the South, especially in the years beginning about World War I and most especially since World War II. I am further of the conviction — indeed, of the faith — that as Southern Christians increasingly come to the awareness that the Church of Christ is His Church they will be given the grace to comprehend that we are all the children of one Father, and accordingly place our racial practices under the judgment of the Kingdom of God.

Index